Exploring England's Heritage

DEVON AND CORNWALL

Andrew Saunders

Published in association with

English ⌗ Heritage

London: HMSO

Andrew Saunders was (from 1973 until his retirement in 1989) England's Chief Inspector of Ancient Monuments and Historic Buildings, firstly with the Department of the Environment and latterly with *English Heritage*. As a former President of the Cornwall Archaeological Society, he has wide knowledge of the history, architecture and archaeology of Devon and Cornwall. He is recognised internationally as an authority on castles, fortifications and artillery, has published widely in these several fields and is Editor of the quarterly journal *Fortress*.

© Andrew Saunders 1991
First published 1991
ISBN 0 11 300025 1

British Library Cataloguing in Publication Data

A CIP catalogue record for this book
is available from the British Library

While the information contained in this book is to the best of our knowledge correct at time of publication, the publisher and author can accept no responsibility for any inconvenience which may be sustained by any error of omission. Readers are also reminded to follow the Country Code when visiting the countryside monuments in this book.

Front cover: St Mawes Castle, with Pendennis Castle in the background. Detail from a watercolour by J M W Turner. Photo: Christie's Colour Library.
Back cover: Botallack Mine. Photo: Ander Gunn.
Frontispiece: interior of Kent's Cavern, Torquay. Photo: Kent's Cavern.

HMSO publications are available from:

HMSO Publications Centre
(Mail and telephone orders only)
PO Box 276, London, SW8 5DT
Telephone orders 071-873 9090
General enquiries 071-873 0011
(queuing system in operation for both numbers)

HMSO Bookshops
49 High Holborn, London, WC1V 6HB
071-873 0011 (counter service only)
258 Broad Street, Birmingham, B1 2HE
021-643 3740
Southey House, 33 Wine Street, Bristol, BS1 2BQ
0272-264306
9–21 Princess Street, Manchester, M60 8AS
061-834 7201
80 Chichester Street, Belfast, BT1 4JY
0232-238451
71 Lothian Road, Edinburgh, EH3 9AZ
031-228 4181

HMSO's Accredited Agents
(see Yellow Pages)

and through good booksellers

Printed in the UK for HMSO
Dd 291298   C80   11/91

Contents

Foreword *by Barry Cunliffe*   *vii*
Acknowledgements   *viii*
Notes for the Reader   *ix*
Introduction   *1*

1 **Prehistory**   *5*
2 **Roman, Early Christian and Anglo-Saxon Settlement**   *15*
3 **Towns**   *25*
4 **Public Buildings**   *37*
5 **Churches and Cathedrals**   *45*
6 **Vernacular Buildings and Rural Settlement**   *61*
7 **Castles and Later Fortifications**   *69*
8 **Country Houses and Gardens**   *79*
9 **Industry**   *91*
10 **Communications**   *101*   .

Select Bibliography   *111*
Index   *112*
Maps   *117*

Foreword

Today as midsummer approaches, Oxford is crammed with tourists. The roads near my office are choked with open-topped buses, their multilingual commentaries extolling the virtues of the city, while the pavements are impassable with crocodiles of visitors, eyes glued on the coloured umbrellas of determined guides. Dons wearing full academic dress attempt to make their way to and from the Examination Schools, to the delight of foreign photographers, and might as well be extras employed by the Tourist Board.

Oxford, Stratford-on-Avon and London together make up the golden triangle – golden, that is, to the tour operators – and millions of tourists are led through their crowded streets each year. The great majority of those who visit Oxford come for only a few hours, then move on to Stratford to stay overnight before returning to familiar London. It is London that takes the brunt. Westminster Abbey will be host to over 3 million, more than 2 million will visit the Tower of London, and then of course there are the museums and art galleries welcoming their annual tidal wave. Tourism, as governments are pleased to remind us, is one of Britain's biggest industries.

Looking at the tired, bewildered faces of the tourists off-loaded and scooped up again outside Oxford's St Giles, I long to grab them and say, 'It's all right – this is *not* what it's about. England is a beautiful, gentle country full of fascinating corners, breathtaking sights – an eclectic mix of insurpassable quality. All you need is someone with vision to show you how to start looking.'

Well, people with vision, as well as the knowledge of our cultural heritage and the ability to communicate, are not in ample supply, but the members of the team assembled to write the eleven volumes of *Exploring England's Heritage* share these qualities in abundance. Each author has a detailed and expert involvement, not only with the region they are writing about, but also with the buildings, the earthworks, the streets and the landscapes they have chosen to introduce us to. These guides are no mere compilations of well-worn facts, but original accounts coloured by the enthusiasm of people who know what makes a particular site so special.

Each volume introduces more than 100 places. Some are well known (who would dare to omit Stonehenge or Hadrian's Wall?); others are small-scale and obscure but no less interesting for that. We are led down alley-ways to admire hidden gems of architecture, into churchyards to search for inscribed stones and along canals to wonder at the skills of our early engineers. And of course there are the castles, the great houses and their gardens and the churches and cathedrals that give England its very particular character.

Exploring England's Heritage does not swamp you in facts. What each author does is to say, 'Let me show you something you might not have seen and tell you why I find it so particularly interesting.' What more could the discerning traveller want?

Barry Cunliffe

Acknowledgements

This book owes much to the research of others, especially to the late W G Hoskins, Aileen Fox, Charles Thomas, Malcolm Todd, Bob Higham, and Bridget Cherry. I am also indebted to many of my former colleagues in the Ancient Monuments and Historic Buildings Inspectorate and to many Cornish and Devonshire archaeologists and architectural historians with whom I have in the past discussed problems relating to sites and their interpretation. I have been fortunate to have had the opportunity to spend a good deal of my active fieldwork in the south-west.

In particular my thanks are due to John Allan of Exeter Museum; to Nick Barton for advice on Kent's Cavern; to my wife, Gillian Hutchinson for her close collaboration throughout the project; to Dawn Flower and Amanda Patton for the drawings and maps; and to Brian Anthony, my editor.

Author and publisher are gratefully indebted to the following institutions and individuals for permission to publish photographs: Batsford, Eric Berry, Colin Bowden, British Library, Britain On View (British Tourist Authority), Brunel Museum, Cambridge University Committee for Aerial Photography, Jo Cox, Devon County Council, English Heritage, Exeter Archaeological Unit, Kent's Cavern, Anthony Kersting, National Library of Air Photography (RCHME, Swindon), National Monuments Record (RCHME), National Trust, Ordnance Survey, Royal Commission on the Historical Monuments of England, Royal Institute of Cornwall and West Air Photography.

We are also thankful to the following for permission to adapt site plans from their original versions (gazetteer-entry numbers are given in bold):
1 Carn Brea: R J Mercer, 'Excavations at Carn Brea, Illogan, Cornwall, 1970–73: A Neolithic Fortified Complex of the Third Millennium BC', *Cornish Archaeology 20* (1981), fig 2; **3** Carn Gluze: Aileen Fox, *South West England*, London, 1964, fig 13, p53; **4** Chun Castle: E T Leeds, 'Excavations at Chun Castle, Penwith', *Archaeologia 76* (1926–7), p205; **6** Hembury Hillfort: Malcolm Todd, *The South-West to AD 1000*, London, 1987, figs 4.1, 6.2; **20** Martinhoe: Aileen Fox, *South West England*, London, 1964, p138; **22** St Helen's: Helen O'Neil, 'Excavation of a Celtic Hermitage on St Helens, Isles of Scilly, 1956–58', *The Archaeological Journal 121* (1964), fig 1, p44; **36** Duchy Palace: N J G Pounds, 'The Duchy Palace at Lostwithiel, Cornwall', *The Archaeological Journal 136* (1979), fig 3, p213; **61** Houndtor: Guy Beresford, 'Three Deserted Medieval Settlements on Dartmoor: A Report on the late E Marie Minter's Excavations', *Medieval Archaeology 23* (1979), fig 2, p103; **64** Tintagel Old Post Office: National Trust guidebook; **91** Charlestown: John Stenglehofen, 'Charlestown', *The Archaeological Journal 130* (1973), fig 15, p278; **94** Finch Brothers' Foundry: R A Barron, *The Finch Foundry Trust and Sticklepath Museum of Rural Industry* (guidebook).

Notes for the Reader

Each site entry in *Exploring England's Heritage* is numbered and may be located easily on the end-map, but it is recommended especially for the more remote sites, that the visitor make use of the relevant Ordnance Survey map in the Landranger series. The location details of the site entries include a six-figure National Grid reference, e.g., SX 888609. Ordnance Survey maps show the National Grid and the following 1:50,000 maps will be found useful: 180, 181, 190, 191, 192, 193, 200, 201, 202, 203, 204.

Readers should be aware that while the great majority of properties and sites referred to in this handbook are normally open to the public regularly, others are open only on a limited basis. A few are not open at all, and may only be viewed from the public thoroughfare. In these circumstances readers are reminded to respect the owners' privacy. The *access codes* in the heading to each gazetteer entry are designed to indicate the level of public accessibility, and are explained below.

Access Codes

[A] site open for at least part of the year
[B] site open by appointment only
[C] site open by virtue of its use, e.g., a theatre, church or cinema
[D] site not open but which may be seen from the public highway

Abbreviations

BP	Before Present
C	Cornwall
D	Devon
EH	English Heritage
LT	Landmark Trust
NT	National Trust

BL	British Library
BOV	Britain On View, British Tourist Authority
CUCAP	Cambridge University Committee for Aerial Photography
DCC	Devon County Council
EAU	Exeter Archaeological Unit
NLAR	National Library of Air Photography, RCHME, Swindon
OS	Ordnance Survey
RCHME	Royal Commission on the Historical Monuments of England
RIC	Royal Institute of Cornwall

Further Information

Further details on English Heritage, the Landmark Trust and the National Trust may be obtained from the following addresses:

English Heritage (Membership Dept), PO Box 1BB, London W1A 1BB

Landmark Trust, 21 Dean's Yard, Westminster, London SW1

National Trust, PO Box 39, Bromley, Kent, BR1 1NH

Introduction

The geology and physical geography of the south-west peninsula is extremely complex and varied. It has had a profound influence on the man-made environment of Cornwall and Devon, setting these counties apart from the rest of England. The formation of rocks and soils inevitably has affected settlement and with it man's exploitation of the land. Emerging like vertebrae down the peninsula are six igneous granite masses: Dartmoor, Bodmin Moor, Hensbarrow, Carnmenellis, West Penwith and the Isles of Scilly. Between them are the metamorphic rocks and sediments including slates, grits, limestones and sandstones. In mid- and north Devon are the Culm Measures which, in the east, are influenced by the New Red rocks producing the distinctive warm red soil, while to the north are heavy, ill-drained clays. Along the south-eastern coastal strip of Devon are the flint-producing chalk cliffs and the greensand, which link the peninsula, geologically, with the main body of lowland Britain.

The south-western landforms owe little to glaciation and rather more to marine erosion and transgression. This is seen most significantly in the transformation in historical times of the Isles of Scilly from a substantial land mass to an archipelago: Charles Thomas's 'Drowned Landscape'. Marine action of another kind has contributed to the accumulations of blown sand (towans) along the north coasts which have buried settlements as late as the 1st millennium AD. At the same time, by projecting into the Atlantic the south-west peninsula allows its inhabitants to share in the traffic of people, artefacts and ideas moving between Ireland and South Wales to the north, and Brittany and Iberia to the south. With such a highly indented coastline of drowned valleys, the sea is always close at hand.

While acknowledging the effect of geography on human settlement and activity, great physical changes have been caused by economic exploitation;

so much so that the landscape we see today is largely man-made. This is especially true for Dartmoor and the other high moors. Some three to four thousand years ago these were favoured places of settlement. Recent environmental studies show that the pollen contained in buried soils and peat profiles provides evidence for the enormous change and destruction which man brought to this land in prehistoric times, and which was combined with the effects of climatic fluctuations. The present desolate, peat-covered wilderness of much of Dartmoor is due to clearance of the earlier oak woodland from the 4th and 5th millennia BC onwards. Deterioration followed; the land became exhausted and ill-drained, so that sphagnum moss took over and blanket peat formed. By the end of the 2nd millennium BC, the moor had taken its present form. Settlement had shifted to the lower ground, and it was only during periods of land shortage, such as that in the 12th and 13th centuries AD, or during the Napoleonic Wars, that the marginal land was temporarily brought back into cultivation.

In more recent times, well within the last thousand years, the coastline has been changed through the choking of rivers and silting of estuaries with the debris of tin extraction. This process went hand in hand with the unrestrained prospecting of mineral-bearing ground; and the very methods of tin streaming, which required the diversion of watercourses and the turning-over of alluvial deposits scarred much of Cornwall and Dartmoor during the Middle Ages. Further denudation of tree cover for timber for tin works or for smelting fuel added to the environmental change. With the development of shaft mining on a large scale, from the 17th century to its serious decline at the end of the 19th, landscape was affected in other ways. China clay extraction has had its distinctive effect, though over more

Ruins of Okehampton Castle, founded soon after the Norman Conquest. EH

1

Tintagel from the north-east. RCHME

restricted areas. Agriculture has had
wider and more insidious implications
for the landscape, by new clearances, by
the erosion of earlier features and
particularly in the patterns of enclosure,
or, more dramatically, in the past ten or
so years, in the removal of field
boundaries. This practice was beginning
to alter the ancient patterns of West
Penwith to such an extent that this
landscape became one of the first to be
designated by government as an
Environmentally Sensitive Area, and
incentives were provided for farmers to
keep to traditional land use.

The earliest evidence for human
activity in a south-west Britain which
was then an extension of the European

land mass is that left by the transient
hunters and gatherers of Palaeolithic
times, and has been found in remarkable
association with extinct animals in the
cave shelters of Kent's Cavern, Torquay
(8, D) and similar caves at Brixham. The
more proficient toolmakers of the
considerably more recent Mesolithic
period, for which fishing had an
increasing place, can be traced to the
fringes of Dozmary Pool, Bodmin Moor,
and elsewhere.

Once man had turned to cultivation
of the land and acquired more
permanent settlements, he began to
leave more permanent evidence of his
activities, including houses and fields
and the means for protecting them,

disposal of the dead, and tangible traces
of his religious beliefs and ceremonial
practices. These 'sites and monuments'
need to be seen in terms both of their
historical and present environment and
not in isolation. This applies as much to
the monuments of the historic periods
as to those of the remoter prehistoric
past.

Geology and the traditional pattern
of agriculture in the south-west have
ensured that there are far greater
numbers of prehistoric survivals, and in
much greater variety, than exist in areas
of equivalent size in lowland England. It
has been said that: 'The 500 square
kilometres of Dartmoor contain what is
probably the most impressive surviving

prehistoric landscape to be found in Britain as the enclosures, huts, cairns, land boundaries (reaves), stone rows and circles were built of the readily available granite blocks and have survived to the present day largely unchanged by subsequent land use' (G J Wainwright and Ken Smith, 'The South Dartmoor Project 1976–1979', *Prehistoric Dartmoor in its context: Devon Archaeological Society Jubilee Conference Proceedings*, 37, 1979, p132). Much the same can be said for parts of Exmoor and Bodmin Moor.

Individually, the visible prehistoric monuments in the south-west fall into five or six broad categories of stone structure and earthwork. There are those associated with death: the chambered tombs, cairns and cist graves. The more enigmatic ceremonial or ritual monuments are the circles, stone rows or single standing stones. The structures of the living remain as isolated or grouped houses, within or sometimes without some form of

This rare combination of Ogham and Roman inscriptions in Lewannick church dates to the late 5th or early 6th century (see entry 18). os

enclosure. The more obvious statements of long-term and external threat are the fortresses of varying complexity, which make use of the natural advantages of hilltops and promontories. Finally, there are the remains of the economic basis for life, whether it is of a subsistence nature or geared towards surpluses enabling trade and exchange beyond the limits of the kin group or the wider immediate community: the pattern of reaves, fields, and stock pounds, and, were we to find them, the quarries for the trade in stone axes.

The visible monuments are, of course, only the most obvious and tangible element in the archaeological record of the prehistoric past in the countryside. They can also be a distorting image because, throughout this period wood was the principal building material, and this does not survive except in special anaerobic circumstances. Evidence for timber structures can only be observed during the course of archaeological excavation or through the quirks of aerial photography or geophysical surveying.

Devon and Cornwall are distinct from the rest of England in a number of ways and in some respects are a foreign land. John de Grandison, soon after his appointment as Bishop of Exeter in 1327, is reported to have written to his friends at Avignon describing the south-west peninsula as 'not only the end of the earth but the very end of the ends thereof' (John Hatcher, *Rural Economy and Society in the Duchy of Cornwall 1300–1500*, Cambridge, 1970, p1). For centuries the social and economic basis was quite different from that of most English counties, with industrial processes leavening, and interwoven with, the solid agricultural base. Then, there was the factor of the Cornish language and the survival in Cornwall of Celtic institutions in a society which had been little influenced by Romanisation, and which had been brought within Anglo-Saxon domination comparatively later than other parts of England. Celtic survivals in Devon are, however, now fairly tenuous, since the eastern part was absorbed into Wessex in the 6th century and in physical terms it merges imperceptibly into Dorset and Somerset.

The impact here of the Anglo-Saxon conquest was great, producing large estates and extensive agricultural colonisation, and, in ecclesiastical terms, the establishment of minster churches. The contrast of Cornwall to this day is real, and most obvious in the place-names, the pattern of churches and other surviving fragments of Celtic Christianity. The Cornish language was in general use until Tudor times and lingered on in the far west into the 19th century. Adam de Carleton, in a letter tendering his resignation as Archdeacon of Cornwall in 1342 after more than thirty-five years in office, confessed himself unable to communicate with the Cornish. It was not just language difficulties: 'The folk of these parts are quite extraordinary, being of a rebellious temper and obdurate in the face of attempts to teach and correct' (John Hatcher, 1970, p2).

With the Norman Conquest, society and its culture changed radically, and the monuments which represent it today relate to the establishment of feudal castles and the widespread building of churches. While major landholders were relatively few in number, the dominating influences were those of the earldom of Cornwall, the Courtenay earls of Devon and the bishops of Exeter. At the time of Domesday, the Count of Mortain was the principal landholder in Cornwall. Richard, Earl of Cornwall (1227–1272), made extensive purchases and exchanges to increase his holding and this concentration of wealth went to the duchy created by Edward III in 1327. The wealth which Devon and Cornwall produced largely went elsewhere. In 1377, £2,219 out of a total revenue of £3,415 left Cornwall, and at least one-third of the total church revenue was taken out. Devon was indeed wealthier, and its cloth trade, as opposed to tin, was not under the control of major magnates but that of the merchants of its towns. The prosperity of Devon increased sharply in the 15th century, in which tin still had its part, and was demonstrated by the building of new bridges and rebuilding of churches.

The building styles of the Middle Ages lingered on much later than in the rest of England. This broadly conservative society was prepared to fight for the old order – whether it was the pre-Reformation Prayer Book in the 16th century or for a despotic monarchy in the 17th – and change largely came about through the effect of industrial and commercial activities. Tin and copper, the cloth trade and the Newfoundland fisheries transformed Devon and Cornwall in the 17th and 18th centuries. This is the society described by Richard Carew of Anthony, whose *Survey of Cornwall* was published in 1602, and by the observant and literate travellers, Daniel Defoe and Celia Fiennes.

The creation of a naval dockyard (later known as Devonport) at the end of the 17th century afforded the south-west closer involvement with national affairs. It would lead to the future dominance of Plymouth in its social and economic life. The roads were improved in the latter half of the 18th century, and then the introduction of railways in the 19th century provided a further revolution, opening up the south-west to its more lasting source of income, the tourist. With the tourist came the poet, the artist and the travel writer.

The selection of 100 'historic sites' to represent this diverse and rich cultural environment is especially difficult. The broad objective has been to make the selection as widely representative as possible while retaining a balance between the particular and the more obvious. This will mean omissions which may seem surprising or wilful, and inclusions which may appear humdrum or obscure. Those sites and monuments which are peculiar to Cornwall and Devon have been given prominence, and emphasis is given to those where extensive access is usually available. This has led to the exclusion of such well-known monuments as Trematon Castle or Powderham Castle. The important town of Barnstaple was omitted because of the effect new commercial development has had on its historic character. The choice is therefore intensely personal and reflects the author's prejudices and affections.

1

Prehistory

The earliest monuments of prehistoric times belong to the comparatively recent period of man's existence when reasonably settled and stable communities began to practise agriculture and to exploit the land on a regular basis. This settled existence in turn brought with it communal activity which produced distinctive methods of commemorating the dead and the construction of elaborate ceremonial monuments. It also stimulated tensions between organised societies which could lead to violence and the need for defended hilltop enclosures. This activity begins to show itself in Devon and Cornwall during the mid- to late 4th millennium BC at the beginning of what is called the Neolithic period. It extended until around the turn of the 2nd millennium BC.

These early farmers buried their dead in communal chambered tombs, and there are indications that some graves were located in and among the fields. Some of the tombs are constructed from enormous slabs of granite and are truly megalithic. In Cornwall they are often called 'quoits'. In west Cornwall there are about twenty, of which Chun Quoit and Lanyon Quoit are among the best known. They also can be found further east, as at **Trethevy Quoit** (13, C), and are associated with long cairns on the fringes of Dartmoor, such as Corringdon Ball and Spinster's Rock. They are in the same category as the long barrows more familiar across southern England. A variant is the group of **Scillonian chambered tombs** (12), together with some on the mainland, described as 'entrance graves'. There are other more complex sites such as **Carn Gluze** (3, C).

Other forms of ceremonial or religious monument are single standing stones (*menhirs*), stone circles and henges, and stone rows. There is, unfortunately, no satisfactory explanation of the functions which these served. As with the large chambered tombs, their construction and organisation represent a great deal of communal effort, and a high degree of political skill. Cornwall has the greatest variety of stone circles (e.g., **The Hurlers**, 7), more than any other region of equivalent size in the British Isles. They also occur on Dartmoor and include a more complex variant of multiple circles, as on Shovel Down and Yellowmead Down. Dartmoor, on the other hand, possesses the greatest number of stone rows (about seventy-five) – more than may be found in the rest of England combined. Those at **Merrivale** (9, D) are good examples.

It has been shown that this period of agricultural expansion entailed a considerable clearance of natural tree cover. Pollen evidence from the one stone row which has been excavated, Cholwich Town (D), on what is now open moorland, indicated that the row was constructed in a woodland clearing. Manufacture of, and trade or exchange, in polished stone axes demonstrated a society beyond the stage of subsistence farming. This seems to have led to unstable political conditions which required the fortification of hilltop settlements as at **Carn Brea** (1, C), **Hembury** (6, D) and elsewhere.

During the 2nd millennium BC, when metal-working technologies had been discovered, there seems to have been greater social tranquility with less need for communal defensive measures. Pressure of agriculture on the higher ground of Dartmoor and Bodmin Moor was intense. This was the peak period for the settlement and cultivation of the high ground, as the elaborate systems of boundaries and fields, or reaves (**Rippon Tor**, 10, D), demonstrate, and it contributed greatly to the increasing soil deterioration. There were two main settlement forms: enclosed hut groups or pounds (**Grimspound**, 5, D) providing the means for confining flocks and herds, and isolated huts and hut groups. House plans were almost universally round with low stone walls on which the roof members were set. There must be a strong presumption for the exploitation

Courtyard-house, Carn Euny. EH

of the very accessible alluvial deposits of tin on the moors, and perhaps of copper and gold, though actual workings of this date have still to be established.

The leading members of these societies achieved considerable wealth to judge from the grave furnishings that accompanied their burials: gold lunulae and other precious objects now to be seen in museums. The burial mounds or barrows, which are the distinctive monuments of the Bronze Age, initially contained single graves. The mounds were often built with greatly diverse ritual and could be massive as at Carne Beacon, Veryan (C) or arranged in numerous and highly visible cemeteries like that at Broad Down/Farway (D) or ranging across the skyline at Taphouse (C) and best seen from the A390.

With the onset of the 1st millennium BC, the high ground had – through a mixture of soil exhaustion and climatic change allowing the formation of blanket peat – turned into the moors that we know today. Settlement and cultivation concentrated on the lower slopes and valleys. Technology improved as iron came into general use alongside bronze by the 7th century BC. This coincided with the dominance of Celtic-speaking people. The circumstantial evidence for tin working and trade now becomes much stronger. There was however, greater insecurity as well as wealth. Defensive works, great and small, became more necessary. These varied from the large communal fortresses, sometimes with multiple lines of ditch and rampart such as **Hembury** (6, D), Woodbury Castle (D) or Castle an Dinas, St Columb Major (C), though in the south-west as a whole there were comparatively few extensive hillforts (e.g., **Chun Castle**, 4, C). Cliff castles (**The Rumps**, 11, C) multiplied, though probably because of the topographical advantages of a deeply indented coastline rather than through the influence of Venetic traders or settlers from Brittany where similar fortifications occur. At the same time there are other forms of earthwork enclosure in great number. In Devon and east Cornwall there are those where the principal enclosure has a number of annexes usually down a hill-slope. In

Cornwall and west Devon there are large numbers of simpler small, circular or oval enclosures which have the descriptive title of 'rounds'. They and their hill-slope counterparts appear to be small settlements of kin groups, were a type which came into fashion during the 3rd or 2nd century BC and were still much inhabited during the Roman period. The prevalent house plan was still circular. An additional feature very local to west Cornwall was a form of souterrain called, in Cornish, *fogou*, or cave, which was usually closely associated with settlements (**Carn Euny**, 2, C). Burial rites generally adopted a flat cemetery form and the stone-lined cists of the Iron Age cemetery at Harlyn Bay (C) can still be seen.

The picture of Devon and Cornwall, the land of the *Dumnonii*, at the point of its incorporation into the Roman Empire is that of a scattered but individually differentiated settlement pattern with a few major communal centres in hillforts. It was a society which lay in the midst of the Irish Sea and Atlantic coastal traffic and trade. The association of St Michael's Mount with the *Ictis* of classical writers and the legends of Phoenician traders may be myth but a major trading port has been archaeologically proved on the eastern side of Plymouth Sound at the promontory site of Mount Batten.

1

Carn Brea
c.3000 BC–15th century AD

SW 684408. Camborne–Redruth. By a rough track from Carnkie, reached by turning S off the A3047 at Pool
[A]

Carn Brea is an elongated hill with three summits separated by two lower saddles. The easternmost summit is surrounded by a massive stone wall linking outcrops of granite. The wall contains many huge boulders, some weighing up to 3 tons. It

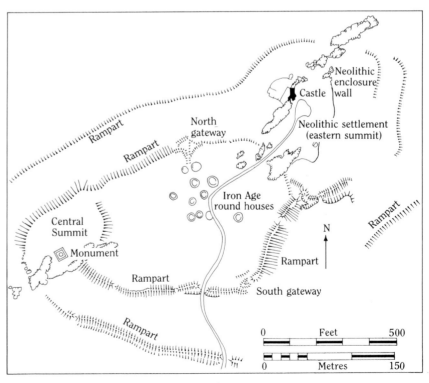

Carn Brea Neolithic settlement (after R J Mercer). EH

must have stood well in excess of 6 ft (2 m) high. This enclosure was about 2 acres in area and appears to have acted as a citadel for a much larger defensive circuit of stone-revetted rampart and a ditch dug down to the bedrock enclosing an area of about 15 acres. Excavations have shown that these defences are of Neolithic date.

Within the larger enclosure were extensive traces of cultivation, and set behind the wall of the inner 'citadel' were a number of terraces upon which timber houses had been built. The excavator believes, on the basis of the number of house sites and the numbers of people needed for the prodigious task of wall construction, that a settlement of 100–150 strong is a reasonable estimate of the population. These people living here in around 3000–2700 BC, were not only farmers but worked stone from a local source into polished stone axes for wider trade and exchange. They themselves received pottery from a source in the Lizard peninsula, 20 miles away, and flint and chert from the Devon/Dorset border.

It is clear from the archaeological record that in the end Carn Brea was attacked from all sides by a very large number of archers. Thousands of flint-tipped arrows were left on the site after the attack and 800 alone were recovered from the limited area of excavation. The defensive wall was deliberately slighted and evidence of burning was widespread within the site. After this the settlement was abandoned.

The hilltop was reoccupied at various times much later. A hoard of Bronze Age metalwork was found in 1744 near the summit of the hill and a hoard of Gaulish and British gold coins from the beginning of the 1st century AD was recovered in 1749. There is a scatter of round-houses of Late Iron Age date, *c*.200 BC–100 AD in the eastern saddle. A medieval strong house ('castle') stands on the eastern summit. It was first mentioned by William of Worcester in 1478 and for a long period was used as a hunting lodge. It has been much modified since. The area has been greatly affected by mining activities in recent centuries. The monument on the central summit is to Lord de

Carn Euny *fogou*. EH

Dunstanville, a landowner closely connected with the local mining industry.

2

Carn Euny Iron Age Settlement and *Fogou*
5th century BC–4th century AD

SW 403288. Sancreed. Signposted from the A30 at Lower Drift. Car park below Brane Farm, then by footpath

[A] EH

The prehistoric settlement, formerly known as Chapel Euny, is situated on the slopes of the hill crowned by the hillfort of Caer Brane. It was first discovered in the early 19th century by miners prospecting for tin, and various excavations were then carried out. Modern scientific excavations took place between 1964 and 1972. The cluster of Iron Age houses and the scant remains of associated fields are the more significant for the presence of the most elaborate of the Cornish souterrains, known by the Cornish word for cave – *fogou*. These are galleries constructed by

lining a trench with dry-stone walling and roofing it with stone slabs which are then usually covered with earth. The passages are often curved and may have chambers leading off them. There are parallels with Breton souterrains and it has been suggested that they may have been introduced into Cornwall from that source.

The *fogou* at Carn Euny has a long sinuous passage with a side passage ('creep') off it at the southern end. At the opposite end of the long passage is another short passage which gives on to a large circular chamber about 15 ft (4.6 m) across. This 'round chamber' was the first part of the complex to be constructed in the 5th century BC. Although the walls are corbelled inwards it was not a fully domed structure and was thought to have been roofed from a central post, though it is also possible that it was left open to the sky.

The long passage was a later stage in the development and the 'creep' was contemporary with it. There was an extension of the *fogou* to the south-west, and the eastern entrance was also a later modification. The long passage was later filled. The function of *fogous* has been the subject of much speculation and the excavations did not provide a solution. On the one hand a comparison with cellars for storage may be made, and on the other there are those who see some kind of ritual significance in their shape and form.

The village in which the *fogou* is situated has suffered extensive damage over the years from cultivation and stone clearance. The excavations have revealed over ten houses belonging to different phases of Iron Age occupation. Three of them are large enclosures of the 'courtyard house' type, the others are smaller and earlier, mostly oval in plan. House walls were frequently shared and interlocking, with much rebuilding. There were four main phases of occupation, distinguished by pottery styles supported by Carbon 14 dating. The settlement began in the 5th century BC and is contemporary with the 'round chamber' of the *fogou*. The second phase belonged to the 2nd century BC, the third starting around 50 BC and lasting until the mid-1st century AD. Finally, occupation continued into the 2nd and 4th centuries when local wares were influenced by Roman pottery styles.

3

Carn Gluze (Ballowall) Chambered Cairn
Bronze Age, c.2000–1500 BC

SW 354313. St Just. One mile W of the town in the direction of Cape Cornwall, but follow the road signposted to Carn Gloose

[A] EH

One of the most remarkable burial monuments of west Cornwall on the cliff edge within sight of Cape Cornwall. This cairn was constructed in several phases with very great sophistication. At the heart of the tomb was a T-shaped pit, cut 7 ft (2.1 m) deep into the rocky subsoil and entered by rough steps, perhaps for an inhumation or for some other ritual purpose. Near this pit were four small, stone-lined cists containing small pots dating from the Middle Bronze Age and perhaps holding offerings rather than cremated human remains. Over all this was an oval, double-walled, corbelled

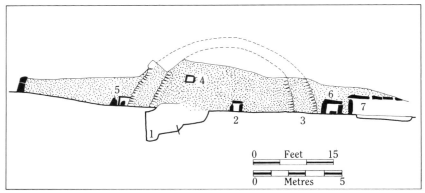

Carn Gluze: reconstructed section (after A Fox). EH

dome about 26 ft (8 m) across and originally about 16 ft (5 m) high. The interior was filled with stone, and in this packing another cist was built containing pottery and the bones of a lamb, probably as a final offering before the dome was sealed. Later, the domed cairn was surrounded by another massive, circular cairn with its external face carefully laid. Later still, an

entrance grave was inserted into the outer cairn on the west side on approximately the same axis as the approach to the primary pit.

The cairn was broken into in antiquity, and it has survived most remarkably, since it was later adjacent to a modern mine and debris partly covered it. It was excavated by W Copeland Borlase and a gang of miners in 1874,

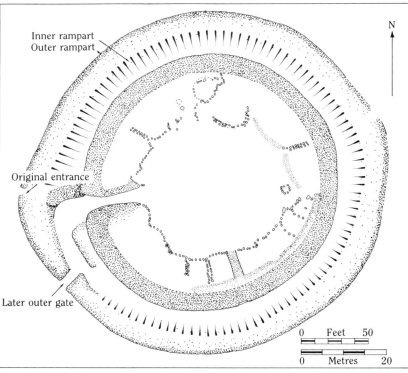

Chun Castle (after E T Leeds). EH

and the measured survey by W C Lukis was published in 1885.

4

Chun Castle
3rd century BC–6th century AD

SW 405339. Morvah. Signposted from the Penzance–Morvah road at Bosullow Common. By footpath from Trehyllys Farm

[A]

While there is a wide variety of Iron Age defended settlements in Cornwall, there are comparatively few true hillforts. Chun Castle is chief among a number of small but very strongly defended forts. It stands on a hilltop commanding an extensive area of the West Penwith uplands and is distinguished from most hillforts in being dry-stone built. This fort is circular with an internal diameter of roughly 160 ft (49 m) and encloses only half an acre (0.2 ha). It is surrounded by two massive stone ramparts about 20 ft (6 m) apart, with traces of inner and outer ditches. The single entrance is staggered in dog-leg fashion so that the outer gate was covered from the inner rampart and the inner gate could not be easily rushed. This was a refinement of its later phase of occupation. The original entrance in the outer rampart was opposite the inner gateway. Beyond the later outer gate are traces of a bank and ditch forming a barbican. In the 18th century the inner rampart was reportedly still at least 15 ft (4.6 m) high. Since then, much of the stone has been robbed to build, among other places, Madron Workhouse.

Excavations took place in the 1920s, producing characteristic 3rd–2nd-century-BC Iron Age pottery. It was also clear that there had been occupation in the Roman period and into the 6th century. Internal circular and rectangular structures arranged against the inner rampart are of more than one date, with the later constructions belonging to the Early Christian era. As well as imported Mediterranean sherds there was 6th-century 'grass-marked' pottery, tin slag and a smelting furnace.

Grimspound from the air. CUCAP

On and built into the main rampart are little pulpit-like features. These were indeed the equivalent of pulpits used in open-air Methodist services in the 19th century.

5

Grimspound
Late Bronze Age, 1450–1000 BC

SX 701809. Manaton. Turn S off B3212 at Shapley Common (4¼ miles NE of Postbridge) along minor road and site is off road to the E after 1½ miles

[A]   EH

Grimspound is among the most substantial of the Late Bronze Age enclosed settlements of Dartmoor. It is situated at a height of 1,500 ft (457 m) above sea level in a fold in the hills between Hookney Tor and Hameldon. A significant factor is the inclusion of Grim's Lake, a tributary of the West Webburn River, within the enclosure which flows below the wall and across the northern interior. The requirement for water immediately to hand suggests that the inhabitants were pastoralists.

The enclosure wall is massively built of large facing slabs coursed horizontally with a core of small stones between the two faces, but it is unlikely that it was intended to be defensible. It still stands 4–5 ft (1.2–1.5 m) high and 9–10 ft

(2.75–3 m) wide, the area within being just short of 4 acres (1.6 ha). The entrance is imposing, incorporating large boulders with a passage 6 ft (1.8 m) wide which is roughly paved. It is on the south, or uphill side. Within the enclosure are 16 circular dwellings grouped towards the south-western half. They are all small, 8½ ft (2.5 m) to 15 ft (4.5 m) in diameter, with walls 3–4 ft (1 m) thick. The walls were probably not much higher than they are now and served as the base for pitched timber rafters sometimes supported by a central post or posts, and carrying a roof covering of turf or thatch. Large slabs set vertically were used as jambs for the narrow doorways which were probably lintelled. Two huts are attached and another two have external porch-like projections screening the doorway. One hut in the centre of the enclosure was inaccurately reconstructed in 1895. To the north of these dwellings are seven smaller circular stone buildings in which there were no hearths and which have been described as store huts. Small stone-built enclosures constructed against the internal face of the surrounding wall are thought to be cattle pens.

Excavations were carried out here by the Devonshire Association in 1894–5 according to the standards of the time. No dating evidence was recovered. It is possible some of the larger 'pounds', such as Grimspound, represent cumulative settlement over a long period of time.

6

Hembury Hillfort
c.3000 BC–1st century AD

ST 112032. Payhembury. N of the A373, 4 miles from Honiton

[A]

Hembury occupies the tip of a spur extending from the Blackdown Hills into the Otter Valley. It is a site of great natural strength and has been used for defended settlement at various times. There have been three main periods of occupation: Neolithic, at the end of the 4th millennium BC; the Iron Age, from

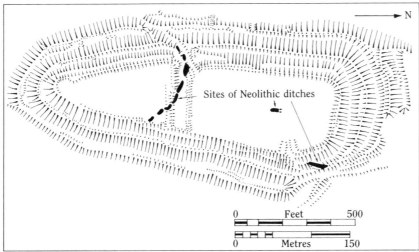

Sites of Neolithic ditches

N

0   Feet   500
0   Metres   150

Hembury hillfort (after M Todd). EH

the c.7th to the 1st century BC; and the Roman, during the 1st century AD.

The earthworks which we see today are those from the Iron Age occupation of the hilltop, but excavations in the 1930s showed that not only was there Mesolithic occupation but, in the 4th millennium BC, there was a defended enclosure. The primary construction was a 'causewayed camp', so called from the short, separate lengths of flat-bottomed ditch which provided the material for a substantial rampart across the centre of the later hillfort. Little of the interior of this early enclosure was examined but an oval or sub-rectangular hut was found near a timber-framed entrance on the western side. This Neolithic settlement seems to have succumbed to attack – at least 120 leaf-shaped flint arrowheads were found chiefly in the ditch – and there was clear evidence of deliberate burning and destruction of the defences.

The visible hillfort was probably built in the early 1st millennium BC, and is one of Devon's most impressive. It has close-set multiple ramparts. The defences are at their highest, consisting of two great ditches and three ramparts, across the neck of the spur which provides the easiest approach. There were two entrances to the fort, both distinguished by a short inturn of the inner rampart, on the east and west sides. On the west, there was an

elaborate timber gatehouse. Recent excavations have demonstrated that the first phase of the defences took the form of a box-rampart, faced and revetted to the rear by timber walls with earth filling in between. The hillfort was probably abandoned some time before the end of the 1st millennium BC and the Roman Conquest.

The hillfort site was subsequently taken over by the Roman army during its initial advance into the south-west. Substantial timber buildings were erected at the northern end of the hillfort, perhaps for barracks and workshops. The gates were remodelled in this period and the site seems to have been briefly occupied about 50–70 AD.

7
The Hurlers
Late 3rd/early 2nd millennium BC

SX 258714. Linkinhorne.
Immediately NW of Minions on the minor road W from Upton Cross off the B3254

[A] EH

If stone rows are a feature of Dartmoor's Neolithic ceremonial monuments, Cornwall has a wide distribution of stone circles. Some twenty-five have been identified. There is a distinct group in

West Penwith. The circles in east Cornwall vary much more in size, and the most interesting are the three circles set close together on a north–south alignment known as The Hurlers. These are among the largest circles in Cornwall and the stones are taller than most. A little way to the west are two more stones, The Pipers, which may be the remains of a fourth circle or of an alignment running down to the River Fowey.

This is one of the few south-western stone circles to have been excavated. The stones in the central circle had been set in pits and well packed with stones. They had also been hammered smooth and the chippings left nearby. In the centre circle of fourteen upright stones, and fourteen marker stones which indicate the sites of standing stones now missing, was a single upright stone placed off-centre. The northern circle with eleven stones still standing, and nine marker stones, had been paved with granite slabs and there was paving between the central and the more ruined southern circle. No dating evidence resulted from the excavation and it can only be assumed at present that there is an association between the circles and other ritual and burial monuments in the vicinity. There is a rough alignment between the circles and the large chambered tomb, the Rillaton barrow, nearby.

In the 16th century, Camden in *Britannia* (1586) wrote that: 'the neighbouring Inhabitants terme them *Hurlers* as being by devout and godly error perswaded that they had been men sometime transformed into stones, for profaning the Lord's Day, with hurling the ball.'

8
Kent's Cavern
c.400,000–100 BC

SX 934641. Torquay, off Ilsham Road and signposted off Babbacombe Road

[A] Finds in Torquay Museum

One of the most important Lower Palaeolithic sites in Britain, producing

Kent's Cavern: artefacts, animal teeth and bones. KENT'S CAVERN

evidence for the very early presence of man, perhaps as far back as 400,000 years ago, is Kent's Cavern, Torquay. It is also one of the best stratified sites for the whole of the Upper Palaeolithic period in Britain. Kent's Cavern is on the western side of the Ilsham valley and consists of a large and complex series of cavities produced by dissolution of the Devonian limestone, and linked together by narrow fissures.

Excavations were begun here as early as 1824, and most notably a year later by a Catholic priest, Father J McEnery. Unusually for the period, he took careful note of the position of, and association between, the man-made stone tools, the bones of extinct animals and human bones; but was unable to publish them. William Pengelly carried out further excavations between 1865 and 1880 and did publish his findings. He found a small group of implements including hand axes in a Lower Palaeolithic stratum together with a very large collection of bones of bear. In recent years, new work has been done on the site and radio-carbon dates obtained for some of the bones, and also uranium dating on stalagmites.

Kent's Cavern was again occupied by Upper Palaeolithic hunters during warmer periods of the last glaciation. The earliest radio-carbon date so far obtained for this phase of occupation is one of 30,900 ± 900 BP (before 1950) from a modern *homo sapiens* maxilla. This is now the oldest hominid to have been directly dated by the radio-carbon method. The date confirms the early arrival of *modern* humans in Britain. A date of 26,210 ± 435 BP was obtained from the tibia of a woolly rhinoceros which may have been associated with a

leaf-shaped point, several scrapers and a saw-edged point. Pengelly recovered several hundred artefacts which included bone and antler tools as well as flint blades and scrapers, amongst them items from the so-called 'Black Band' stratum. A bone piercer from the 'Black Band' has been dated to 12,320 ± 130 BP, and may, by implication, date a barbed point from the same level. The main animals of prey were probably wild horse, red deer and larger ungulates such as the aurochs. Bones of geese, swan, grouse, and ptarmigan also occur but it is not known whether these were introduced to the cave by humans or other predators. The barbed points may have been used to hunt land mammals as well as fish.

The cavern continued to be used as a shelter in more recent prehistoric times. Neolithic and Iron Age potsherds have been found there.

There is guided access to the caves but the faunal remains and stone implements are best seen in the Torquay Museum.

9

Merrivale Stone Rows
Late 3rd/early 2nd millennium BC

SX 554747. Walkhampton. S of the B3357, Tavistock–Princetown road, E of Merrivale Bridge

[A] EH

The group of Neolithic ceremonial monuments at Merrivale is one of the

finest of such groups and the most accessible on Dartmoor. The catalogue of monuments in this complex runs to two double stone rows and one single alignment, a small stone circle with two single standing stones near it, and a number of barrows and cairns associated with commemoration of the dead. There is also a particularly fine group of large prehistoric round huts of later date close by.

This is clearly one of a series of foci of ritual or ceremonial significance constructed, no doubt over a considerable period of time, around the end of the 3rd millennium BC. The stone monuments were erected at a time before the peat cover over Dartmoor was established. Stone rows have been described as the most distinctive monuments of prehistoric Dartmoor in particular. There are at least seventy known examples. They have not been satisfactorily dated or interpreted. One row has been excavated without, however, producing any dating evidence. It is clear that stone rows in general have undergone several phases of construction and were often built in association with cairns and barrows.

The northern of the Merrivale double rows is 596 ft (182 m) long, and the mean width between the rows is about 3 ft 6 in (1 m). Its eastern end is closed by a blocking stone. The stones themselves are small, the largest being little more than 3 ft (1 m) high. The southern double row overlaps the other at both ends and is not quite parallel to it. Its length is 865 ft (263.5 m). Very nearly half-way along the row is a ring of

Merrivale stone rows. EH

stones, the kerb of a barrow, 12 ft (3.7 m) in internal diameter, which interrupts the row. The east end is closed by a blocking stone. Both rows are roughly aligned east and west. The single row has a cairn at its northern end, and continues for 138 ft (42 m) in a roughly south-westerly direction, and is at an angle to the southern of the two double rows.

10

Rippon Tor Reaves
Bronze Age, mid-2nd millennium BC

SX 746755. SE of Hemsworthy Gate off the B3387 between Widecombe-in-the-Moor and Haytor Vale

[A]

During the Bronze Age, somewhere about 1700/1600 BC, an extensive system of land boundaries was laid out over much of Dartmoor. This seems to have been a single decision because the boundaries appear to be interdependent. The physical process was gradual and investigations have shown that the boundaries began as fences or earth banks but in time they became more permanent in the form of stone walls. The local name for these boundaries, defining field systems and wider land divisions, is reaves. Reaves may extend for miles across the moor in parallel with one another and they may cross land with little regard to the character of the terrain. They will usually finish with a cross 'terminal reave' on the upper slopes leaving the higher land for unenclosed grazing. Their existence over a wide area of Dartmoor (and they are now being recognised on Bodmin Moor and elsewhere), as well as similar forms of extensive forms of land division in other parts of the country, appears to indicate a high degree of social organisation. Reaves on Dartmoor form patterns which suggest the territorial arrangements of distinct communities. Each of these territories tended to be about 2 or 3 miles (3–4 km) in breadth and to include a single block of enclosed land laid out on a common axis. Their original sizes are hard to estimate since

large portions of the reaves have been incorporated into more recent field systems still in use today, or have been destroyed by cultivation.

The Rippon Tor system is the largest known field system in Britain, and it has been estimated that it may have covered a minimum of 3,300 ha with perhaps a further 1,400 ha, though its original extent to the south-east is unknown. It runs across the valley of the East Webburn and includes the later settlement of Widecombe-in-the-Moor itself. The reaves run in a north-west/south-east alignment and end on a terminal reave, roughly at right angles to the system on the upper slopes of Hameldown. The Dartmeet reave system meets it at right angles and marks the division between territories. Within the reave system as a whole are clusters of houses and settlement enclosures. The Rippon Tor system includes several

settlement areas, the best known of which is Foales Arrishes. Like the reaves themselves, the stone walls of the circular huts often have wooden predecessors. The analysis of this Bronze Age 'landscape' so far points to a large population living in dispersed farming settlements in a highly organised society with strong overall political control.

11

The Rumps
2nd–1st centuries BC

SW 934812. Polzeath, St Minver. By footpath from car park at Pentireglaze off road to New Polzeath

[A] NT

Headlands on precipitous cliffs can be economically fortified with defences

Rippon Tor reaves from the air. CUCAP

across the neck, and the coastline of Cornwall and Devon offers this advantage with some frequency. There are many promontory forts, or 'cliff castles' as they are often called, and they generally appear to be of Iron Age date. The most elaborately defended is that at Trevelgue Head, Newquay (C), which has six lines of defences. They have been described as being 'among the most striking and distinctive prehistoric works in the south-west' (Malcolm Todd, *The South-West To AD 1000*, London, 1987, p163). They seem to be fortified settlements of the same family as hillforts in an inland context. Previously they have been thought to be strongholds of coastal traders but in fact their hazardous situation usually makes them unsuitable as trading posts.

Of the promontory forts along the northern Cornish coast, The Rumps is among the most impressive and has had the advantage of recent archaeological excavation. This was concentrated upon the defences. There are three ramparts and ditches, which still survive as substantial earthworks, cutting off the interior which contained a number of hut platforms. One circular hut was excavated as well as the entrance to the fort. Three phases of construction were identified in the excavation.

12

Scillonian Chambered Tombs
Late 3rd–mid-2nd millennium BC

Isles of Scilly, principally St Mary's

[A] EH

The chambered tombs or entrance-graves of the Isles of Scilly are said to 'form one of the most remarkable groups of burial monuments in Europe'. Up to fifty survive, and many more will have been destroyed in the past. They are strikingly uniform in plan. Most of them are circular, with the base of the cairn retained by a kerb of massive stones on end or horizontally laid in rough courses. The rectangular chamber is similarly built and extends to the edge of the mound with an opening in the surrounding kerb. The chambers

Bant's Carn burial chamber, St Mary's, Isles of Scilly. EH

are roofed with large granite slabs. In some instances the cairn stands on a larger, circular, kerbed platform.

Even allowing for the fact that the present fragmented archipelago was a single substantial island in the 2nd millennium BC, the concentration of chambered tombs in such a small area is astonishing by mainland standards. The tombs also tend to be concentrated into distinct cemeteries. There are three main groups: along the eastern side of St Mary's, and two linear cemeteries on Sampson and Gugh. Other smaller groups are on Bryher and St Martin's with individual graves scattered elsewhere. Sometimes they are constructed against a rock outcrop or cairn. The upper cairn at Bant's Carn was constructed on the corner of an early terraced field.

Several tombs have been examined, most recently at Bant's Carn on Halangy Down, St Mary's (SV 910124) – perhaps the grandest of all – as part of the replacement of a fallen capstone. This is one of the tombs with a low, revetted outer platform. Other prominent tombs on St Mary's, at Porthellick Down and at Innisidgen, have been cleared of vegetation and made accessible. At Knackyboy Cairn, St Martin's, in 1950, the interior was found to be largely intact. It contained parts of twenty-two urns, six of them standing in two rows of

three near the inner end of the chamber and containing cremated bones. It has been estimated that the chamber's contents represent the remains of at least sixty individuals. Around, and partially over the urns was a mixture resembling the contents of a domestic midden including ash, charcoal, cremated bone, pottery sherds, beads and bronze fragments. The pottery and other objects found here and elsewhere have an end date somewhere in the mid- to late-2nd millennium BC. This suggests that the practice of collective burial continued to operate in Scilly long after it had gone out of use on the mainland.

The question inevitably arises: why such a concentration of chambered tombs in this small area? Gone are such notions as the 'islands of the dead'. It is suggested that some graves acted as markers for the land of the founding kin groups and were set among the fields if not on existing field boundaries. Charles Thomas in *Exploration of a Drowned Landscape* (London, 1985, p140), suggested that in a confined island community certain elements of ceremonial can become exaggerated. One might go further in supposing that the inbuilt conservatism of an island community, little affected by outside influences, meant an abnormally prolonged ritual practice which required the building of more and more new tombs as well as the continuing use of existing ones.

13

Trethevy Quoit
Late 3rd millennium BC

SX 259688. St Cleer. W of the B3254 from Liskeard to Launceston. Turning to Darite and Tremar, signposted

[A] EH

One of the finest stone burial chambers in the south-west, Trethevy Quoit is situated above the 700 ft (213 m) contour on a hill just off the southern edge of Bodmin Moor. In 1584 it was described by John Norden as 'a litle howse raysed of mightie stones, standing on a litle hill within a feilde' ('Description of Cornwall' (MSS), *c*.1610). There is still a slight mound around the chamber. Seven granite orthostats (stone slabs vertically set on edge) form a closed chamber and an antechamber. A single granite capstone 18 ft (5.5 m) long covers both chambers. It has a very steep pitch due to the collapse of the western supporting stone. The stone dividing the main chamber from the antechamber lacks a lower corner and provides a gap perhaps for access between the two. The capstone has a hole near its highest corner which is probably artificial.

Such megalithic tombs are believed to belong to the Neolithic period, perhaps of the late 3rd or early 2nd millennium BC. There is no record of any excavation or finds here.

Trethevy Quoit. EH

Roman, Early Christian and Anglo-Saxon Settlement

In the south-west there was no substantial cultural division between the pre-Roman Iron Age and the four centuries during which the institutions of the Roman Empire were imposed elsewhere. Apart from some fairly limited military activity during the 1st century AD, only one Roman town was established, and that hallmark of Romanisation, the country-house estate, or *villa*, was almost but not quite absent. The enclosed farming settlement, the 'round', was still the norm in Cornwall, though there was a shift towards a more oblong form of dwelling in place of the traditional round-house. Courtyard houses were adopted in west Cornwall (**Chysauster**, 14). The name used by the Romans to denote this territory was *Dumnonia*, of which *Isca* (Exeter) was the official capital. Within this tribal grouping of the *Dumnonii* were the *Cornovii* from whom Cornwall eventually got its name.

Much has been learnt recently about the development of Roman Exeter into a cantonal capital from the fortress established by the II Legion Augusta in the 50s AD. The remains of the legionary bath-house were found in the open area west of the cathedral, but are now reburied. The later Roman city expanded beyond the limits of the fortress and the existing town walls, and elements of today's street plan stem from it. More too is coming to light about the extent of the Roman military presence outside Exeter in the period 55–80 AD. The sites of three auxiliary forts are now known in Devon: Bury Barton (Lapford), North Tawton, and another near Okehampton. In Cornwall, only one is known at Nanstallon, near Bodmin. It has been partially excavated. Along the north coast of Devon are two signal stations built to keep watch on the seaborne activities of the Silures of South Wales (eg, **Martinhoe**, 20). Apart from the signal stations and masonry in the Exeter town wall there is, however, little

that is Roman readily visible. One class of monument with as much as five examples in Cornwall is the milestone, or more correctly, record of road maintenance, which survives in unexpected places such as Tintagel and the far west. Excavation has provided our knowledge on Roman Exeter and on the civil settlements which have been discovered in the region, such as the *villa* at Holcombe and a few other Roman sites in east Devon, or of the solitary house, possibly of a Romanised local official, at Magor in west Cornwall.

Following the official withdrawal of Roman armies and imperial administration from Britain in the mid-5th century, there is a long period for which historical and archaeological information is scant. There are references to kings of *Dumnonia* such as Constantine during the mid-6th century and memorials on stone using Latin terms and script. The slight and tantalising survivals of the early-medieval period are those pertaining to the establishment of Christianity from Celtic sources during the 5th and 6th centuries, and to the contemporary, perhaps princely, establishment at **Tintagel** (23, C). External influence seems to have come from two directions: through commercial contacts with north-west France and the Mediterranean world, and missionaries from Wales and Ireland. The appearance of high-quality tableware and oil and wine jars which originated in the eastern Mediterranean at such sites such as Tintagel show that there were centres of high status ready to trade in exotic goods. This was a period of considerable movement of people and ideas, from south Wales and Ireland into Devon and Cornwall, from Cornwall into what is now Brittany and parts of Iberia, and growing Anglo-Saxon pressure from Wessex.

Early Christianity in the south-west can best be seen in Cornwall where there

Chysauster. EH

Tintagel Castle from the west. EH

are remains of earth-banked enclosures, 'enclosed developed cemeteries', known as *lan*. This prefix among present place-names is an indication of early Christian centres. Stones with the Christian symbol using the initial letters for Christ in Greek (*chi-rho*) cut on them are other indications of early Christianity, as are the inscribed memorial stones, such as **King Doniert's Stone** (16, C) and those found at **Lewannick** (18, C). About twenty ecclesiastical establishments which took on a Celtic monastic form have been identified with some certainty in Cornwall and there were others in Devon. At Exeter, however, the Christian influence derived from the Roman mission established at Canterbury, and from West Saxon political power. Minsters were established here and at other places in east Devon in the 7th century. Exeter was the place where St Boniface received his training in 670–90. Remains of early Christianity are scarce and belong to the 8th century. Now that the deteriorating remains of the chapel of St Piran have had to be reburied for their own protection, the most visible example is that on **St Helen's** in the Isles of Scilly (22). The widespread use of carved crosses as Christian foci, as at **Copplestone** (15, D) or at **St Neot** (50, C), was a development of the 10th and later centuries.

In everyday life, changes were taking place in this nebulous post-Roman period. It is evident that there was a shift to more open farming settlements from the earlier enclosures known as 'rounds'. This is marked by a place-name shift from the *ker* applied to these enclosures to the *tref* and the more common prefix *tre*. Such Celtic place-names are almost only preserved in Cornwall – as the West Saxon penetration of Devon, and with it the use of English, was well advanced by the end of the 7th century. Cornwall – to Anglo-Saxons the land of the west Welsh – retained its own cultural identity for much longer. Military resistance was maintained until the West Saxon victories in the 9th century. 'Kings' such as Doniert or Dumgarth, continued to exist in Cornwall towards the end of the century, but under Athelstan, King of Wessex, Cornwall seems to have been administratively absorbed into its English neighbour after his military campaign of 936.

Political and social stability in the 10th and 11th centuries was threatened by destructive Viking raiding. Alfred, King of Wessex was the first to develop a system of fortified centres or *burhs* to act as resistance centres and also, it seems, to encourage markets and urban life. There were four in Devon: **Exeter** (26), Barnstaple (Pilton), **Totnes**

(Halwell) (32) and **Lydford** (19). Reorganisation of the church was also part of the West Saxon political settlement. Monasteries were revived under the reformed Benedictine rule, especially at Exeter and Tavistock; the unconventional Celtic monastic establishments were converted into collegiate churches, and it was in association with these, particularly Bodmin and St Stephens (Launceston) where the formal markets were established. Bishoprics were established at Crediton, Devon, in 909 and **St Germans** (51) in Cornwall in 926. Both sees were subsumed into that of **Exeter** (47) in 1050.

Very little remains in tangible form from this period prior to the Norman Conquest, apart from rare ecclesiastical structures such as the crypt at **Sidbury** (52, D), the elaborately decorated crosses (**Lanivet**, 17, C) or the burhgal defences of **Lydford** (19, D). Archaeological evidence for the nature of ordinary settlement scarcely exists. The 10th–11th-century settlement of **Mawgan Porth** (21, C) is therefore all the more remarkable.

14

Chysauster Courtyard-house Village
2nd century BC–5th century AD

SW 472350. Madron. Signposted from the B3311 at Badger's Cross. Footpath from car park

[A] EH

A particular type of Late Iron Age/Romano-British unenclosed settlement with courtyard-houses as the dominant house plan is found only in West Penwith and the Isles of Scilly.

The courtyard structure was usually oval in plan with a massive, stone-faced, surrounding wall of earth and rubble, and often 6–9 ft (1.8–2.7 m) thick. A doorway gave access to a central, open courtyard which was often paved, and around the courtyard a number of rooms were constructed against or into the enclosing wall. These rooms usually numbered three or four, though up to seven are known. The rooms themselves may have been circular, or long and narrow, with small recesses in the outer wall thickness. A large round or oval room was commonly found opposite the entrance containing a hearth, and which may be assumed to have been the main living area. This room often had a socket stone in the floor to take a roof support, and sometimes there were stone-lined boxes set into the floor. Some of the other rooms round the courtyard may have been for milking or tending animals. The better preserved houses show a high standard of construction: the masonry facing is laid to rough courses, interiors are often paved and have drains covered with stone slabs. The door at the main entrance was often hinged and pivoted in a stone socket.

Over twenty-five hamlets containing three to ten houses of this type have been located. There are more courtyard houses standing alone or within some kind of enclosure. The settlements are generally situated on hill-slopes close to one of the hillforts which dominate the high ground. They are often associated with terraced fields and these, together with the stone querns from hand mills found in the houses, indicate that the inhabitants grew cereal crops as well as rearing stock. There are often small enclosures, or garden plots attached to the houses.

Chysauster is the largest and best known of the courtyard-house settlements with good evidence for an associated field system. It is extremely well preserved with the walls standing up to 5–6 ft (2 m) high. It has also been excavated. Eight houses are arranged in pairs, as it were, along a street, and there are at least two more houses separate from the main group. An additional feature is an underground chamber known in Cornwall as a *fogou* or cave. That at Chysauster has not been examined in recent times and has had to be sealed for safety reasons. Its purpose is uncertain (*see Carn Euny*, 2, C).

Chysauster had a long life beginning in the 2nd century BC. However, it is clear that occupation continued throughout the Roman period and new buildings were being constructed in the 2nd and 3rd centuries AD. It provides a good example of a distinctive mixed-farming settlement in this distant part of Roman Britain.

15
Copplestone Cross
10th century

SS 771026. Colebrooke. At the junction of A377 with A3072 in the centre of the village
[D]

The late Saxon cross-shaft stands at the junction of the parishes of Colebrooke, Crediton and Down St Mary on the main

Copplestone cross. EH

Exeter–Barnstaple road. The *copelan stan* was an important boundary marker and is referred to in a charter of King Edgar in 974. It is not associated with a churchyard and its erection may be due to the Crediton bishopric. The granite shaft, which must have been brought at least 10 miles (15 km) from Dartmoor, stands 10 ft (3 m) high with interlace ornament decorating each of its faces. A niche inserted later near the top may have contained a small figure.

16
King Doniert's Stone
9th century

SX 236688. St Cleer. On a minor road between Redgate and Common Moor, 1 mile NW of St Cleer
[A] EH

A large, tapering but nearly rectangular cross-base, which bears the inscription *Doniert rogavit pro anima* 'Doniert has asked [prayers?] for [his] soul' within a panel on the broader face, stands within a walled enclosure beside the road. Side panels are filled with coarse interlaced ornament. It is supposed that Doniert is the same as *Dummnarth rex Cerniu*, 'King of Cornwall' whose drowning is recorded for the year 875 in the *Welsh*

Reconstruction drawing of Chysauster. EH

King Doniert's stone. EH

Annals. The stone has long been known as one of the curiosities of Cornwall and was illustrated by Norden in his *Description of Cornwall* (completed *c*.1610).

Alongside it is a taller broken cross-shaft with a panel of interlaced ornament. Both cross-bases have mortices for a shaft or a cross-head.

17

Lanivet Crosses and Hogsback Gravestone
5th/6th–11th century

SX 039644. Lanivet. Church in village off the A391

[A]

Lanivet is at the hub of early routes crossing from north and south as well as along the main spine route through Cornwall. This may have a bearing on the fact that the parish contains an unusual number of crosses in fields and at roadsides. The churchyard itself has its share of early memorials. A pillar stone of the 5th/6th century is by the south porch in the church. It is inscribed *ANNICU*. There is a tall cross-shaft to the west of the tower with primitive incised decoration including a male figure. There is also a fine wheel-cross with interlaced ornament and a cross-slab with the cross partly in relief and partly incised.

Additionally, there is the best example of only four coped or hogsback-shaped tombstones in Cornwall. These

have some similarities with the type of gravestone found in the Scandinavian parts of northern England – usually long narrow blocks, high in proportion with their width, often having a curved top with representations of shingles which reinforce their house-like appearance. The Lanivet example has a key pattern on the sides and top and an interlace motif at the ends. On the top, or 'roof', the key pattern is closed at each end by bear- or dog-like beasts. There is therefore the suggestion here and in other parts of Cornwall of some degree of Viking settlement in the 10th or 11th centuries.

18

Lewannick Churchyard and Inscribed Stones
Late 5th/early 6th century

SX 808276. Lewannick village *c*.5 miles SW of Launceston. Signposted from the A30

[A]

The earliest signs of Christianity in Cornwall are the *chi-rho* inscriptions and a number of other inscribed stones. Among these is a pair of memorials at

Inscribed stone in Lewannick churchyard. E BERRY

Lewannick, one now in the church and the other in the churchyard. These suggest influences both from the Mediterranean region and from the north, from Ireland in particular.

The Lewannick stones employ both Roman capitals and ogham lettering. Ogham script was evolved in southern Ireland and occasionally occurs in Wales and England. It consists of unconnected vertical strokes across an angle of squared stone. It can be fairly closely dated, and in this case suggests that the churchyard at Lewannick would have been in existence by the late 5th or early 6th century. The stone now standing within the west end of the church is inscribed *'IACIT VIIAGNI'* (Here lies Viiagnus) and that on the south side of the churchyard, *'INGENAUI MEMORIA'* (The memorial of Ingenauus). The use of the word *memoria* is interesting since it is a technical term especially common in North Africa and occuring at only two other places in Britain.

The earliest form of the place-name is Lanwennac (*c*.1120). The personal name element, in this case, Gwenek, may be that of the secular founder, the first priest, or a saint. Gwenek is equivalent to the Breton saint, Guenoc. The prefix *lan* relates to an early ecclesiastical enclosure, often a cemetery, sometimes a monastery or church. The word *memoria* on one of the Lewannick stones implies a special grave within the cemetery.

Where the *lan* survives today as a physical feature it is often represented by the embanked enclosure of a churchyard, frequently but by no means exclusively, round or oval in shape. Since they have been used for burials over many centuries, the enclosed area is generally several feet above the ground level outside. The ditch outside the enclosing bank often becomes a lane running round the perimeter. Lewannick churchyard with its traces of external bank and its interior high above street level provides one of the best examples of this type of early Christian enclosure in Cornwall.

Right: cross-shaft in Lanivet churchyard, west of the church. RIC

19

Lydford
10th–11th century

SX 510848. Signposted from A386
Tavistock–Okehampton road

[A] EH

Lydford lies on the western edge of
Dartmoor. While it is not on any main
road it does occupy a highly defensible
position on a wedge-shaped promontory
with the deep gorge of the River Lyd on
the south and a very steep-sided valley
on the north-west. It appears in an early
10th-century list of *burhs*, or fortified
towns, created by King Alfred and his
successors to protect the Saxon
kingdom of Wessex, and was the most
westerly. In the late 10th and early 11th
centuries it was a place of some
importance, and a Danish Viking raid up
the Tamar and Tavy was driven off at
Lydford in 997. The town was one of the
four original boroughs of Devon (the
others being Exeter, Barnstaple and
Totnes) and like them it possessed a
royal mint. Its coins are known from the
reign of Ethelred II (979–1016) to that of
Edward the Confessor (1042–66). Like
the other boroughs it had an early
Norman fortification planted within it.

Lydford is likely to have been a place
of significance before it became part of
the strategic thinking of the Saxon kings
of Wessex. The church is dedicated to St
Petrock, the most popular of the Celtic
saints in the south-west. Excavations in
the castle produced a scrap of pottery of
a sort derived from the eastern
Mediterranean in the 5th or 6th century
AD, and found in some profusion at
Tintagel. It may denote a site of high
social status. Not far away at Sourton,
beside the main east–west road (A30) is
an inscribed stone with three lines of
Roman capitals which have been read as
PRINCIPI VIRIVCI AVDETI. The use of
the word *princeps* implies someone of
power, perhaps a local ruler, with his
seat in the close vicinity during the 6th
century.

The physical remains of the Saxon
fortified town are impressive. Cutting off
the promontory is a substantial earth
bank, which is best seen in the field

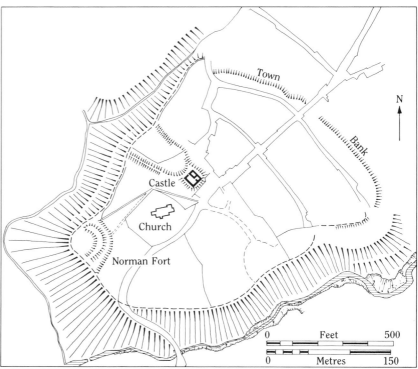

Lydford Saxon town and Castle. EH

behind the Nichol Hall. Excavation has
shown that there were two main phases
in the defences. The initial construction
was a rampart consisting of alternate
layers of turves and saplings on which
was a fighting platform made of
substantial squared timbers. In the later
phase, the front of the rampart was faced
with mortared granite blocks. The line
of turf-built rampart continued round
the edge of the promontory below the
early Norman castle and under the
bailey rampart of Lydford Castle.

Inside the defences are the elements
of the early street plan. The principal
street, as today, runs down the spine of
the promontory, past the castle and
church, to the gorge. At right angles to
it can still be seen three pairs of parallel
side-lines which are probably part of the
original layout. The first of these lanes is
immediately behind the cross rampart,
and others can still be detected between
later houses. Excavation has shown
further fenced subdivisions at right
angles to the late-Saxon street grid,
serving as property boundaries.

20

Martinhoe Fortlet
1st century AD

SX 664494. Martinhoe. Approached
by a track leading NW from the
village, thence by footpath across
fields

[B]

There are two early Roman fortlets, or
signal stations, on the Exmoor coast on
either side of Lynmouth: Old Burrow to
the east and Martinhoe to the west. They
are among the most conspicuous Roman
military works in the south-west. Both
were clearly sited to observe the Bristol
Channel and South Wales. They are not
intervisible and others may still be found
in what might be a system of observation
points. They are similar in size and in
the form of their defences. The fortlet
proper is square with double ramparts
and ditches. It is enclosed by a roughly
circular outer rampart and ditch about
70 ft (21 m) distant from the inner

Martinhoe Roman signal station (after A Fox). EH

A   postholes for gate
B   ovens

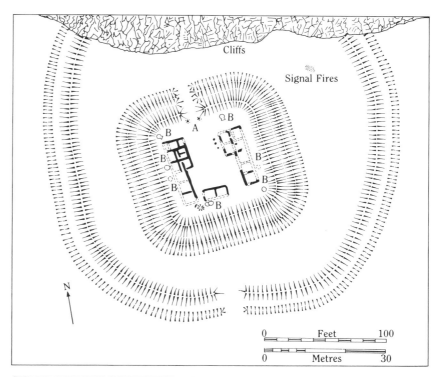

work. The entrances in the two earthwork enclosures are on opposite sides for greater security.

The fortlet at Martinhoe has been excavated in recent years. It appears to have been occupied during the Neronian and early Flavian period (54–75 AD). The garrison was 80-strong, a 'century', accommodated in two parallel ranges of wooden barrack blocks divided into small rooms. There were additional rooms at one end for the officer, a 'centurian', in charge. Ovens were let into the back of the turf rampart. Another small building was placed at right angles to the barracks and may have been used for workshops. A possible place for signal fires was located towards the cliff edge within the outer enclosure.

21

Mawgan Porth Early Medieval Settlement
10th–11th century

SW 850673. St Mawgan. B3276 to Mawgan Porth. On the uphill edge of a miniature golf course N of the road to St Mawgan

[B]

Mawgan Porth is at the mouth of the Vale of Lanherne which, in the early Middle Ages, must have been a broad tidal inlet. On the north side, and now lying overgrown on the edge of a miniature golf course, is an exceedingly rare monument – the partially excavated remains of a settlement belonging to the 10th and 11th centuries AD. It was discovered by chance in an evaluation of the site prior to proposed building development in 1949. More extensive excavations took place in the 1950s.

The significance of the site chiefly lies in the detail of the buildings from a period of history about which little is known in terms of physical remains. The most fully excavated of at least four complexes of buildings (three of which

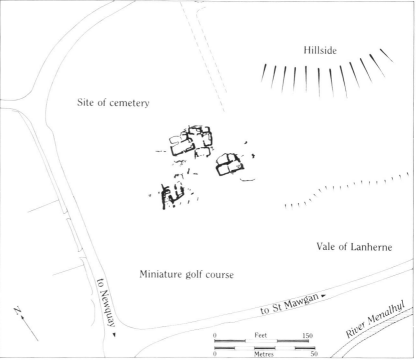

Mawgan Porth. EH

have been substantially excavated) consisted of four main structures, each rectangular, and set around a central rectangular courtyard. The principal building was similar to later medieval long-houses in the south-west in that cattle were housed at the lower end with people living at the higher end, and all under the same roof. The byre had a drain that ran out in the south-west corner. The living-room had some degree of order. It had a floor that was smooth and flat unlike the broken and eroded floor of the byre. In the angles on either side of the end door, which opened into the courtyard, were box-beds enclosed by slate slabs set on edge. Small 'boxes' also defined by slates on edge set along other walls seemed to be storage bins. There was a central hearth. This room had an annex to the north with a small back room opening off it. Other rooms around the courtyard also showed signs of domestic use with box-beds and hearths, but they were not all constructed at the same time. A little way downhill to the south was another

arrangement of houses around a courtyard of similar form, and there was another group of buildings to the south-west. The settlement had a life of about a hundred years. There was no dramatic end, and it seemed to the excavator that the inhabitants had simply packed up and left at leisure.

Uphill and to the west of the settlement, and surprisingly close to it, was a burial ground containing the skeletons of men, women and children. Twenty-three graves were excavated and it can be assumed that there were more.

22

St Helen's Oratory
8th–12th century AD

SV 901169. St Helen's, Isles of Scilly. Access by arrangement with boatman

[B]

St Helen's is one of the small islands along the northern edge of the

Scillonian archipelago. It was known as *Insula Sancti Elidii* during the Middle Ages. It is now chiefly remarkable for the Early Christian settlement on its lower southern slope. As a site associated with an early 'saint', it was reverenced and maintained during the 11th and 12th centuries. It is still one of the best surviving examples of an early ecclesiastical establishment in England.

The settlement has been partially excavated, and subsequent research has pointed to two main phases of activity. The first is represented by a small rectangular building with a doorway in its long south side. It is complete with internal benching and, at the east end, a raised step supports the remains of an altar which, on its south side, had a stone-lined cavity probably intended to contain a holy relic, presumably of the founder, St Elidius. This building is seen as an oratory or chapel, very likely of 8th-century date. The possibility of a timber predecessor was not examined in the excavation, though an earlier structural phase of this kind is sometimes found elsewhere, and this has been suggested for the similar chapel on the little island of Tean close by. Elsewhere, within a roughly oval stone enclosure wall, were up to six graves, neatly edged with granite slabs, and also a circular stone-walled hut or cell. This conjunction of circular hut, tiny chapel and burials all within an enclosure is paralleled at other Early Christian sites in Western Scotland and Ireland.

The second phase dates from the 11th century when the site seems to have possessed a resident cleric, and a more substantial church was built within the enclosure to the south-west of the oratory. A little later, during the first half of the 12th century when the site was the responsibility of Tavistock Abbey, the church was enlarged by the addition of a northern aisle, perhaps, it has been suggested, to enclose the founder's grave and encourage pilgrimage to the site. This may explain why the early hut was also restored at the same time. A new entrance was made in the now more convenient eastern side so that the faithful could have easier access from the church. The

The oratory and settlement at St Helen's, Isles of Scilly (after H E O'Neil). EH

Natural granite boulders
Walling

enclosing wall was now brought closer to link with the round hut, and within the circuit were three small rectangular houses providing for those clerics serving this place of pilgrimage.

23

Tintagel Castle
Late 5th/early 6th–13th century

SX 050890. Tintagel. Footpath from the village, then by steep steps to the Island

[A] EH

Tintagel is one of the 'wonders' of the south-west. Its coastal setting is spectacular and it is a place around which legends grow. Geoffrey of Monmouth, who wrote *History of the Kings of Britain* in about 1139, made Tintagel the palace of Gorlois, Duke of Cornwall, where the future King Arthur was conceived, but stories widespread in medieval Europe had Tintagel as the palace of King Mark, and gave it a place in the Tristan and Isolde legend. The 19th-century poems of Alfred, Lord Tennyson have helped to sustain the Arthurian legend to the present day. The visible remains too are clouded in uncertainty. The last half-century has witnessed two quite distinct interpretations of the earliest remains, one claiming it to be a Celtic monastery, and the other, the seat of a post-Roman chieftain. The common factor behind both literary legends and archaeological interpretations is the fact that this is a site of very great significance in the immediate post-Roman/early Christian period.

The latest feature is the castle and it is the most obvious 'monument'. It is now believed that the castle was built by Richard, Earl of Cornwall, and younger brother of Henry III, shortly after acquiring the manor of Bossiney, which included Tintagel, in exchange for other lands in 1236. It was little more than a lordly seaside residence, rather than a castle of military significance. Although the 'chasm' separating the Upper and Lower Wards on the mainland, and the hall and residential block on the Island, was not so great then as now, it is still an idiosyncratic design. With the death of

Tintagel Castle. EH

Richard in 1272, the castle was only fitfully maintained and in 1540 Leland described it as a ruin.

The more difficult problem lies with the clusters of small, low, rectangular structures on cliff terraces or on the plateau of the Island, especially around the chapel. Many of these were exposed and consolidated during the 1930s when they were assumed to be the remains of a large Celtic Christian monastery. This interpretation is still to be found in current literature but there is now an alternative point of view. This argues that there is in fact nothing on the site which positively supports the case for a monastery of the 5th to 7th centuries. There are now known to be many more buildings (at least 170) as a result of observations made following a disastrous fire in 1983, and they represent a considerable sequence in both structure and time. A factor which must influence any interpretation is the presence in very large numbers of broken wine and oil jars, fine red dishes and tableware, derived from late 5th- and 6th-century North Africa and the Aegean. Such luxuries imply a site of

very high status, and coupled with the traditions on which Geoffrey of Monmouth built his story of King Arthur, is this indeed the seat of a post-Roman chieftain or petty king? It might also explain why Richard of Cornwall was so anxious to obtain the site in 1236. Was he consciously identifying himself with the legendary King Arthur by building himself a romantically sited 'castle' on a site associated with the tradition?

Another factor has to be brought into the 'mystery' surrounding Tintagel and that is the church on the cliff, distant from the present village, and the two late Roman 'milestones', one of which is in the church. Why was there a road near this inhospitable stretch of coast and away from the main routes? The church is a well-preserved Norman structure in its own right but the churchyard contains early burial mounds. Two were opened in 1942, and were found to contain slate-lined graves; they may be the clue to the earliest manifestations of Christianity at Tintagel, rather than the castle site and its traditions of early kings.

3

Towns

Remove Plymouth, Exeter, Exmouth and the conurbation of Torbay and there are no towns in Devon and Cornwall with a population greater than 20,000. Yet the south-west is full of small market towns. Villages in the more familiar English sense are uncommon. These small towns are essentially either inland markets or coastal trading ports serving a dispersed settlement pattern. Nearly all, however, were deliberate creations rather than settlements which grew up spontaneously, and were initially populated by as many foreigners as local people.

The factor influencing the creation of new markets was the lack of a market within a radius of 6 miles. This was the argument put forward by petitioners from St Austell in the 1630s: 'There is neither markett or faire within the mannor, but the town is fitt for both especially being soe remote from markett townes' (A H Shorter, W L D Ravenhill and K J Gregory, *Southwest England*, London, 1969, p119). The nearest markets were Tregoney, Grampound and Lostwithiel, all said to be 6 miles away. A market was granted in 1661 and this had a corresponding effect on its neighbours. By 1716 Tregoney was said to be 'a poor market town of good note before St Austell was made a market', and the burgesses of **Fowey** (28, C) had a similar complaint. This pattern of interlocking circles of 5- or 6-mile radii can be plotted across the south-west, with substantial gaps only in areas of harsh upland country with sparse settlement like Bodmin Moor or Dartmoor. Physical barriers such as estuaries divided the hinterland, leading to the development of medieval towns on opposite sides of a harbour: **Fowey** and Polruan, **West** and **East Looe** (25, C), and **Dartmouth** (24, D) and Kingswear.

Exeter (26) retained something of its urban nature following the breakdown of Roman administration in the 5th century. Other than Exeter, the emergence of towns in the south-west in

the 10th century arose from the defensive needs of the West Saxon kings in the face of sustained Viking attack. The four fortified centres, or *burhs*, were well-sited from the point of view of their defence – Exeter with its Roman town walls at the head of the Exe estuary was by the year 1000 already a major city, Pilton (D) on the north coast on the Taw, Halwell (D) on the south between the Avon and the Dart, and Lydford (19, D) as the western outpost. Cornwall was excluded from this defensive strategy.

The *burhs* had an economic purpose as well. As a result Barnstaple succeeded Pilton, and **Totnes** (32), Hallwell, as towns. Lydford has traces of a planned street system (though it was to be an urban failure) and all four were official mints. The development of markets linked to particular population centres came later to Cornwall through the initiative of the more important religious establishments (Bodmin, **Launceston** (29) (St Stephen's) and St Germans (51)). The Domesday Book indicates that Bodmin was a borough in 1066 with Helston possibly as another.

The change of political and economic masters arising from the Norman Conquest saw the exploitation of the money revenues of markets and fairs as a useful addition to labour services owed from land. The Count of Mortain was adept at bringing existing markets into his own control (Launceston and Trematon (C), as well as establishing new ones (Liskeard (C)). Other lords established markets at an early date (Okehampton (D) and Tregoney (C)). Throughout the 12th century, leading landholders, religious and lay, sought to improve their finances by creating markets and fairs on their estates, though long-term success could not be guaranteed. Among the earliest towns were those at the head of estuaries or navigable rivers which could be reached by water transport and could serve an inland market. The silting of the estuaries with the detritus of tin streaming eventually cut off these places

A medieval street in East Looe. RCHME

from the sea. **Truro** (33, C) therefore succeeded Tregoney and was in its turn disadvantaged by Penryn and later **Falmouth** (27, C).

By the 13th century, especially under John, the Crown was increasingly willing to grant formal charters to towns allowing a considerable degree of self-government and freedom to set and exact tolls. This had taxation advantages for the royal revenues. For this reason many of these towns sent members to Parliament from the 14th century onwards, and at this time there were thirty-seven boroughs in Cornwall and ninety-one in Devon. The control of the tin industry too demanded centres where tin could be assayed and taxed. Stannary or coinage towns were established (Ashburton, Chagford, Plympton, and **Tavistock** (31) in Devon; Bodmin, Lostwithiel, Helston, and Truro in Cornwall). Administrative needs could require an urban base: the stannary courts and prison were held at Lydford (40), which doubled up as the centre for the administration of the Forest of Dartmoor. The earldom of Cornwall moved its administrative and financial base to Lostwithiel at the end of the 13th century. Stimulated by the Bordeaux wine trade and the export of tin and cloth, coastal towns advanced in wealth and power. Few medieval south-western towns were walled, namely: Barnstaple, Totnes and Exeter in Devon, and Launceston in Cornwall. Coastal ports organised defences of different kinds: Fowey, **Plymouth** (30) and Dartmouth.

The economic upturn for cloth manufacturing in the 15th and 16th century saw a rebirth of Devonshire towns. Exeter was the most important but other centres were Tavistock, South Molton and Totnes and there was a consequent rise in civic pride in such places as Tiverton and Cullompton. The Newfoundland fisheries revived Dartmouth, and in the 16th and 17th centuries there was an increase in the number of incorporated towns. Devon had more than Yorkshire by the end of the 17th century, and was only second to Cornwall in its notorious number of parliamentary boroughs. Other industries had their influence, such as

shipbuilding at Topsham (D) and Appledore (D). With tin and copper mining as the predominant industry in 18th- and 19th-century Cornwall, urban centres of a new kind sprang from earlier settlements, together with new ports for the export of minerals and import of coal and lime. New towns were created at Falmouth and at Dock (Devonport) to serve Atlantic commerce and the needs of a naval base. In the 18th century Dock became the largest

town in Devon, and eventually became part of Plymouth.

Another form of urban growth began in the mid-18th century – the seaside resort. By the 1790s, Exmouth (D) was the most frequented watering place followed by Sidmouth (D), Dawlish (D) and Teignmouth (D). Because the Royal Navy made a practice of anchoring in Tor Bay before the construction of the Breakwater made Plymouth Sound safer, Torquay became fashionable for

Butterwalk, Dartmouth, before wartime bomb damage and later restoration. RCHME

the wives of naval officers and subsequently a favoured place for retirement. The north coast developed later, though Lynmouth (D) had its wealthy visitors in the early 19th century. The coming of railways influenced the fortunes of towns greatly, particularly through the development of mass tourism. This affected the south-coast towns most but it also saw the making of places like Ilfracombe and Newquay. The railway also killed many old market towns which could not be reached by train and which were replaced by new settlements on the lines.

While Exeter, Plymouth and, on a smaller scale, Truro and Barnstaple, dominate their particular regions, the urban structure as a whole is presently in a state of flux with the decline of the old centres as places of bulk shopping and as 'out of town' hypermarkets or malls develop in their place.

24
Dartmouth

Townstall is the parent settlement of Dartmouth on the hill behind the present town. Originally, the major port on the River Dart was Totnes. Yet from the early 13th century, the name Dartmouth was applied to the harbour town which grew from two riverside settlements either side of an inlet known as the Mill Pool. Hardness was to the north, and Clifton to the south, both connected by the mill dam now known as Foss Street. The Pool was reclaimed after 1815 and provided the site for the market-place. The reason for the early-medieval urban development towards the mouth of the estuary was the value of the deep water anchorage. It was here that the English contingent for the Second Crusade assembled in 1147 and again in 1190 for the Third Crusade. Around 1200, a borough was formally created. The town gradually expanded to the south along the waterside and the suburb of Southtown was established by the 14th century.

Dartmouth came into commercial prominence with the growth of the wine trade with south-west France and the counterbalancing growth of the Devon cloth trade. In 1346, the port was able to supply 31 ships for the siege of Calais. The most notorious of the medieval merchants was John Hawley, who was probably the model for the Shipman in Chaucer's *Canterbury Tales*. After a decline during the later Middle Ages, prosperity was regained in the period 1580–1643. This arose from the development of the Newfoundland fishing trade and a revival of the cloth trade. It led to the construction of the New Quay further out into the river in 1584–5. Some of the new buildings fronting this quay still remain such as the refronted Castle Hotel and the Butterwalk. The present line of the waterfront is an embankment of 1885.

Dartmouth could never compete with other south coast ports as a potential naval base because of the narrow entrance to the Haven, nor as a trans-Atlantic terminal, though for twenty years in the late 19th century there was a fast and regular steamship service to South Africa and Australia. Poor railway communications was another problem. One lasting development was the establishment of the Royal Naval College, first in training ships in the harbour in 1863, and later in the grandiose structure built by Sir Aston Webb in 1902–5.

The defences at the mouth of the Haven are described elsewhere. Within the town is a fort of the early 16th century at Bayard's Cove protecting the inner harbour. In the church are fine 15th-century screens and a west gallery of 1633. There is a brass to John Hawley (d.1408) and his two wives. The south door bears remarkable ironwork of the late-14th century, probably repaired in 1631, in the form of a sprouting tree with the trunk crossed by figures of two leopards. The town is still full of good buildings and retains much of its early street plan. The only complete medieval house in Dartmouth is the Cherub off Higher Street. Many of the late-medieval and Tudor merchants' houses, including John Hawley's, later used as a guildhall, were demolished to make Newcomen Road as a new exit from the town in 1865. Also demolished in this scheme was the house of Thomas Newcomen,

The Old Cottage Restaurant, East Looe.
E BERRY

the designer of the first industrial steam engine in 1712. The oldest surviving Newcomen engine is preserved as a memorial to him in Coronation Park.

25
East Looe

East and West Looe, separated by an estuary which forms a harbour, are among the many planted boroughs introduced into Cornwall in the early Middle Ages. First mention of them is in 1201. By 1411, they were joined by the earliest of the estuary bridges of Devon and Cornwall. When Celia Fiennes crossed it in 1698 the bridge had 14 arches. 'This is a pretty bigg seaport', she wrote (*The Illustrated Journeys of Celia Fiennes 1685–c.1712*, ed. Christopher Morris, London, 1982, p203). This bridge was pulled down in 1853 and the present one stands about a hundred yards upstream of it. Fishing is still the important industry despite the distractions of tourism.

The remarkable feature of East Looe is its planned grid of streets which retain their medieval pattern because their narrowness has virtually excluded the motor car. The town was sited on a sand spit on a former course of the river. Springing off the main street parallel to the river are four closely set parallel streets whose functions are indicated by the names Higher, Middle and Lower Market Streets. Most of the houses had cellars, or ground floors which were 3 or 4 ft below street level. Many of the houses were timber fronted, richly carved and with decorative plastering. The side walls were of stone, and thus a means of fire prevention. Several of these houses can be recognised though others will be disguised by later frontages. One is dated 1555, another 1632 with six-light oriel windows on the first floor. The Guildhall is thought to have been built c.1500. There is now no visible trace of the 18th-century gun batteries at Churchend. Likewise, the town's political representation dwindled in the 19th century, with the abolition of its two Parliamentary seats in 1832.

26
Exeter

Exeter as a historic town has undergone three major disasters in the course of the last fifty years. The first was the German bombing in May 1942 when some 38 acres of the built-up area suffered total destruction or serious damage. The other two were self-inflicted: further destruction and dismal rebuilding in the course of regeneration in the 1950s, and a further bout of destruction of historic buildings and street plan in the 1970s and 1980s in the cause of inner city redevelopment. As a result, one may find individual buildings and some areas of great interest, but what was once one of the country's major historic towns is now only a gathering of fragments.

Exeter's origins lie in a Roman legionary fortress established in the 50s AD on a steep-sided ridge above the lowest bridgeable crossing of the Exe. The impressive legionary bath-house was discovered by excavation below Cathedral Green and backfilled. After c.75 AD, the cantonal capital of *Isca Dumnoniorum* was created on the site of the fortress. This was the only Roman town in the south-west and its role as

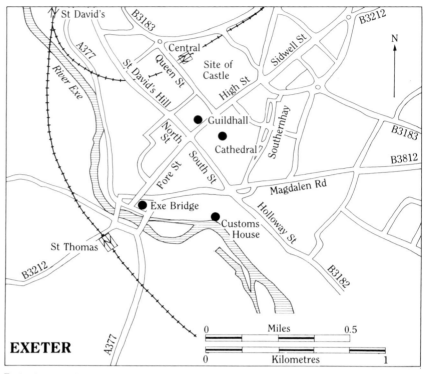

Exeter town centre map. EH

the regional capital continues to this day. The town expanded in the 2nd century and its walls have remained to influence the development of urban life throughout the Middle Ages. Roman masonry can still be seen (underpinned by medieval and later facing) in the length of City Wall to the west of South Street.

Despite the breakdown of Roman administration in the 5th century, urban life of a sort continued. Exeter was one of the four 9th-century fortified towns (*burhs*) in Devon. Although the bishopric did not move to Exeter until 1050, there had been a monastery here in the 680s at which St Boniface was educated. The Norman Conquest saw the planting of a castle in the northern corner (Rougemont) of the walled town. The surviving gate-tower is of great interest in view of its early date and the Saxon style of its triangular-headed windows. The Cathedral (47) and those monuments of civic success – the Guildhall (39), Exe Bridge (101) and the Customs House (38) are described

elsewhere in this book. The wealth of medieval Exeter merchants still appears in a few individual houses. The parish churches were mostly rebuilt in the 14th and 15th centuries as a result of the City's increasing prosperity. The 15th-century Tuckers' Hall was the guildhall of the weavers, fullers and shearmen, and represents the source of much of that wealth. Wynyard's Almshouses (1463), much restored in the 19th century, lie off Magdalen Street.

Among the early religious buildings are the remains of the west range of the 11th-century St Nicholas Priory (The Mint) and St Pancras Church. Many of the medieval churches were small and on cramped sites, leading to the erratic siting of towers. The wealth of the cathedral establishment is more obviously seen in the opulent houses of various dates around the Cathedral Close. Many of these are basically medieval, constructed on a courtyard plan, and contain elaborate and decorative carpentry in their roof construction. The 'Law Library' at no. 8

is a particularly good example. An initiative of the Cathedral establishment was the system of underground passages, or conduits, parts of which are accessible, which were cut to provide a direct water supply to the precinct in the 13th century.

Exeter's prosperity in the 16th and 17th centuries was based on the textile trade and its position as a port. Restriction of the river by the building of weirs, together with the development of larger ships, had seen its role usurped by Topsham, lower down the Exe. In 1566, a canal was completed which by-passed the obstacles and was the first in England to employ a pound-lock. A new quay and warehouse were created, and later the 17th-century Quay House was built to allow loading of cargo under cover. Customs rights were acquired by the end of the 17th century, and the splendid Customs House was the result.

Daniel Defoe commented not only on Exeter's trade and manufactures but also as a town 'full of gentry and good company' (*A Tour through the Whole Island of Great Britain*, Everyman Edition, London, 1974, p222). Commercial prosperity declined in the 18th century with the industrialisation of the cloth trade but Exeter kept its place as a social centre. The Assembly Rooms (Royal Clarence Hotel) were built in 1769, and the Palladian Sessions House occupied the interior of the castle in 1773. The Devon and Exeter Hospital had been built in Southernhay in 1743. Associated with these public improvements were new brick-built houses and terraces in the London manner. Bedford Circus is no more but there are still good examples to be found. New suburbs in Regency style, such as Pennsylvania Park, grew up around the turn of the century.

New markets were built in the 1830s, and the facade of the neo-Greek Higher Market has been retained amid drastic modern developments. The Royal Albert Museum and Art Gallery of 1865 in a Venetian Gothic style dominates Queen Street which was a new road towards the north. An earlier improvement in communications was the building of a cast-iron bridge in 1835 across the valley of the Long Brook, to avoid the steep descent and ascent of the old road to the north, which Queen Street came to replace. The modern road solution carves through the south-west quarter of the old town in brutal fashion.

27
Falmouth

The town of Falmouth is a relatively modern creation. Its charter of incorporation was granted in 1661 and the first urban glimmerings were little more than fifty years earlier. It owes its existence to the value of the Haven as one of the largest and secure natural harbours in the British Isles, and to the decision to fortify the entrance in 1539 as part of Henry VIII's scheme of coastal defence.

The only settlement then was the manor house of the Killigrews, Arwennack, a fragment of which still remains. Little changed until Sir John Killigrew was persuaded by Sir Walter Raleigh to develop a town which would cater not just for the garrison of Pendennis Castle but also for the ships using the haven. In spite of opposition from the long established town of Penryn a little higher up the Fal, royal permission was obtained for building

Exeter Castle gatehouse. EAU

Falmouth Custom House. E BERRY

four inns at Smithick or Pennycomequick in 1613. This move was given impetus in 1626 by the start of a mail service between Pendennis and Plymouth and thence to London. After the Civil War, a market and two annual fairs were permitted. The customs collection was also moved from Penryn. In 1661, the town took the name of Falmouth, and from then on its population grew quickly. Development was further influenced by the establishment of the packet station in 1689, which was a transatlantic and Iberian communications service lasting until 1850. By the 18th century, Falmouth was the largest trading port in Cornwall. The coming of the railway in 1863 brought a new industry, tourism, and the building of the Falmouth Hotel in 1865, close to the railway station and in a commanding position overlooking the sea, took advantage of it. After the First World War ship repairing was developed on a large scale and this has remained a major industry.

The early town lay at the foot of a steep hill to form a long, narrow main street described in 1859 as 'of a mean appearance straggling along the side of the water'. In the 19th century the town expanded at right angles up the valley known as 'The Moor'. The modern town faces both the harbour and the sea with the docks and Pendennis in between.

The church of King Charles the Martyr of 1662–4 followed upon recognition of urban status. It is a curious mixture of classical styles and the traditions of late Cornish gothic. There are other 17th-century survivals, such as the house in Bell's Court now occupied by the Maritime Museum. Some good 18th-century buildings are

in Church Street, Bank Place, and at the far end of Arwennack Street and the beginning of Grove Place, where there is a handsome brick-built terrace using chequerboard patterns with vitrified brick headers. Of the public buildings, the early 19th-century Custom House with Greek Doric portico and its large brick stack for burning contraband tobacco gives meaning to Custom House Quay. In Church Street is the Royal Cornwall Polytechnic Hall of 1833. Of private houses the most significant is Marlborough House built at the beginning of the 19th century by Captain Bull of the West India Packet Service. Early-19th-century stucco terraces face Flushing. The growing resort developed the sea frontage behind Gyllyngvase, and was accompanied by tropical gardens and the construction of Castle Drive round Pendennis Head in 1865.

28

Fowey

To Celia Fiennes, Fowey was 'a narrow stony town the streetes very close' (*The Illustrated Journeys of Celia Fiennes*, p204). It takes its name from the river and owes its foundation to the neighbouring Tywardreath Priory. The prior granted the town a charter in 1190. It is likely that from the start it

had a cosmopolitan population, and even in 1439 there were 27 alien householders in the borough. During the 14th century, the town prospered greatly and it was able to send as many as 47 ships and 770 men to the king's fleet at the siege of Calais in 1347. Fowey acquired a reputation for trade and piracy. It is not very surprising that retaliation followed. On at least two occasions in the 14th century and, more particularly, in 1457, the town was attacked and burnt. As a result, the successors to the stewards of Tywardreath Priory, who had built Place House beside the church, fortified the house against future attacks. A pair of square blockhouses (that on the Polruan side still remains nearly to full height) guarded the ends of a chain boom across the harbour. In the following century, St Catherine's Castle was constructed at the harbour mouth. These defences continued to be maintained so that in an appeal for special privileges in 1684 to Charles II the townspeople could say that the defences and the town were 'very ruinous through the damage of the late wars [1667]' (Charles Henderson, *Essays in Cornish History*, Oxford, 1935, p40).

The medieval town consisted of a long winding street parallel to the water from the bottom of Lostwithiel Street to the Bodinnick ferry passage. Early maps indicate that the river bank was walled.

Fowey, with the church and Place House on the left. E BERRY

The present church dates from after 1336 when its predecessor was destroyed in a raid. It is unusual for Cornwall in that it retains its 14th-century style. The tower and the porch were added in about 1460. Place House has been associated with the Treffry family since the 15th century. Although strongly fortified with a substantial tower, which is shown on a 1540 map of south-western coastal defences, the house was virtually rebuilt in the early 19th century in a romantic gothic style.

There are within the town a number of interesting buildings. The Old Town Hall has late-medieval windows and was thought to be the remains of a chapel of St Mary. At a later date it was used as a town prison and now serves as town museum. On the Town Quay, the house now called 'Frenchman's Creek' which has a late-medieval roof has been suggested as the early Havenor's Hall. The Ship Hotel in Lostwithiel Street has Elizabethan panelling and vaulted plaster ceilings. It was then the town house of the Rashleigh family. Below The King of Prussia is the old market-place fronted by granite columns.

In the 19th century, expansion took place southwards towards the sea, and hotels and lodging houses established themselves here. Close to the passage to the Polruan ferry is a large square, creeper-covered house which was for long the home of 'Q', Sir Arthur Quiller Couch, whose 'Troy Town' novels did so much to endear the town to Edwardian tourists. The arrival of the railway had the effect of turning the northern part of the town into an industrial area, and Fowey became a major port for the shipping of china-clay.

29

Launceston

Dunheved, as Launceston was previously known, was the creation of Robert, Count of Mortain. By 1086, he had removed the existing market from the canons of St Stephen's, on the hilltop a mile to the north, to his castle. In time, the name, Lan Stefan, was also acquired by the new town. By virtue of its association with the earldom of

Cornwall, Launceston was paramount, and it remained the county town until 1838 when the assizes, and later the county gaol were transferred to Bodmin. As well as being deprived of its courts and parliamentary status (together with the suburb of Newport it sent four members to Parliament until 1832), in more recent times it has lost its two railway stations but is more happily by-passed by road. As a result, the town has kept its shape and character from former days.

When Richard, Earl of Cornwall, rebuilt the castle in the mid-13th century, he walled the town at the same time. There were three gates of which only the South Gate still remains. Launceston was the only walled town in Cornwall. The most picturesque approach, and much favoured by late-18th-century landscape artists, is from the north, through St Stephens. At the bottom of the hill is Newport where a simple packhorse bridge alongside a ford crosses the River Kensey. On the other side of the river is the church of St Thomas containing a large and elaborate Norman font, and behind are the fragmentary remains of the Augustinian Priory. The traveller must then climb the steep hill into the town. This street was so precipitous that a new road was cut along the hillside below the castle bailey in the 1830s.

Inside the town, apart from the looming presence of the castle, the chief feature is the church of St Mary Magdalene. It was originally a chapel of St Stephen's but was made parochial in 1380. A new church was begun in 1511 at the expense of Sir Henry Trecarrel, leaving the earlier west tower intact. This is the most lavishly decorated church in Cornwall, its granite built south and east walls completely covered with carved ornament, religious symbols and secular heraldry. Inside is a fine carved and painted pre-Reformation pulpit.

At the end of the 16th century, Carew describes the inhabitants' new increase of wealth, as expressed in recently repaired and enlarged buildings. Something of this state of affairs can be seen in the slate-hung jettied houses in the High Street and the Square. A

St Mary Magdalene, Launceston. E BERRY

century later, Celia Fiennes, after remarking on the (now demolished) Town Hall in the Market Place, says, 'there is in this place 2 or 3 good houses built after the London form by some Lawyers, else the whole town is old houses of timber work' (*The Illustrated Journeys of Celia Fiennes*, p213). The assizes did indeed keep the prosperity of the town alive through the 18th century and this shows in its buildings. King House, near the Southgate Arch, was the birthplace of Philip Gidley King, Governor of New South Wales and the developer of Tasmania. There is a group of red brick 18th-century houses on either side of Castle Hill of which the most spectacular is Eagle House. It contains extensive rococo decoration in papier mache. Lawrence House is now a museum. The White Hart is the most substantial of the coaching inns and has as its entrance a late 12th-century romanesque doorway removed from the priory.

30

Plymouth

The wide peninsula at the head of the Sound separating the rivers Tamar on the west and Plym on the east, consists of a limestone cliff breached by three, deep, tidal inlets: Stonehouse Creek on the west, Sutton Pool on the east, and Mill Bay with Sour Pool in between. This has been an important influence on the creation of the largest conurbation in the south-west. Not until 1914 were the three towns of Devonport, Stonehouse and Plymouth united within the single local authority of Plymouth.

Mount Batten, east of the Cattewater at the mouth of the Plym, was the site of a late prehistoric and Roman entrepôt of great significance. However, the earliest recorded settlement was the fishing village of Sutton, north-west of Sutton Pool. Henry I granted part of this royal estate to Plympton Priory (Sutton Prior) and part to the Valletorts (Sutton Vautort). Neither developed in the same way as Dartmouth or Fowey because the great anchorage of the Sound was open to the prevailing south-west winds. Nevertheless, in 1355, the Black Prince launched his last French campaign from here. Sutton Prior was created a borough in the mid-13th century and the name Plymouth came to be used for the port. By the end of the 15th-century, it had become a successful trading town, and in Tudor times was a naval base in the wars against Spain, playing its celebrated part in the actions against the 1588 Armada. Its late-medieval defence was what Leland described as 'a strange castle quadrate, having at each corner a great round tower'. This does not survive, but in a map of 1540, walls and towers are shown along the whole length of the Hoe. The towers at Devil's Point and Firestone Bay still remain. St Nicholas (now Drake's) Island in the Sound was also fortified. Little is left of medieval Plymouth, but some notable Tudor and Stuart houses still exist in the Barbican.

After the Civil War, in which the town had been held for Parliament, the significance of Plymouth Sound in Atlantic trade or warfare gave added impetus to the development of a permanent naval base. A massive new fort, the Royal Citadel (76), supplanted an earlier Elizabethan fortification on the east end of the Hoe, and a dockyard was established on the Hamoaze at the mouth of the Tamar. Dock (after 1824 to be known as Devonport) came into being by 1692, and by 1815 had a population nearly half as large again as Plymouth.

Stonehouse, in between, was always smaller than the other two towns and became enveloped by the spread of naval and military buildings, in particular the great hospitals on either side of the Creek. It was a popular residential area for naval officers. Durnford Street, its main street, still has modest late-18th-century terraces as well as the Royal Marine Barracks (1779–85). The

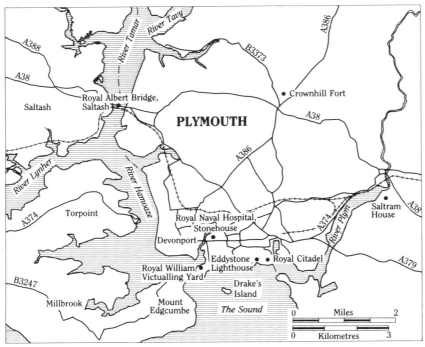

Plymouth area map. EH

Kerr St, Plymouth, with Town Hall, Doric column and Odd Fellows Hall (formerly Civil and Military Library). RCHME

construction of the Breakwater by Rennie between 1812 and 1847 was a magnificent feat of civil engineering which was to create a large and sheltered anchorage and an important adjunct to the naval base.

The corresponding growth of the town of Devonport was greatly influenced in the early 19th century by the architect, John Foulston, who put his neo-classical stamp on the Three Towns as Nash did for London or Grainger for Newcastle. Most of Foulston's civic buildings in Ker Street survive, though in the most depressing surroundings. There is the Town Hall with its four-column Greek Doric portico of 1821, the Doric column commemorating the change of name to Devonport (1824) and the extraordinary Egyptian style Civil and Military Library (1823). The dockyard itself was full of monumental and innovative buildings. Unfortunately, only two houses of the grand terrace built for the Commissioner and the senior dockyard officers in 1692 survive from the last war. With the need for expansion, Morice Yard was laid out in 1719–24 for the Board of Ordnance. The North Yard of 1848 catered for the steam navy. The grandest of all the dockyard buildings is Sir John Rennie's Royal William Victualling Yard (98) at Stonehouse (1826–35).

Plymouth was, however, terribly and permanently maimed by bombing in 1940–3. The whole of the city centre was wiped out. A brave decision was taken in 1943 to rebuild a model city to a plan drawn up by Professor Patrick Abercrombie and J Paton Watson, the city engineer, with no regard for the former street pattern. Apart from the Barbican which somehow escaped the worst of the bombing, few of the old landmarks remain. The Guildhall and St Andrew's Church, the largest medieval church in Devon, though gutted by fire, continue their former roles. The ruin of the 17th-century gothic Charles Church remains as a war memorial but largely inaccessible in the centre of a roundabout. The new road system in fact has had a devastating effect on such of old Plymouth that does survive. The architecture of the new centre reflects

concepts of the Modern Movement modified by 'Festival of Britain'. The balance between comparatively low buildings and the width of Royal Parade and Armada Way is not a success.

31
Tavistock

It is generally agreed that Tavistock is one of the most interesting and attractive of Devon's inland towns. It has a spacious and picturesquely castellated 19th-century centre where much use was made of a greenish volcanic stone from the neighbouring quarries of Hurdwick. The town has been profoundly influenced in its planning and architectural style by its two previous owners: the Benedictine abbey, until 1539, and from the 16th century until 1911, the Russells, earls and dukes of Bedford.

The abbey was founded by Edgar, King of Wessex, in 974, and in time became the wealthiest and largest in the south-west. In 1105, the abbey obtained a market for the settlement outside its precincts. A formal borough was created before 1185. Very little remains of the abbey today, although its former existence between the parish church and the River Tavy to the south has greatly influenced the layout of the town. The position of the Abbey Church and the cloister is fixed by the surviving late-13th-century masonry in the parish churchyard. The west gate of the abbey and formerly part of the abbot's lodgings, the so-called Betsy Grimbald's Tower, is in the vicarage garden. There is a length of precinct wall along the river bank. The Great Gate of the abbey is in Abbey Place, restored in 1824 by John Foulston and since 1829 used as the Tavistock Library. Part of the abbey infirmary is now used as a Christian

Fitzford Cottages, Tavistock. RCHME

Brethren Chapel. The original market-place lay to the north-west of the Great Gate and it is here that the earliest houses can be found. The parish church is mainly an early-16th-century rebuilding.

In other respects Tavistock is almost entirely a 19th-century town. The Duke of Bedford remodelled its centre during the 1840s. He built the Guildhall and Tudorised (Sir Jeffrey Wyatville) the Bedford Hotel which had begun life as a merchant's house in about 1725 on the site of the abbey refectory. Part of the urban replanning was the provision of a pannier market with shops fronting the new Duke Street and approached from the Town Hall (1860). He laid out the new Plymouth road with its associated villas and, in the 1850s, built several hundred miners' houses to the south of the town along the Yelverton road and elsewhere on the outskirts.

Tin, and later copper, mining was an essential basis for Tavistock's prosperity from at least the 12th century. In 1305, it was established as one of the four stannary towns of Devon. As Dartmoor tin streams declined in importance during the 16th-century, Tavistock was able to take advantage of the cloth boom. From the early 18th century copper mining developed, reaching its peak in the early 1860s when Devon Great Consols at Blanchdown was one of the richest copper mines in the world. Mining was also long-established around Mary Tavy on the south-western edge of Dartmoor. One of the formerly numerous engine houses is preserved at the site of Wheal Betsy, which was mined for lead, silver and zinc.

Tavistock is also famous for the birthplace of Sir Francis Drake, at Crowndale about a mile to the south. The statue to him at the southern approach of the town is by Boehm. The Tudor gatehouse nearby was moved to this site in 1871.

32

Totnes

After Exeter, medieval and Tudor Totnes was the wealthiest town in Devon and this is demonstrated today in its

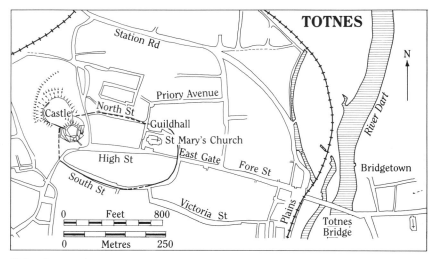

Totnes town centre map. EH

Totnes Castle keep from the north-west. EH

buildings and character. It is the most rewarding, visually and archaeologically, of all the small towns in the south-west. Its origins lie certainly in the 10th century, and it was one of the five Devonshire boroughs recorded in the Domesday Book. Its significance lay in its position as a port at the highest navigable point, and lowest bridging place, on the Dart estuary.

The extent of the Saxon *burh* was continued by the medieval town walls (the line is still traceable by way of North Street and South Street). There was a single main street dividing the oval enclosure with side lanes running off at right angles. The western end of the High Street was diverted off its alignment towards the south when the Norman castle was planted part inside, part outside the limits of the defensible enclosure after 1066. The East Gate of the town survives and spans the High Street. It was remodelled in the 19th century, and was seriously damaged by fire in 1990. The High Street continues as Fore Street in an easterly, downhill direction to the river, and the town quay and this area constituted a 13th-century suburb to the original town nucleus. A rival borough, Bridgetown, was established on the eastern side of the river, by the 13th-century lords of Berry Pomeroy. It was not incorporated into the Borough of Totnes until 1835.

Totnes was granted by William the Conqueror, together with 107 other Devon manors, to Juhel or Judhael, who built the castle in the most commanding position. A stone shell-keep now crowns the steep motte. On the north side of the church stood a small Benedictine priory founded by Juhel in *c*.1088. Its buildings were demolished soon after the Dissolution and the 16th- and 17th-century Guildhall was built on the site. This contains the panelled Court Room, with a painted plaster coat of arms dated 1553 above the mayor's chair. On the first floor is the Council Chamber, with the town prison below.

Totnes's prosperity was based on the cloth trade and it also exported tin. From the mid-17th century, however, the town did not keep up with developments in the textile industry and the merchant community declined. Daniel Defoe's description of it at the beginning of the 18th century is of a good country market town, and a 'residential' town 'especially for such as have large families and but small estates' (*A Tour through the Whole Island of Great Britain*, p225).

This peak of prosperity is represented by its buildings. A recent survey has shown that 66 houses date to before 1700. A feature of this period is the covered walk (Butter Walk) on the north side of the High Street formed by a series of stone pillars carrying the overhanging storeys of the houses. On the south side of the street, the house fronts are slate-hung to keep out the penetrating rain. Many of the houses have panelling and richly decorated plaster ceilings. Fore Street also has pleasant 18th- and early-19th-century buildings of which the Royal Seven Stars Hotel is a good example.

33

Truro

Truro is the only place in Cornwall which has long had pretensions to being the 'county' town. Its importance as an inland port during the Middle Ages was confirmed by a charter of *c*.1173 recognising its borough status. The borough was very much the creation of Richard de Lucy, a close adherent of Henry II. In the 13th century, Truro had an annual fair and a weekly market; it was also a 'coinage' town for tin. In 1295 it was one of the five Cornish boroughs to send representatives to Parliament. Over the course of centuries the higher reaches of the Truro river were clogged with mining debris, and by the late 17th century Truro's position as a port was in decline. Its role as a market, however, continued. Truro was by no means the most prominent of Cornish boroughs but by the 18th century, as the expansion of tin and copper mining

Strangways Terrace, Truro. RCHME

brought with it wealth and bankers, it had become the social capital of the county. More substantial claims to pre-eminence arose in 1877 when it achieved the title of city. Since then the county administration was established here, and it has finally become the capital of Cornwall with the move of the Crown Courts from Bodmin to the site of the short-lived castle.

The old town lay at the confluence of two rivers, the Kenwyn and the Allen, to form the Truro River, a tributory of the Fal. A feature of its broad cobbled streets was running water in the gutters. Boscawen Street is the principal street. Its width is deceptive since it formerly had a row of houses down the middle. Architecturally, Truro's distinction developed from the 18th century. Great merchant houses, such as the Mansion House (1751) and Prince's House (1737), near the former quay, the Assembly Rooms and Theatre (1772) at High Cross, of which only the Bath stone facade with its medallions of Shakespeare and Handel survives, and, Lemon Street (1795) at right angles to Boscawen Street are the chief witnesses.

Lemon Street is the most sophisticated Georgian street-scape in Cornwall, with three-storeyed, stone-fronted houses in uniform style, closed at its top by the Lander Monument. This is a Doric column supporting the figure of the African explorer, Richard Lander, sculpted by Nevill Northey Burnard in 1852. Nearby is the Infirmary, the nucleus of which was built in 1799.

With the turn of the 19th century, stucco was used instead of granite facing for private houses. Strangways Terrace (1835) off Lemon Street is an impressive sequence of houses looking over the town. In the centre is the charming late Georgian crescent, Walsingham Place. There are good examples of early-19th-century non-conformist architecture and among public buildings are the Royal Institution of Cornwall, housing the county museum, and the Market Hall of 1846 in Boscawen Street. When the Cathedral (57) came to be built in 1880, the south aisle of the old church of St Mary's was retained and incorporated into the new edifice. The latest addition of architectural distinction to the town is the new Crown Court.

4

Public Buildings

Devon and Cornwall have many public buildings which bear their own regional stamp. The presence of a large, semi-royal landowner (Duchy of Cornwall), and an independent community embracing all those connected with the extraction and marketing of tin (the Stannaries of Devon and Cornwall), during the Middle Ages gave rise to conditions and circumstances peculiar to these counties. Civic buildings reflecting urban pride, ostentation and the furtherance of trade, and particularly administrative buildings covering assessment and collection of taxes or other revenues, and the application of justice and its penalties were subject to local conditions. Also affected, but less directly, are schools, hospitals and almshouses, and finally the broadly social, ranging from assembly rooms and libraries to seaside amenities.

Large towns with sufficient wealth and civic pomp to stimulate major architectural display are really only two in number, and both Plymouth (30) and Exeter (26) were too grievously damaged by bombing in the Second World War for much to have survived. The translation of Dock to Devonport (1821–24) can still be glimpsed in John Foulston's Doric Town Hall and Column. His Union Street linking the three towns of Plymouth, Stonehouse and Devonport was a brave gesture of urban planning. Neo-classicism is the style most frequently associated with formal townscapes and this was applied extensively to Devonport and Plymouth in its residential terraces as well as its public face. Foulston's Royal Hotel, Theatre and Assembly Rooms, Library and Athenaeum, severally embodied the Grecian temple facade but have now gone. Nevertheless, his neo-classical influence extended beyond Plymouth to Tavistock (31), to Teignmouth (D) and to Penzance (D). **Exeter Guildhall** (39, D) has a more exuberantly primitive classicism of 1592–5, but it does represent the transition of the medieval

corporate hall towards the civic buildings of the last and present centuries. Elsewhere, there is little of distinction, apart perhaps from Truro City Hall in the Italian Renaissance style of 1846.

The smaller towns of the south-west paid more attention, during the early 19th century, to the provision of new market buildings in place of the old open markets in the streets. Foremost was Exeter with its Higher and Lower Markets of which the Grecian facade of the former still remains. Barnstaple (D) has a distinguished pannier market of the 1850s. It also has in Queen Anne's Walk an early-18th-century exchange consisting of a Tuscan colonnade facing the quay. Market buildings abound, sometimes in restrained architectural compositions or in forceful situations such as at Penzance (C), and some, displaying feats of ingenuity in roof construction, as at St Austell (C).

The numerous ports in the south-west required customs houses of which the grandest internally as well as externally is that at Exeter. At Plymouth, the Old Customs House, of 16th-century date, was replaced by that of 1810. Most unusual are those buildings required to meet the needs of the earldom/duchy of Cornwall in the administration of its seignorial responsibilities and control of the revenue of the stannaries. In the 12th and 13th centuries this led to specialised buildings rarely seen in other parts of England. The now very fragmented **Duchy Palace** (36, C) at Lostwithiel is the only purpose-built medieval 'office block' in the country. Likewise, **Lydford Castle** (40, D) provides a complete example of a medieval courtroom and prison which served not just the Devonshire stannaries but also that other great medieval institution, the Forest Law. Elsewhere, the assizes required substantial buildings. That in Exeter of 1774 occupies much of the castle interior. Bodmin (C) has a neo-classical courthouse of 1837–8, and also the ruins

Exeter Guildhall early this century. RCHME

37

of the former county prison of 1855 with a gatehouse of Burges-like medievalism. The new Crown Courts at Truro are the latest in this type of building.

The provision of schools was a not uncommon act of charity for their birthplace by those who had made their fortune. **Week St Mary** (43), in a remote part of north Cornwall has a late-medieval college, and **Blundells School**, Tiverton (35, D) of 1604 is one of the most impressive for size and design of its date. Another form of philanthropy is the school building of 1841 for the children of Heathcote's Tiverton lace workers. Kelly College, Tavistock (D), founded by Admiral Kelly in 1867 in the period of public school development, bears with it a substantial gothic frontispiece. In rural areas there are frequently schools and master's houses picturesquely grouped.

The Royal Naval Hospital, Stonehouse (35, D) provided a model for hospital reformers, particularly the French, and it influenced the Military Hospital on the opposite side of Stonehouse Creek. Elsewhere, the new hospitals of the 18th century were Palladian style buildings such as the Royal Devon and Exeter in Southernhay and the Infirmary at Truro. Of more radical design was the Exe Vale Hospital at Exminster (D) (1842–5) built by the Devon architect, Charles Fowler, as the County Pauper Lunatic Asylum with wards radiating from a central service block in a semicircle. Almshouses are often linked by arcaded fronts as at Tiverton (D), Barnstaple (D) as well as **Moretonhampstead** (34, D), and external galleries at St Germans (C) and at Polmear (C).

Buildings for social gatherings, cultural pursuits and less serious entertainment were increasingly in demand from the 18th century onwards. The late-medieval church houses had a communal function and in some way were the predecessor of the village hall. A good example is that at Holcombe Rogus (D). Assembly rooms, however, were to appeal to Georgian gentry. Those in Exeter (1769) claimed to be the first building in England to be called an 'hotel'; Truro's came three years later. Institutions for scientific and literary bodies and museums appeared in the 19th century. The most distinctive of these were those in the Grecian or Egyptian style (**Egyptian House**, 37) by Foulston. The ubiquitous Passmore Edwards free libraries are associated with the Truro architect Silvanus Trevail. Buildings directly pertaining to watering places and later to the more general resorts, other than hotels of which King Arthur's Castle Hotel, Tintagel (C) is the most dramatically situated, are less common than might be expected. The Esplanade at Sidmouth (D) dates from 1835–8, the Grecian baths at Ilfracombe (D) from 1836, and Paignton has a small pier of 1878, leaving the **Torquay Pavilion** of 1911 (41, D) as the best of seaside vulgarity.

34
Almshouses, Moretonhamstead
1637

SX 754861. In village centre
[D] NT

Murray's Handbook for 1859 describes the houses in Moretonhamstead as 'mean and thatched, and, with the exception of the *poor-house*, which has an arched arcade of the 17th centy., there is nothing worth notice in the town save an old cross and elm tree at the entrance of the churchyard.'

The building of almshouses during Elizabethan and Stuart times was widespread among the propertied classes. It was a means whereby charities might also serve as public memorials to their founders. Here the founder's identity is not displayed but, outside the major towns in Devon and Cornwall, the almshouses at Moretonhampstead are among the most noteworthy.

The ground floor of the two-storey building is fronted by a loggia or arcaded walk of eleven round-headed bays with the central bay as the entrance. It is distinctively built in large granite ashlar, including the stubby moulded columns, and its roof is thatched. It is dated 1637 above the entrance but despite the attempt to use classical forms, the details are in late-medieval and Tudor style.

Blundells School, Tiverton. A F KERSTING

Almshouses, Moretonhampstead. RCHME

35
Blundell's School, Tiverton
1604

SS 957125. Near the Loman bridge SE of town

[D]

Tiverton has benefited from a remarkable number of charities and benefactions, particularly from its Tudor merchant clothiers. The Greenway Chapel and the almshouses in Gold Street are prominent architecturally and there was another school founded by Robert Chilcott, Blundell's nephew, but the most influential of all the benefactions was the school founded by Peter Blundell in 1599.

The Old School was built in 1604 and was planned for 150 boys, an exceptional size for a school of this date. The building was converted into dwelling houses in 1882 when the school moved to another site. The school stands within a large walled enclosure. The single long range is divided into three by two two-storey porches. The three groups of three windows originally lit the dining hall and two other open halls for the upper and lower schools, the master at one end, the usher at the other, in a plan common to other schools of this date. These two halls were divided from each other by screens and had seats ranged along the long walls as specified in Blundell's will. The cupola between the two schoolrooms was reconstructed in 1840. The windows were lowered and the buttresses added in 1882. At the rear of the school building were projections containing the two-storey master's house, the kitchens and a room for the usher.

36
Duchy Palace, Lostwithiel
c.*1290*

SX 105597. The Quay, E of A390

[D]

The Duchy Palace at Lostwithiel is perhaps the most unusual medieval building in Cornwall and certainly one of the most significant. Its title is misleading. It was in fact a complex administrative centre for the earldom, and later Duchy of Cornwall. Unfortunately it has been disgracefully neglected and damaged in the past and its mistreatment continues to this day.

Great Hall — 18th Century — Modern — Convocation Hall

0 Feet 15
0 Metres 5

Duchy Palace, Lostwithiel (after Pounds). EH

Richard, Earl of Cornwall and brother of Henry III, acquired the land which became the manor of Restormel from the extensive estates of Isolda de Cardinham in 1268–9. On Richard's death in 1272, his son Edmund acquired adjacent blocks of land near Lostwithiel in order to make this the centre of the administration of the earldom instead of Launceston Castle. The reason for this move was both economic and geographical. Lostwithiel was more central to the major medieval tin-producing area of Blackmoor, and the town was at the head of the then-navigable part of the River Fowey. The Duchy Palace was built *c.*1290 immediately behind a quay on the river frontage.

The functions of this complex were varied. It was the administrative centre of the duchy lands in the south-west. Here were the duke's Steward; the Receiver, the collector of the duke's revenues; the Feodary, who supervised the feudal rights and perquisites; the Havenor, who looked after the duke's maritime privileges and customs fees; and the Auditors, who kept the duchy accounts. The county court was also held here and it was where the Knights of the Shire were elected until the Reform Act of 1832. Lastly, Lostwithiel was for long a coinage town where tin was assayed, stamped and weighed for export.

An engraving of 1734 shows the very ruined condition of the buildings, which indeed were already in a poor way in 1540. The engraving does, however, enable an understanding of the surviving buildings. At the heart and facing the quay was the Great Hall, an eight-bay structure with cellars and storage underneath. In about the middle of the 18th century, the three northern bays (but not the north wall) were taken down, and this is the reason for the substantial gap in the facade. At the north end of the range is a smaller hall known as the Convocation Hall, from having been used as the meeting place of the tinners' representatives after the decay of the Great Hall. This was smaller in size than the other hall but much more substantially built, and was probably of three storeys. The stannary

buildings were to the west of the Great Hall and nearer the town. They included a blowing-house for assaying purposes and a weighing-house. There was also the stannary prison in this area but these buildings have not survived.

What does survive is fragmentary and not improved by modern adaptations. The Convocation Hall is the most substantial relic since it has been in the hands of the Freemasons since 1878. It has been much altered, the lancet windows were replaced with Victorian gothic tracery and the north gable rebuilt as a hipped roof.

37

Egyptian House, Penzance
1835–6

SW 474303. Chapel Street
[D] LT

The most remarkable building in Penzance's Chapel Street is the 'Egyptian Hall', as it was described at the time, built for John Lavin, a mineralogist, as a museum, shop and dwelling house in 1835–6. After years of neglect the building has been recently

Egyptian House, Penzance. BOV

Exeter Custom House. A F KERSTING

restored by the Landmark Trust, and has been redecorated in its original style following the stripping of later coats of paint from its Coade stone mouldings.

It is very late in the brief fashion for the Egyptian style in architecture. P F Robinson built the Egyptian Hall, Piccadilly, London in 1811–12 (now demolished), and John Foulston built the Civic and Military Library in Ker Street, Devonport in 1823. A similar early-19th-century building is to be seen in Hertford. The Penzance building has close similarities with that at Devonport, and Foulston was still working in Devon and Cornwall in the 1830s, but it is not listed among his works and its authorship must remain uncertain.

38

Exeter Custom House
1681

SX 920922. The Quay
[B]

On 28 May 1678, a committee was set up by the City 'for erecting a new customs

house and cellars in such place and such manner as they shall think fit', following the reorganisation of the Custom Port, enlargement of the facilities on the Quay, and the further improvement of the Exeter Canal which originated in 1564. It was built in 1680–1 on the Quay at the expense of the city, to a design by Richard Allen, about whom nothing more is known. This handsome building is nevertheless one of the best of its kind in the country. Its brick construction is early for Exeter. It has two storeys, five bays and a central pediment.

The building was shared between the officials of the Board of Customs and Excise and the city customs officials. Originally it had an open arcade at ground level but this was filled in during the 18th century. The original staircase remains, and the baroque plastered ceilings by John Abbott of Frithelstock (the most eminent of the Devonshire plasterers of the time) which were completed in 1681 are the most noteworthy internal features. The Long Room has an oval centrepiece with a wreath of flowers, masks and snakes all in very high relief.

39

Exeter Guildhall
14th–16th century

SX 919926. W side of High Street
[A]

The most important secular building in Exeter is the Guildhall, boldly projecting on its granite columns into the High Street. It is without doubt the most pretentious civic building in the south-west, and the most ancient. The site has been occupied by a hall since at least 1160 but the present building dates from 1330 and was remodelled in 1468–9. This is the date of its impressive arch-braced roof of seven bays which has details in common with the other elaborate late-medieval roof structures in and around Exeter, such as the 'Law Library' in the Cathedral Close and the great house of Bowhill. At the Guildhall the principal trusses rest on painted carved stone corbels.

The round-arched, porticoed, Elizabethan street frontage belongs to 1593–6. Heavy and crudely moulded brackets above the Tuscan columns at street level support superimposed composite columns separating three, eight-light mullion and transom windows. The strapwork ornament in Beer stone was originally coloured and gilded. The present balustrade is not the original; that was removed in 1718.

Exeter Guildhall, after recent cleaning and repair. J COX

41

40

Lydford Castle
12th–18th century

SX 510847. In village. Signposted
from A386

[A] EH

Despite its superficial appearance and
title, Lydford Castle is a castle in name
only. It was in fact a court house and
prison serving the Forest of Dartmoor
and the tin industry (Stannaries) of
Devon during the Middle Ages, and
fitfully thereafter, into the 18th century.
Lydford was superseded as a judicial
centre as a result of the improvements of
Sir Thomas Tyrwhitt at Princetown and
the establishment of Dartmoor Prison
there in 1806.

An earlier Norman earthwork and
timber castle is at the tip of the fortified
promontory, south-west of the church.
Its occupation did not extend beyond the
mid-12th century. The title 'castle' was
transferred to the later structure in the
village.

In 1195 a strong house for detaining
royal prisoners was built within the
town. Archaeological excavation has
established that beneath the present
tower was a square, free-standing
building with massively thick walls, and

Torquay Pavilion. RCHME

at least two storeys high since there was
no ground-floor access. This building
can still be seen in the lower walls
within the tower, its ground-floor
windows blocked or partially unblocked.
Its outer wall face can be traced on top of
the mound. This earlier building was
ruined perhaps about fifty years after its
construction. It was then patched up in
order that its ground floor should be the
base for another thinner-walled tower
on top. The ground floor was filled in,
apart from a cellar in the northern

corner, and was surrounded by a deep
ditch with a mound concealing the
outside of the earlier building. A small
bailey was added, enclosed by ditches
and banks. It now took on the
appearance of a small traditional castle.
The drastic remodelling was done in the
mid-13th century, probably on the
instructions of Richard, Earl of
Cornwall, in whose charge the
Stannaries and the administration of the
Forest of Dartmoor lay. He also revived
the town of Lydford by establishing a
Wednesday market in 1267. The prison
remained in use into the 17th century,
and there was a major renovation during
the 18th century when the spine wall
across the interior was rebuilt and larger
windows inserted on the upper floor.

The hall or courtroom was on the
upper floor, approached by stairs from a
lobby immediately inside the entrance.
On the other side of the cross-wall at
this level was a smaller room which was
probably subdivided to provide
accommodation for the keeper. Below,
at entrance level, a door from the lobby
opened into a large room which may
have been the common prison. Smaller
rooms leading off it had distinctly
harsher amenities and, entered from a
trapdoor, was the cellar or pit in the
northernmost corner for the lowest sort
of felon. It was in this pit in 1510 that
Sir Richard Strode MP was, in his own
words, 'imprysoned in a dongeon and a

Lydford Castle. EH

deepe pitte under the ground in the castel of Lidford . . . the which prison is one of the most annoious, contagious and destestable places wythen this realme'.

41

The Pavilion, Torquay
1911

SX 918635. By Torquay harbour

[C]

The only substantial contribution to seaside architecture in the south-west, other than hotels and esplanades, is the Pavilion beside the harbour at Torquay. This is a light-hearted confection of cream and green Doulton stoneware panels over a steel frame, with a dome surrounded by a statue, corner turrets like copper-roofed bandstands, and art-nouveau ironwork around the roof promenades. The interior has an elaborately plastered barrel-vault and a splendid civic coat of arms in a roundel supported by trumpet- and lyre-carrying angels. All this was designed by the

borough's engineer and surveyor, H A Garrett, in 1911.

42

Royal Naval Hospital, Stonehouse
18th century

SX 466547. Stonehouse High Street, Plymouth

[D]

Just as the Royal Naval dockyards influenced the development of industrialisation during the 18th and early 19th centuries, so did the Navy set new standards in hospital design. Hospitals in the modern sense of the word for the 'Sick and Wounded' were first built for the Admiralty in Minorca (1711) and Gibraltar (1741–6). In 1741 there were proposals for three naval hospitals in England, at Gosport, Queenborough and Plymouth. Nothing happened until 1746 when a hospital for 1,500 patients was begun at Haslar, outside Gosport. Plymouth followed somewhat later in 1758 but the hospital

at Stonehouse was medically much in advance of Haslar. The layout was the earliest example of a hospital on the pavilion plan with ward blocks separated to avoid the spread of disease. It apparently had a critical influence on French hospital reformers.

The architect was Alexander Rovehead. Ten three-storey blocks were arranged formally round a central courtyard, interspersed by four single-storey pavilions which were probably intended for kitchens and messrooms, and all linked by a covered colonnaded passage. The focal point, placed on the entrance axis, was the administrative block and chapel, its main elevation provided with a pediment with a clock tower and bell cupola above.

The hospital was built to the south of the now filled-in Stonehouse Creek, so that the patients could be brought directly in ships' boats to the hospital jetty. This led directly to a building which acted as a bath-house and clothing store. The whole was enclosed by high stone walls so that the sailors recruited by press-gangs could not escape.

The Stonehouse hospital was smaller than Haslar. The first specification was for 600 patients, later increased to 960. By 1795, 1,200 were divided among 60 wards. The terrace for the senior medical staff was begun in 1763. Although there was some bomb damage in the Second World War (one block was destroyed) the hospital remains very much as completed.

43

Week St Mary College
16th century

SX 238977. Week St Mary. Signposted E of A39. In centre of village, E of church.

[B] LT

Week St Mary still has some of the attributes of the borough it was in the Middle Ages. The earthworks of a castle remain beside the church which itself has some architectural pretension with double bands of carved decoration around its granite tower. The present

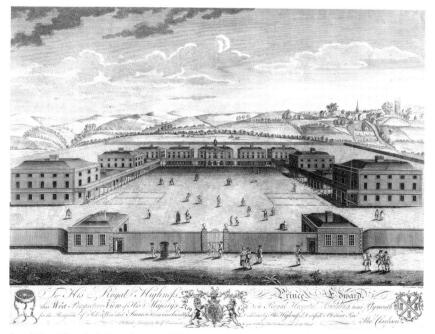

Royal Naval Hospital, Stonehouse, *c*.1770. BL

43

Week St Mary College. E BERRY

'town' has its market square, two greens, shops and temperance hotel. It also has the remains of an early-16th-century college founded by a local girl who acquired great wealth in later life, and returned to her roots.

Richard Carew who, a century later, must have known the story well, recounts that 'St Mary Week was the birthplace of Thomasine Bonaventure, I know not whether by descent or event so called, for whiles in her girlish age she kept sheep on the foreremembered moor, it chanced that a London merchant passing by saw her, heeded her, liked her, begged her of her poor parents, and carried her to his home. In process of time, her mistress was summoned by death to appear in the other world, and her good thews, no less than her seemly personage, so much contented her master that he advanced her from a servant to a wife, and left her a wealthy widow' (*The Survey of Cornwall*, 1953, pp188–9). She married another London merchant who also died leaving her his property and finally she married Sir John Percival, Lord Mayor of London, who left her a good deal more when he died. She gave or bequeathed this wealth to many charities, including the founding of this school and chantry in 1506.

The foundation document stated that the priest of the chantry was also to teach children freely in the school. He was supported by a schoolmaster, and the services of a laundress were also stipulated in the foundation. It was said in 1546 that 'ye sayde Chauntrye is a great comfort to all ye countrie, for yt they yt lyst may sett their children to borde there and have them taught freely, for ye wch purpose there is an house and offices appointed . . .' (R and O B Peter, *Histories of Launceston and Dunheved*, Plymouth, 1885, p344).

The surviving part of the college, which previously had lodgings for schoolmasters, scholars and assistants, is on one side of a walled and battlemented courtyard, and was later used as a farmhouse. The house has a fine door with a carved tympanum with a plain shield amidst foliage. Now owned by the Landmark Trust, the house serves as a holiday cottage.

Because the college was associated with a chantry it too suffered when chantries were suppressed in 1547. This was much regretted for as Carew describes: 'divers the best gentlemen's sons of Devon and Cornwall were there virtuously trained up in both kinds of divine and humane learning under one Cholwell, an honest and religious teacher, which caused the neighbours so much rather to rue that a petty smack of popery opened a gap to the oppression of the whole . . .' (*The Survey of Cornwall*, p189). Officially it was said that 'the school was in decay, by reason it standeth in a desolate place, and far from the market, for provision of the said scholars' (Peter, *Histories of Launceston*, pp334–5). The revenues were transferred to support the school at Launceston.

5

Churches and Cathedrals

Few medieval churches in Devon or Cornwall escaped rebuilding during the 15th and early 16th centuries, so there is a pervasive late-gothic, 'perpendicular' style running through the peninsula.

Common distinguishing characteristics can be adumbrated for many churches: a west tower, a long nave in five or six bays, with one or two aisles of similar width as the nave, and of equal or nearly equal height. Clerestories are rare. Sometimes nave aisles are projected eastwards to flank the chancel where they may provide subsidiary chapels. Nave and chancel are often the same height, and internally, the only division between the two was a rood screen, now not always present, and a chancel arch is therefore unusual. Roofs are generally of the waggon type, with curved braces to every rafter, and, frequently, carved bosses at main intersections. Naturally there are exceptions. A tower is almost universal, though not always at the west end. Some are placed transeptally, perhaps due to the influence of **Exeter Cathedral** (47, D). Spires are rare, and there are less than a dozen in Cornwall, usually dating before 1400. In Devon, there are two main groups of spires, around Kingsbridge in the south-west and a few in the north. A feature greatly developed in Cornwall in the 15th century was the porch, varying from the single-storey to two and three storeys in wealthier districts. Surface enrichment in granite is a Cornish rather than Devon practice and is at its most exuberant at Launceston. The remarkable collection of figure sculpture on the tower of St Austell may be dated to 1478–87. In Devon, this form of enrichment can reach even greater sophistication as at **Cullompton** (49) where, in addition to sculpture and armorials, there is a profusion of pinnacles and detailed tracery in belfry windows which indicates an influence westward from Somerset. As with the Greenway Chapel at Tiverton (D), surface decoration could be a vehicle for the donor's personal ostentation.

Within these late-medieval churches there can be a wealth of fittings which escaped the 16th- and 17th-century reformers. Devon rood screens are renowned. The tradition for fulsomely carved screens had its exemplars in Exeter Cathedral and at **Ottery St Mary** (53, D). But these, exceptionally, are of stone. Elsewhere they are of timber. Most of the Devon screens carried a loft supported on elaborately decorated coving. **St Nonna, Altarnun** (55) in Cornwall has particularly fine woodwork and besides its screen running right across the nave and aisles, there are seventy-nine carved bench ends of *c*.1523. Launcells (C) has over sixty bench ends, many with renaissance motifs, and which like those of Devon are square-ended. It also has a fine set of encaustic tiles.

There are, of course, many indications of earlier church building. Only the crypt at **St Giles, Sidbury** (52, D) presents a visible survival of a pre-Norman church. E H Sedding in his *Norman Architecture in Cornwall* noted that in about 140 out of the 200 or so medieval churches in the county there is some evidence of Norman work. Much of the evidence takes the form of residual fonts and doorways. There are more than 100 Norman fonts in Devon, and also there are some early towers which have been retained in later rebuildings. It is clear that church building was at its height in the second half of the 12th century and perhaps is a physical embodiment of the parochial organisation put in hand by Bishop Bartholomew. These churches tended to be cruciform in plan, with naves often aisleless. Sometimes residual transepts can be found amidst the later rebuilding, as at **St Morwenna, Morwenstow** (54, C). Evidence for 13th-century buildings is uncommon. Exeter Cathedral epitomises the decorated styles of the 14th century but it does not seem to have had great influence beyond the city. There are isolated examples of

14th-century work, and places such as Lostwithiel (C) and Fowey (C) appear to be subject to infuences from wider afield.

Monasticism has left little trace. Among the eight Cornish monastic houses, only the Augustinian priory of **St Germans** (51) survives to any extent, although something of the plan of that at Launceston has been recovered. One feature of Cornish church life was the collegiate church. There were at least eight, many with roots beyond the Norman Conquest (**St Neot**, 50). Collegiate churches elsewhere, like Ottery St Mary, usually had more conventional origins. Monastic remains survive little better in Devon. It is possible to reconstruct the plan of the great Benedictine house of Tavistock, otherwise, the badly ruined remains of **Torre Abbey** (56, D) provide the best example. Private chapels exist in some number associated with but not necessarily attached to the larger houses. There is a corresponding lack of chantry chapels in the churches.

Despite the upheavals caused by the onset of the Reformation, leading to popular revolt in the Prayer Book Rebellion, and later to the martyrdom of the local seminary priest, Cuthbert Mayne, Protestantism took hold. The Society of Friends gained considerable strength in Cornwall in the 17th century

(**Come-to-Good Friends' Meeting-House, Kea**, 46). Devon was receptive to the Baptists, Unitarians and Congregationalists. The restored 17th-century Loughwood Baptist Chapel, Dalwood, (D) is an example of this. But, unlike Cornwall in the 18th, Devon did not respond substantially to Methodism until early in the 19th century. Meanwhile, the established church maintained its position, and the 1660s saw the building of two new churches, both dedicated to King Charles the Martyr, at Plymouth and Falmouth. Both buildings continued the stylistic traditions of perpendicular gothic. The conventions and forms of classical architecture appeared in memorials and church monuments, from Prior Vyvyan's (1533) tomb chest at Bodmin (C) to the splendid Jacobean achievements at **All Saints, Holcombe Rogus** (45, C). At a more vernacular level are the slate-carved figures prevalent in east Cornwall during the first half of the 17th century. Other elaborate slate memorials are similarly widespread in Devon.

The tradition of open-air preaching is maintained today at **Gwennap Pit** (48, C). The effect of the evangelism of John Wesley and his brethren, together with that of other nonconformist sects has left its mark on the landscape of the south-west. Whether in the small towns,

especially in mining and industrial areas, or at isolated cross-roads deep in the countryside, the chapel is just as distinctive a feature as the abandoned engine house. Especially in north-east Cornwall and north-west Devon the local sect of Methodism, the Bible Christians, founded in 1815, had their own humble chapels which contrast with the large, grand and often ornate town chapels of the Weslyan Methodists and others. The number of chapels of all kinds was prodigious. It has been estimated for Devon that there are, or have been, more than 1,000 buildings belonging to one or another of the nonconformist denominations. Many have become redundant while the longer lasting have frequently been reordered internally.

The full-blown Gothic Revival came in the mid-19th century, together with the High Church Bishop Phillpotts. Some of the leading architectural names of the century designed new churches in the south-west, particularly in the newer seaside towns and the suburbs of Exeter and Plymouth. G E Street's first essay on his own was at Biscovey, Par (C) in 1849; George Gilbert Scott carried out major restorations at Barnstaple and Exeter Cathedral, and William Butterfield excelled himself at **All Saints, Babbacombe** (44, D). Local architects included the Seddings – the brothers E and J D and nephew E H, who practised a restrained gothicism. Less felicitous was J P St Aubyn. The climax of 19th-century church building came with J L Pearson's **Truro Cathedral** (57), a monument of great distinction even though stylistically out of step with Cornish architectural traditions.

44

All Saints, Babbacombe
19th century

SX 925654. Torquay. St Alban's Road, Babbacombe

[C]

It has been said of the 'High Victorian' architect, William Butterfield, that his 'works of the 1860s and early 1870s seem to be his most individualistic, of a

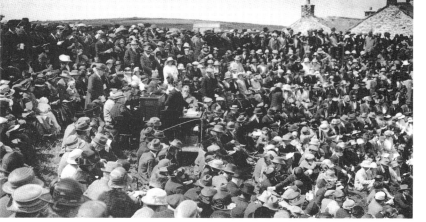

Above: Whit Monday service at Gwennap Pit, 1925. RIC

Left: west front of Exeter Cathedral. A F KERSTING

polychrome splendour often defying description' (Roger Dixon and Stefan Muthesius, *Victorian Architecture*, London, 1978, p208). In 1865 he was engaged to design a new church at Babbacombe, a recent and wealthy suburb of Torquay. It was consecrated in 1867 by Samuel Wilberforce, Bishop of Oxford, with the construction of the east end, and it was completed in 1874. All Saints, Babbacombe, is considered to be one of Butterfield's most important churches, and in the profusion of coloured stone, tile, and polished marble, and the overall texture and polychromy of the interior, it is perhaps the culmination of his style.

In addition to the architecture and its associated surface decorative treatment, Butterfield's furnishings are an integral part of the design and complement this remarkable and idiosyncratic church. The font and the pulpit are distinguished by overlapping arcading and the use of a variety of coloured marbles. He was also responsible for the lectern, candlesticks and altar cross. In addition, he designed the memorial brass to Anna Maria

Hanbury (d.1877) who, with her husband, had paid for the building of the tower and its bells. The stone reredos with its fine mosaics is by Salviati.

45

All Saints, Holcombe Rogus
15th–17th century

ST 056191. Holcombe Rogus. Signposted from the A373 from Tiverton at the junction with the M5 **[C]**

The church cannot be appreciated in isolation from Holcombe Court, in Hoskins's words 'the finest Tudor house in Devon' (W G Hoskins, *Devon*, Newton Abbot, 1972, p410), or the Church House in its characteristic position on the boundary wall between the church and the Court. Below this group lies the village on the sloping ground to the south. The elevation of Holcombe Court from the gate presents a hall with two large, six-light, transomed windows and a three-storey entrance tower. The 'long

Bluett Pew, All Saints, Holcombe Rogus. J COX

gallery' has the earliest dated plaster ceiling in Devon since it bears the name of Roger Bluett who died in 1566. The Church House belongs to the early 16th century. Like others which survive in Devon, and Poundstock in Cornwall, it combined the function of village hall which was probably on the first floor, and accommodation for a priest. It is now the property of the Landmark Trust.

The church is principally of the 15th century. It is remarkable for its associations with the great house and for the memorials of the Bluett family. Most obvious within the nave is the rare and magnificent example of a Jacobean family pew. This is a large, arcaded, screened enclosure with a cornice composed of a series of medallions carved with scenes from the books of Genesis and Exodus.

The Bluett Chapel was on the north side of the chancel. It contains spectacular 17th-century alabaster monuments. That to Richard Bluett (d.1614) and his wife is the most flamboyant. The two effigies lie beneath a coffered arch supported on Corinthian columns. Above the columns are figures, and on the arch which supports an armorial achievement, is strapwork from which lions' heads spring. Sir John Bluett (d.1634) and his wife lie recumbent under a heavy pediment and their eight children are ranged in order beneath them.

The church also possesses good 18th-century memorials, in particular that to the Revd Robert Bluett (d.1749), and has a wealth of incised memorial slabs, ledger stones of high quality, which deserve more protection than they currently have from chair legs, not to mention erosion under foot.

All Saints, Babbacombe. RCHME

46

Come-to-Good Friends' Meeting-House, Kea
18th century

SW 813404. Kea. Signposted from the A39 at Carnon Downs

[C]

Quakers were established in Cornwall from the earliest years of the Society. Their founder, George Fox, and some associates were indeed imprisoned in the North Gatehouse of Launceston Castle in 1656. Except for a few partial survivals among pre-19th-century Methodist preaching houses, the only notable buildings of Protestant dissenters in Cornwall are the Friend's meeting-houses at Marazion and that known as 'Come-to-Good'. This was an industrial area with both tin and copper mines, and, in 1840, a smelting-house for silver. The building stands back from a lane which was formerly one of the main routes from Truro to Falmouth.

The meeting-house was built in the first decade of the 18th century. The Journal of Thomas Gwin recorded his attendance at the first meeting for worship on 13th June, 1710. It is a small rectangular building with whitewashed cob walls and a hipped thatched roof. The original entrance in the south wall between buttress-like projections has been replaced by one in the west end. Its interior has been described as a perfect example of its type with plain woodwork, open-backed benches and a raised platform for the ministers facing the loft or gallery. The simple platform is of an unusual type for it occupies only part of the east end of the meeting-house. Usually there are two tiers, sometimes three, giving accommodation for elders, overseers and recorded ministers. The loft was an addition of 1717. It is supported by two posts and reached by a steep, narrow stair in the corner. There is no ceiling, the roof being open to the thatch.

At either end of the building are two additions: a thatched linhay for carts and for tethering horses under cover, and a recently built porch providing a room beyond the present doorway into the

Elders' bench, Come-to-Good Friends' meeting-house, Kea. E BERRY

building. The meeting-house is surrounded by a small green enclosure which has been a burial ground, and there is a stone mounting-block to the east side, near the entrance.

47

Exeter Cathedral
12th–15th century

SX 922925

[C]

The cathedral stands just to the east of the earlier Christian focus. This lay in the early Christian cemeteries which overlapped the north-eastern corner of the Roman forum. A minster church was established here in the 670s, refounded by Athelstan in 932, and destroyed by the Danes in 1003. The minster church was rebuilt by Cnut, and this building, remains of which have been established archaeologically, became the parish church of St Mary Major when the Norman cathedral was begun. This church was replaced in 1864 and was itself demolished in 1971.

The see was not transferred from Crediton to Exeter until 1050, and with the installation of a Norman bishop, William Warelwast, the Conqueror's

nephew, in 1107, an entirely new cathedral was begun. The outstanding survivals of the Norman building, whose nave was completed in about 1160, are the two great transeptal towers which impinge so significantly on the Exeter skyline. The cathedral was a collegiate rather than a monastic foundation so there are few associated external structures. There was a cloister, later destroyed in the 17th century. The chapter house, however, survives and is a memorial to the administrative reforms of Bishop Brewer (1224–44).

The rebuilding of the Norman cathedral, which started at the east end with the addition of the Lady Chapel, took more than a century, between the 1270s and the 1380s, ending with the great image screen of the west front. This lengthy rebuilding was nevertheless comprehensive and followed a uniform design with the result that Exeter has greater stylistic consistency than any other English gothic cathedral apart from Salisbury. There is an emphasis here on surface texture and colour which goes beyond that developed at Westminster Abbey and Lincoln Cathedral. The magnificent tierceron ribbed vault, 300 ft (91.5 m) long, unites the structure. The multiplication of unpolished Purbeck shafts on the piers, give what has been described as 'a rippling effect', and together with the carved corbels and bosses, all provide a feeling of great richness and warmth. Bishop Bronescombe (1258–80) was the prime mover. The Lady Chapel and the whole eastern arm were constructed by 1320. The new west end began in 1329, and the main work must have been completed so that Bishop Grandison could be buried in his little chapel behind the west front in 1369. The carving of statues for the image screen continued, however, into the 15th century.

The internal details and furnishings are of very great interest. Much of the carved stonework was coloured and recent cleaning has helped to bring this out. Most visually striking from the nave is the richly carved, arcaded stone pulpitum completed in 1324, with the organ case of 1665 above. The stepped sedilia in the choir have light and open

Gwennap Pit, 1890s. RIC

moulded canopies of great elaboration. The bishop's throne and its canopy, of 1313–16, is of spectacular grandeur and, although constructed of oak, it has the same intricate architectural detail as the sedilia. These and the pulpitum are the work of Thomas of Witney, a craftsman who had earlier worked at Winchester Cathedral. A survival from the previous century is the set of forty-eight 13th-century misericords originally in the stalls set in the Norman choir and then re-used. They form the oldest set in England. In the nave, above the north arcade, is the Minstrel's Gallery or rather the sculptured balcony of a hidden room large enough to hold an orchestra or choir, and originally erected for the Palm Sunday ceremonies. Fourteen angels carrying different musical instruments occupy recesses in the balcony.

Throughout the building there are points of archaeological and historic interest too many to adumbrate here: chantry chapels, monuments to early bishops and to later laymen, and wall paintings. The great east window should be mentioned. It was glazed in 1391 and incorporates much of the glass from an earlier scheme of 1304. In general, the process of repair and restoration currently proceeding is greatly adding to knowledge, and this process has applied particularly to the understanding of the complex development of the west front.

48

Gwennap Pit
19th century

SW 716417. Gwennap. At Busveal, 1 mile E of Redruth by minor road from A393

[A]

With the tradition of non-conformist open-air preaching in Cornwall so widely established, it is appropriate that the most famous preaching pit of all should be included among the more conventional churches and chapels.

Like other early travellers, John Wesley found on his first visit to Cornwall in 1743 that the country west of Truro was full of tin and copper mines and in the Gwennap area there were 'unparalleled and inexhaustible mine workings all around'. He returned many times to Gwennap, but the places where he preached have not been identified with certainty. He first made use of Gwennap Pit in 1762. He had spoken to an open-air meeting at Redruth on the Sunday afternoon but 'the wind was so high at five that I could not stand in the usual place at Gwennap. But at a small distance was a hollow capable of containing many thousand people. I stood on one side of this amphitheatre towards the top, and the people beneath and on all sides, and enlarged on those

words in the Gospel for the day'. Wesley described it as 'a round, green hollow, gently shelving down, about fifty feet deep' in which the audience was 'commodiously placed, row upon row'.

The hollow which provided such an effective auditorium lay between Busveal and the former Cathedral Mine. It probably was the result of mining subsidence and may have been more extensive than it is today to judge from the estimates of congregations of 20,000–30,000 at a time. Wesley preached at Gwennap Pit eighteen times in 1762–89, and it continued to be used by Methodist preachers thereafter.

In 1806, a group of miners, with the support of the local Methodist societies, obtained permission from the landowner to remodel the pit into a more regular form 'in memory of Mr Wesley'. This gave the Pit its present appearance with thirteen concentric rings of continuous seating. Around the top was a wall, which has the form of a grassy bank with two stepped entrances on opposed sides. The preaching place, two-thirds of the way up, is marked by two granite uprights. The first service was held on Whit Monday, 18 June 1807 and the tradition of the Whit Monday event continues today.

Beside the entrance to the Pit is Busveal Chapel, opened in 1836. This simple building epitomises much of West Country Methodist architecture. It contains copies of the highly dramatic and imaginative engraving of William O Geller's 1845 painting of Wesley preaching in the amphitheatre, and other memorabilia.

49

St Andrew, Cullompton
15th–16th century

ST 022073. Cullompton. On the east side of the town

[C]

The prosperity brought to Devon by the wool trade reached its peak at the end of the 15th and the beginning of the 16th centuries, and is demonstrated in the rebuilding of parish churches on a grand scale. Tiverton and Cullompton are among the best examples of this display of individual wealth and civic pride.

Cullompton was a collegiate church before the Norman Conquest and was given to Battle Abbey by William I. It later went to the Priory of St Nicholas at Exeter. The nave and chancel of the present building, however, belong to c.1450. The aisles were added about the year 1500, the Lane Chapel is dated 1526, and the west tower was built in 1545–9. The tower has the range and quantity of decoration more often associated with Somerset towers. Above the west window are three large carved panels with the Crucifixion and the Virgin and St John with elaborate shafts flanking the panels, and a multitude of pinnacles on the parapet and on the offsets of the buttresses.

Just as Tiverton church has the Greenway Chapel and Ottery St Mary the Dorset Aisle, so Cullompton has the Lane Aisle. The clothier, John Lane, extended the south aisle for nearly all its length with great richness of detail. The buttresses are decorated with references to his wealth: ships, cloth shears and teasel frames as well as his merchant's mark. He ensured that no one entering the church should be unaware of his munificence, with a well-placed inscription along the west wall of the aisle. Inside, the piers separating his aisle from the south aisle have panels and niches with thirty-two figures of men in Tudor dress, each holding a scroll. The chapel is fan-vaulted and the springers are carved with angels holding various emblems, including a number with John Lane's merchant's mark. The pendants have, as well as emblems of the Passion, symbols of his trade. The brass is now missing from his tombstone but there is an inscription to him and his wife.

The church as a whole has a superb panelled and coloured wagon roof on angel brackets, and with cross-ribs to all the twenty-four panels in each bay. The roof runs uninterrupted for the whole length of the nave and chancel. Unusually for Devon there is a clerestory above both nave and chancel. There are other splendid examples of carved woodwork. The rood screen has eleven bays, three for each aisle and five for the nave. The fan tracery of the coving supports a fine carved cornice of three orders. The colouring on the east side is original; that on the west was recoloured in 1849 at the time of the restoration of the church. Above the screen is the rood beam, and in the south aisle is a Golgotha – two baulks of oak carved in the fashion of rocks, skulls and bones which served as the base for the crucifix and for the figures of Mary and John on either side. It was, before the Reformation, set up on the rood beam. In the east bay of the north aisle are old, high-backed box pews in the Moores Chantry chapel, and across the whole of the west end is a Jacobean gallery on Ionic columns.

Rood screen, St Andrew, Cullompton. RCHME

51

50
St Anietus, St Neot
14th–16th century

SX 186678. St Neot. On the SW edge of Bodmin Moor. Signposted by minor roads from the A38, W of Doublebois

[C]

St Neot has been described as 'one of the most interesting and beautiful places in Cornwall' (Henderson, 'Parochial History of Cornwall', p169). It is Cornwall's second largest parish and the church-town is particularly attractive. Certainly the remarkably complete set of early-16th-century stained glass in the fifteen windows gives it a reputation of more than local significance.

The church has its origins in a Celtic monastic establishment, and a college of priests was in existence at the time of the Norman Conquest. A holy well, rebuilt in 1862, lies 300 yards from the church and has legendary associations with the patron saint. There is in the churchyard a cross-shaft richly ornamented with interlace patterns, perhaps the finest of its kind in Cornwall. The much later medieval lantern cross came from St Kew.

The nave and south aisle of the church belong to the 15th century and make an impressive crenellated composition from the south. The oldest part of the present building is the west tower, probably of the previous century. The glory, however, lies in the stained glass, although now much restored, and renewed in about 1830 by John Hedgeland. The earliest of the windows, and the least restored, is the Creation Window at the east end of the south aisle. One of its scenes shows Seth placing in Adam's mouth the seeds from which the wood of the Cross would eventually spring. This was a legend familiar to the Cornish of the late Middle Ages and was dramatised in the Cornish-language cycle of mystery plays written at Glasney College, Penryn. The story of the Flood in the next window shows the ark as a three-masted ship of around 1500. It seems that the original intention was to show a series of Old Testament stories but this had to be abandoned due to lack of funds. Instead, the principal families of the parish were pressed into contributing and became responsible for particular windows and for the subject matter of the glass. The Borlase window shows St Christopher and St Neot, St Leonard and St Catherine with the Borlase family underneath. This is followed by that of the Martyns and the remaining windows

on the south side by the Motton, Callaway and Tubbe families. Many of the windows show local saints, including St Patrick – not the patron saint of Ireland, but a hermit who lived on Drake's Island in Plymouth Sound. The most famous of all is the St Neot window on the north side, given by the young men of the parish, which illustrates a series of events in the life of the saint. The west window of the north aisle

The Young Women's Window, St Anietus, St Neot. RCHME

relates to the life of St George. The east window in the chancel, however, is entirely the work of Hedgeland as are the two in the organ chamber and that beside the south door.

51
St Germans Priory
12th–16th century

SX 359578. St Germans. Signposted from the A38 at Tideford

[C]

In the year 926, King Athelstan created a Cornish diocese following the conquest and absorption of Cornwall into the Anglo-Saxon kingdom of Wessex. This act followed the English model and matched the new bishopric created at Crediton, Devon, in 909. A monastic establishment after the fashion of the Celtic Church already existed, and along with St Petroc's at Bodmin, both represented the more important ecclesiastical centres in Cornwall. Nothing remains of this period.

There were just five early bishops of Cornwall. The last was Burhwold who died in 1043. The see then passed to his nephew who was already Bishop of Crediton. On his death in 1046, Leofric, named by King Edward the Confessor to be Bishop of both Cornwall and Crediton, moved his see to Exeter in 1050. From then on Exeter was the ecclesiastical capital of Devon and Cornwall, until the establishment of the Bishopric of Truro in 1876.

The earlier monastic house was converted into a college of secular canons in order to fit more appropriately into the organisation of the Anglo-Saxon church. This was later converted by Bishop Bartholomew (1161–84) into a priory of regular canons of the Augustinian order in the mid-12th century. The present buildings owe their origins to this period of ecclesiastical reform. Remains of the north range of the priory's claustral buildings and the undercroft of the Prior's Lodging lie below the house of Port Eliot alongside the church.

The nave of the early church was flanked by narrow aisles and their roof

St Germans Priory: west door. RCHME

lines can be seen at the west end. The nave clerestory had single windows spaced above the centres of the piers. At the west end of the nave there was an additional bay flanked by twin towers. Between them, at an upper level, a wooden gallery must have run across the west wall. The stair in the south tower is the only one in Cornwall of Norman date. The external elevation of the west end is the most striking romanesque composition in Cornwall. The nave is preceded by a projecting portal of seven orders. It has chevroned and roll-moulded arches and jambs with alternating colonettes and chevroning. The gable has the rare feature of a cross. The lower parts of the two towers are still 12th-century. The upper parts of the north tower are 13th-century and move from the square plan to an octagon with lancet windows. The upper parts of the south tower are a 'perpendicular' rebuilding.

In the 15th century, the south aisle was greatly widened and the porch rebuilt, linking with the chapel at the east end of the aisle which had been added a century before. After the dissolution of the priory, the chancel, which had extended some 50 ft (15.2 m) east of the present building and had been used by the canons, fell into disrepair and collapsed in 1592. After a fire in 1803, the old north aisle of the church was pulled down and was replaced by the Eliot family pew, designed by John Soane who worked on the house for John, the second Lord Eliot, later created Earl of St Germans, from 1804–6. Of the monuments in the church the most important is that of Edward Eliot (d.1722) by Rysbrack which occupies the lower part of the north-west tower and is, according to Pevsner, 'the most ambitious C18 monument in Cornwall'. Also of note is the stained glass by Burne Jones (1896) in the east window.

52

St Giles, Sidbury
?10th–15th century

SY 140917. Sidbury. On A375 N of Sidmouth

[C]

One of the most interesting churches in Devon, Sidbury retains, unusually, elements from before the Norman Conquest. Restoration of the chancel in 1898–9 revealed, below the floor, a Saxon structure which has been interpreted as a free-standing mausoleum or shrine. It was about 10 ft (3 m) square, half-buried in the ground and entered by a short flight of steps, and was perhaps the memorial of the founder of the church. The upper part of the building had been destroyed when the early-12th-century chancel was erected and the lower portion filled in. The only other pre-Conquest survival is a small fragment of a cross-head.

Although the external impression is that of a richly decorated 15th-century 'perpendicular' building, the church originates in the early 12th century. Its subsequent development, however, cannot be followed with certainty. There is a vertical break in the masonry on the

Nave, west gallery and organ, St Giles, Sidbury. RCHME

Plate 1 *The Cornish coastline with The Rumps in the background.* NT/JOE CORNISH

Plate 2 *All Saints, Babbacombe. The north aisle and chancel arch.* JO COX

Plate 3 *The temptation of Eve. A detail from the Bluett Pew at All Saints, Holcombe Rogus.* JO COX

Plate 4 *Saltram House saloon chimney-piece, attributed to Thomas Carter the Younger.* NT/ROB MATHESON

Plate 5 *Restormel Castle.* EH

Plate 6 *Tintagel Castle. The inner ward.* EH

Plate 7 *St Michael's Mount.* NT/HOWARD PHILIPS

Plate 8 *Lily pond at the front of Knightshayes Court.* NT/ANDY WILLIAMS

Plate 9 *Launceston Castle.* EH

Plate 10 *Castle Drogo. View to the north of main entrance.* NT/CHARLIE WAITE

Plate 11 *Postbridge Clapper Bridge.* JO COX

Plate 12 *Royal Albert Bridge, with Tamar road bridge behind.* EH/PATRICK BROWN

south wall of the chancel which suggests a short chancel, which may have been part of a cruciform plan. There are round-headed windows of early form with their heads cut out of single stone blocks. The chancel was extended later in the 12th century, and a corbel table with grotesque heads unites the two parts at roof level. The ashlar of the east wall has a fine chequer-pattern surface decoration cut into it which is still romanesque in character. The west tower belongs to the early 12th century. It has shallow buttresses without offsets rather like pilaster strips, and another strip up the middle of the sides. The upper part of the tower was taken down in 1843–5 in preparation for restoration and two full-length statues of a saint and a bishop, probably of 12th-century date, were found and are now in niches on the west wall. The ground floor of the tower is a rib-vaulted room with the ribs resting on four carved corbels: two lion masks, one maned lion and an atlas figure. Aisles were added later to the nave.

There was substantial reconstruction of the church in the mid-15th century when the aisles were rebuilt, the walls of the nave raised, and fine wagon roofs inserted throughout the church. The manorial records of Salcombe state that in 1445 there were no returns from Dunscombe quarry since it had been handed over to the parishioners of Sudbury for work on their church. Extensive repairs were carried out early in the 17th century by John Stone, freemason, possibly the father of the famous Nicholas Stone.

Internally, there is an interesting series of wall paintings of various dates especially those round the 13th-century windows in the north wall of the chancel. There is a possible St Christopher on the tower arch, and a 16th-century vine-scroll above the chancel arch. The handsome painted gallery is dated 1754. The chancel fittings in Arts and Crafts style are by Walter Cave, whose family lived at Sidbury Manor. The choir stalls, altar (in the form of a Jacobean table), and alms-desk and box belong to 1899. The reredos (1904) and altar frontal (1905) are also by Cave.

53

St Mary, Ottery St Mary
13th–16th century

SY 098956. Ottery St Mary. S of the A30, approached by the B3177 from the E and by the B3174 from the W

[C]

Edward the Confessor gave the manor and hundred of Ottery to the cathedral church of Rouen in 1061. A church was dedicated here by Bishop Bronescombe in 1260. Later, Bishop Grandisson purchased the estate from the Rouen chapter in 1335, and two years later obtained royal licence for the foundation of a college for secular priests which was suppressed in 1545. Historically and architecturally the church is amongst the most important in Devon.

Whether the church retains elements from Bronescombe's time has been much debated. It is generally held nowadays that it is essentially of the mid-14th century but the plan is oddly old-fashioned, especially the pair of

Lady Chapel Screen, St Mary, Ottery St Mary. RCHME

transeptal towers. Grandisson seems to have deliberately recreated his cathedral here in reduced form. Its collegiate status dictated an eastern arm considerably longer than the nave.

The vaulting provides the most interesting architectural detail. The lierne vault of the choir has been compared with work at Wells and Bristol rather than Exeter. The vaults of the Lady Chapel, crossing, transepts and nave differ from the predominant curves of the choir with their use of straight lines to form crosses and stars. The carved, figured, roof bosses are thought to be the work of carvers responsible for the nave vault at Exeter. The outer north aisle of the nave has a fan-vault with pendants consisting of openwork bars. The aisle was provided by Cicely, Marchioness of Dorset, c.1520, for the use of the parishioners. Its vault closely resembles the Lane Aisle at Cullompton. The north porch is of three storeys with the ground floor also fan-vaulted. This and the south porch were additions of the early 16th century. A general restoration was carried out by Butterfield in 1849 which provided new seating and redecoration, much of which has since been removed or concealed.

The medieval furnishings are of very great interest. The gilded wooden lectern was given by Grandisson and is one of the earliest eagle lecterns in England. The stalls have misericords with Grandisson's coat of arms. The reconstruction of the reredos, also of Grandisson's time, was completed by Blore in 1833. The parclose screens, though not *in situ*, are among the earliest wooden screens to survive in Devon. In the nave are two richly canopied tombs of the bishop's brother, Otto de Grandisson (1358) and his wife Beatrice (1374). Between the chancel and the north aisle is the tomb of John Haydon of Cadhay (1587), first governor of the church after the Dissolution. At the east end of the Dorset Aisle is the full-length standing figure in armour of John Coke (1632). The north tower has a weathercock fitted with two trumpets which formerly produced a whistle.

The collegiate buildings were ranged round a small cloister to the south of the

North arcade of the nave, St Morwenna, Morwenstow. RCHME

56

nave and have now gone. The houses of individual canons were grouped around the churchyard but are now very much altered. Among the property transferred to a body of governors in 1545 was the schoolhouse of Grandisson's foundation, refounded as 'The King's New Grammer School'. John Coleridge (1719–81) was vicar of Ottery and master of the grammar school. His son, Samuel Taylor Coleridge, the poet and philosopher, received his earliest schooling here.

54

St Morwenna, Morwenstow
12th–15th century

SS 205154. Morwenstow. Signposted along minor road from A39

[C]

The church stands isolated, except for the vicarage and the glebe farm nearby, in a valley falling towards the sea. The Cornish historian Charles Henderson wrote: 'It is difficult to see why the Normans should have erected so fine a building at this remote place', and also: 'Few churches can surpass Morwenstow in romantic situation or architectural interest' ('Parochial History of Cornwall', *The Cornish Church Guide*, Truro, 1928, p167).

This is one of the best preserved Norman churches in Cornwall. Unusually it is aisled, and three bays of the north arcade survive on thick circular piers with scalloped capitals. The arches have zig-zag and beak-head decoration and, in the spandrels, projecting heads of men and beasts. The eastern two bays have early pointed arches on circular piers. In the 15th century, a south aisle and tower were added and the Norman south door was removed to the new wall. The doorway has colonnettes and zig-zag decoration on the arches. On one of the capitals are two birds and on the other fir cones. The Norman font, by comparison, is very primitive with a simple cable moulding round its foot.

In other respects, the church is of considerable interest, especially for its carved woodwork. The waggon roofs are original and some of the bench ends have early-renaissance motifs. The rood screen of c.1575 was taken down and later reassembled with cast-iron tracery by the vicar, R S Hawker, in 1845.

The other component of Morwenstow is the impact of the eccentric Hawker (vicar, 1834–75) on the church and parish, besides his well-known poems and concern for shipwrecked mariners and for animals. This appears most emphatically in physical terms in the vicarage which he built in 1837, now a small hotel. The house was so placed that it faced only 'the Church and the Sea, the suggestions of both which are boundless' (Piers Brendon, *Hawker of Morwenstow: Portrait of a Victorian Eccentric*, London, 1975, p87). He adapted a model for 'a Clergyman's house, on a moderate scale' which he found in T F Hunt's *Designs for Parsonage Houses*. His own embellishments were the chimneys, built to resemble the church towers of places where he had previously lived. The kitchen chimney must have been altered or put up later since it was

shaped like his mother's tomb. Over the front door was an inscription:

A House, a Glebe, a Pound a Day,
A Pleasant Place to Watch and Pray.
Be true to Church – Be kind to poor,
O Minister, for ever more.

55

St Nonna, Altarnun
12th–15th century

SX 223814. Altarnun. NE of Bodmin Moor and 1 mile N of the A30 at Five Lanes

[C]

St Nonna's church carries the epithet 'Cathedral of the Moors'. Although it has a magnificent Norman font, with bearded heads at each corner and large rosettes between, the church today is almost wholly of the 15th century. It is a fine example of the period and its tower is one of the tallest in Cornwall, but its chief point of interest is its remarkable carved fittings. The rood screen is complete and runs right across the nave

Bench ends, St Nonna, Altarnun. RCHME

and both aisles. Each section is divided into two 'lights' with 'perpendicular' tracery. Additionally, there are over seventy carved bench ends by Robert Daye which show, besides the symbols of the Passion and renaissance motifs, large figures of angels and more humble scenes such as a man playing bagpipes, a fiddler, a fool and sheep grazing. One bench end is 'signed' by Robert Daye but the date is illegible. The work was probably carried out between 1520 and 1530. The altar rail crosses all three altars and is dated 1684 with the names of the vicar and churchwardens spelt out above each baluster. The barrel roofs have carved ribs and bosses.

Altarnun also has great significance for Methodists. John Wesley and his companions stayed nearby in a house at Trewint on the main road on their first and later journeys to Cornwall. In the centre of the village is a simple Georgian Methodist meeting-house with an external stair and stables below. It is now a dwelling house. Over the door is a profile bust of Wesley (1836) by the Altarnun-born sculptor, Nevil Northey Burnard (1818–1878), who became fashionable in London but who eventually died penniless in Redruth workhouse. A plaque in his memory has been fixed on his birthplace next door to the chapel.

56
Torre Abbey, Torquay
12th–16th century

SX 907637. Off the sea front W of the harbour

[A]

The Premonstratensian abbey at Torre was founded in 1196 by William de Brewer and settled by canons from Welbeck Abbey in Nottinghamshire. When the abbey was dissolved in 1539, its net income was the largest of any of the English Premonstratensian houses. Much of the abbey was left to decay but the south and west claustral ranges were converted to a residence by Thomas Ridgeway after 1598. It was bought by Sir George Carey in 1662 and remained with the family until the 1930s when it was acquired by the Corporation of Torquay to become a museum and art gallery. The Careys had enlarged and altered the house in the late 17th and 18th centuries.

The greater part of the abbey remains, including the severely ruined church and east range. The southern and western sub-vaults were incorporated into the later house. The gatehouse beside the kitchen is the most complete survivor and is of 14th-century date, carrying coats of arms of the abbey, the Brewers and their successors the Mohuns. In what was once an outer court is the great buttressed tithe barn, perhaps of the 13th century. Its roof has been reconstructed.

The church, now almost entirely destroyed, was partly excavated in 1911. It was cruciform in plan with a square-ended, aisleless presbytery of three bays, short transepts with two eastern chapels, and a nave of six bays. The northern aisle has been established recently to have been part of the original plan. The masonry of the crossing piers has fallen and the massive fragments have been left as they fell. The entrance to the chapter house of five, richly moulded round-headed orders and nook shafts, flanked by round-headed windows, is the most rewarding architectural survival.

57
Truro Cathedral
19th century

SW 825449.

[C]

Truro Cathedral was the first Anglican cathedral to be built since Wren's St Pauls in the City of London. Moves towards the revival of the ancient diocese of Cornwall began in 1847 when a Bill for the formation of three new dioceses (including one for Cornwall) failed to get through Parliament. Efforts continued, and in 1876 sufficient subscriptions and endowments had been assembled for the Home Secretary to steer a Bill to conclusion authorising the foundation of the bishopric. The first bishop was Dr Edward Benson, later to become Archbishop of Canterbury. He was installed and enthroned in St Mary's Church, Truro, that church being constituted the cathedral church of the diocese.

At the first Diocesan Conference in 1877, steps were taken to provide a suitable cathedral on the site of St Mary's Church. John Loughborough Pearson was selected as architect on the strength of his successful design for St Augustine's, Kilburn. 'My business is to

West side of gatehouse, Torre Abbey. NMR

think what will bring people soonest to their knees', was Pearson's self-imposed task, and his plans were presented and accepted in 1879. The foundation stone was laid in 1880, and after seven years the work had advanced sufficiently for the consecration to take place. The central spire was finished in 1903 and the western spires in 1910.

The comparison which is most frequently made of Truro is the way Pearson's conception soars above the narrow streets like many old cathedrals of France. Indeed Pearson drew deeply upon French gothic in much of his architecture. This shows at Truro, particularly in the spires and towers. The building is generally in the Early English idiom. It is vaulted throughout, for Pearson was well aware how essential vaults were for achieving success in the gothic style. Externally, there is great emphasis on verticality. Internally, there is a gradual increase in decoration from the sparse nave towards the east end, and the change in bay sizes and the pattern of the vaulting in the choir and sanctuary help to focus attention on the high altar and the carved stone reredos behind. The choir stalls and bishop's throne were designed by Pearson himself.

Pearson was strongly opposed to the total demolition of the medieval church of St Mary and the south aisle was allowed to remain as an aisle to the choir. This aisle, of 1504–18 is externally one of the most ornate gothic structures in Cornwall, and in its massed surface decoration it comes close to the ultimate exuberance of St Mary Magdalene, Launceston.

Truro Cathedral from the south-east. BATSFORD

59

6

Vernacular Buildings and Rural Settlement

Vernacular buildings must always be seen in the context of their broad landscape. Landscape and settlement interact with one another and both are determined by their inheritance from the past. The mainly dispersed settlement of the south-west is due to patterns laid down in prehistory and to the different traditions brought by Anglo-Saxon colonisation. The medieval economy of Cornwall, and to a great extent that of Devon, was unlike that of most English counties. It was industrial as well as agricultural, it involved seaborne trade and fishing. There were few substantial landlords and the rural structure lacked many of the ingredients of full-scale manorialism. The agricultural base was mixed, with good arable land in the Exe valley, between the Teign and the Dart and in southern parts of mid- and east Cornwall. Elsewhere, pastoralism was more suitable (**Trowlesworthy Warren**, 67, D). Devon became more fully exploited agriculturally during the 15th century. Relics of commonly farmed open fields are surprisingly numerous. **Braunton Great Field** (58, D) is one of the principal national examples for the continuance of this system of farming. The Forrabury Stitches, near Boscastle (C), is another on a smaller scale. For much of the south-west an in-field, out-field system operated. This entailed a fairly small permanently cultivated area close to a settlement and worked in conjunction with a much larger area extending into the marginal land. The out-field might be grazed or parts of it cultivated from time to time. The roughly rectangular field patterns of the Bronze Age, fossilised on Dartmoor and other uplands, can also be seen as the underlying basis for the complex patchwork of now small irregular plots which have evolved in the course of medieval and later agriculture in parts of the extreme south-west, on the Lizard and the Land's End peninsula, especially

in the neighbourhood of **Zennor** (68, C).

The materials used in vernacular building reflect the underlying geology. While in towns timber framing was often necessary, in the countryside the basic, traditional material was cob. Cob is a clay earth tempered with small stones, straw and often cow dung and hair, thrown up in layers above a stone base and tamped by foot. This was used well into the middle of the 19th century until mass-produced bricks, and, more recently, concrete blocks, provided a cheap alternative. Around the moors granite 'moorstone' was for the taking, slates and similar stone elsewhere as available. The common roofing material was thatch of Devon combed wheat-reed, and also turf or heather. Slate was much used from the Middle Ages on since this was a material readily available in east Cornwall and the South Hams. It has to be remembered that the buildings in traditional materials which survive today are those of the relatively wealthier members of contemporary society. The poorer elements lived in crude and simple huts which had little durability.

The origins of the medieval house in the south-west go back at least to the 10th-century settlement at Mawgan Porth (21, C), where the 'long-house' and suggestions of a courtyard arrangement have been recorded. This can then be followed to the 13th-century settlement at **Houndtor** (61, D) and other excavated sites in Devon and Cornwall, and through to the roofed (habitable) 'long-house' at **Sanders** (66) at Lettaford (D). The 'long-house' is essentially a building which has a cattle byre at one end and living-rooms for humans at the other, all under the same roof but separated by a cross-passage.

Developing in parallel was the hall-house, without an integral byre, but with the same sequence of rooms in line and a main living room or hall (**The Old Post Office, Tintagel**, 64, C, and

Houndtor medieval village. EH

61

Kirkham House from the rear, showing the restored first-floor gallery. EH

Kirkham House, Paignton, 62, D). In his *Survey of Cornwall* Carew described the manner formerly adopted by the Cornish gentry: 'to plant their houses low, to lay the stones with mortar of lime and sand, to make the walls thick, their windows arched and little, and their lights inward to the court, to set hearths in the midst of the room for chimneys, which vented the smoke at a louvre in the top . . .' (p124). Elsewhere in the *Survey*, when describing the buildings of the yeomanry he wrote of: 'walls of earth, low thatched roofs, few partitions, no planchings or glass windows, and scarcely any chimneys other than a hole in the wall to let out the smoke' (p138). The improvements associated with the 'Great Rebuild' in the 16th and 17th centuries led to the addition of upper floors over the subsidiary rooms, often jettied out into the hall space; the insertion of chimneys and the increasing importance of the parlour which sometimes involved throwing out a wing at right angles to the main building. Entrances were given some architectural pretension and courtyards were walled as at **Leigh Barton** (63, D). There was a movement towards internal refinement with painted and moulded screens and decorative plaster ceilings. The two-unit plan of ground floor and chambers above eventually led to a plan form two rooms

deep instead of the single line. By the 18th century, vernacular houses were conforming to a more familiar regularity of room size and fenestration.

Outside the house were the barns, the linhay or open-fronted cattle shed, the enclosed shippon or byre, the ash-house, and perhaps, a stable and round-house for the horse gin. The ancillary buildings of a Dartmoor hamlet are well demonstrated at Lettaford. The major surviving medieval barns belonged mostly to the larger ecclesiastical institutions. The remaining dovecotes or culver-houses (Crafthole (C) and Trevanion, Wadebridge (C)) are circular. There are still about twenty dovecotes in Devon. Windmills were generally a manorial institution in the Middle Ages; and a revival of interest in the late 16th and early 17th centuries, coincided with an increase in agricultural production. A few towers still stand. More common are water mills.

Peculiar to Cornwall are holy wells and the *plen an gwarry* (amphitheatres). Both have religious connotations though the Christian aspect may have replaced something earlier. Many springs are associated with the name of a saint, and there are about forty which have some form of building over them. These can range from a simple well-house to sometimes full-blown chapels (**Dupath Well Chapel**, 59, C). The

amphitheatres known as *plen an gwarry* are recorded as places for the performance of Cornish mystery plays. They are as likely as not to be adaptations of the earthworks of Iron Age enclosed settlements (**St Piran's Round**, 65, C).

Particular forms of town house evolved in the south-west, best seen in the south-coast towns such as **Totnes** (32), **Dartmouth** (24) and **Plymouth** (30). Characteristically, they are timber-framed with stone side walls (for fire prevention) with the gable end to the street and entered from a side passage. They were usually taller than one storey and were often of three. This was a fashion which extended to small inland towns as well as the larger towns. Plan forms could vary but a distinguishing regional type involved a back-block behind, separated by a small courtyard from the shop and hall in front but often connected to the main house by a gallery at an upper level.

Industry has had its own effect on the pattern of settlement and of housing. The landscape of west Cornwall is dominated by the cottages of miners and mining villages and their accompanying chapels. The same is true of the more recent china clay landscape north of St Austell. An early 19th-century development at **Halestown** (60), St Ives, was a planned town for mine workers which combined philanthropy with ballot rigging. Model industrial housing, again for miners but on a more extensive scale and with greater architectural sophistication, was that of the Duke of Bedford at **Tavistock** (31, D). At Tiverton (D), housing for the Heathcoats' laceworkers mirrors, on a much smaller scale, the northern model industrial villages of Saltaire and Port Sunlight.

58

Braunton Great Field
Medieval

SS 475356. Braunton. SW of town from A361

[D]

The Great Field (350 acres or 142 ha in extent) is bounded by the River Caen, which enters the Taw estuary, and Braunton Marsh, which was reclaimed early in the 18th century. It remains one of the very few open fields in the country which is still cultivated in common on the medieval strip system. As at Laxton in Nottinghamshire, the patterns of unhedged strips covering a large area of the countryside are the last remnants of this form of agriculture. At Braunton, the divisions between the strips are marked by low grass baulks and sometimes large beach pebbles at the ends of the strips rather than by a furrow as they commonly were in the Midlands. The Great Field was referred to in a document of 1324 which recorded a particular holding of 26½ acres in 25 different strips. In 1840 some 600 strips were cultivated by as many as 60 different people. In 1986, there were 140 strips still farmed commercially.

In the Middle Ages, the occupancy of the strips was divided up between the community to ensure an equable division between good and poor land. There is considerable evidence in the south-west for the early, widespread use of open field cultivation, but it was going out of use during the course of the Middle Ages with the enclosure of fields, and generally did not survive into the 18th and 19th centuries.

59
Dupath Well Chapel
15th century

SX 375693. Callington. 1 mile SE of Callington by minor roads SE off the A390 or NW from the A388

[A] EH

The late Henry Jenner estimated that 'In Cornwall there are considerably over a hundred natural springs or wells which, having appropriate names attached to them or special qualities attributed to them, may be accounted as "holy", though their sanctity is not necessarily always of Christian origin' ('The Holy Wells of Cornwall', *The Cornish Church Guide*, Truro, 1928, p249). Many are named after saints or are associated with churches. Many were believed to have particular healing qualities. Dupath Well was one of those resorted to for any

Dupath Well Chapel. EH

illness. About forty wells in Cornwall have buildings over them, most are simple, small, gabled houses. Some cover buildings take the form of chapels with altars associated with them. There are others with smaller but elaborate cover structures. Of the latter, Dupath is one, and is perhaps the most ornate.

Dupath belonged to the canons of St Germans and the square granite structure probably belongs to the late-15th century. There is a sunken basin at the far end and the water, coming in from the front, runs into the basin presumably for bathing purposes and overflows outside the building. The steeply pitched roof is composed of granite slabs and is vaulted internally. The chapel is crowned with a bellcote-like turret with carved pinnacles over the entrance. There are also pinnacles at the corners of the entrance front.

60
Halestown
19th century

SW 506386. St Ives. E of the B3311, 1½ miles SW of St Ives

[D]

This is a planned industrial village built in the 1830s by a James Halse, solicitor, politician and mining adventurer, to house several hundred, of his

Braunton Great Field from the air. CUCAP

Village shop, Halestown. E BERRY

workpeople. He was Tory member for St Ives between 1826 and 1838, and the project was reputed to be not so much philanthropy as a design to secure the franchise of his employees under the property qualifications of the 1832 Reform Act, and so increase his chances of being returned again to Westminster.

About eighty houses and cottages arranged in widely spaced pairs and threes were laid out along three roughly parallel 'streets' each with a substantial garden. A cross-street still has its well-defined stone gutter. The quality of the design and construction of the buildings is very high. In addition to the nearby tin mine, the village had a ropeworks. There was a chapel for Wesleyan Methodists (now converted into flats), an inn, and a school house with a residence for the master.

61
Houndtor Medieval Settlement
12th–13th century

SX 744788. Manaton. N from B3387, 1½ miles E of Widecombe-in-the-Moor. Parking-place at cross-roads W of Hound Tor then by footpath

[A] EH

The abandoned medieval hamlet lies at about the 1,000 ft (305 m) contour just below Hound Tor. It consists of a cluster of rectangular structures within an early field system and was occupied in the 12th and 13th centuries. It is likely that the hamlet was an extension from other holdings in the valley in the vicinity of the modern farm of Great Houndtor. Pollen analysis has shown that at some

time in the 14th century local cereal production ceased. The arable was converted to permanent pasture in the last two hundred years or so.

The hamlet comprises four long-houses, four smaller houses, a shed, and three corn-drying barns associated with small closes or gardens. The houses show considerable variation in both plan and size. The long-houses usually had an inner room as well as a living-room, and a byre separated from the cross-passage by a wall. One house has an additional inner room. The living-rooms were heated from central hearths. The use of the lower rooms as byres is established by the central drains. One large house, which had two smaller houses associated with it within a common yard and enclosure wall, was given the title of 'manor house' by its excavators, although there is no documentary evidence for the existence of a manor house at Houndtor. One of the four smaller houses had evidence of a central drain towards the lower end suggesting

that cattle were kept under the same roof, and generally they appeared to be simple homesteads of lower status. The three barns with built-in corn-drying ovens and associated malting kilns lay in a line to the north-west of the settlement itself.

There was some archaeological evidence for an earlier form of settlement on the site. Three sunken-floored structures were sealed by the later houses, but the presence of early stake and turf structures and the suggestion that the settlement was originally of Saxon date are a matter of debate. A separate farmstead, some 340 yds (371 m) north-west of the hamlet was built within a prehistoric pound and made use of the remains of hut circles within it.

The fields around the settlement are part of a palimsest built up over many periods of farming, broadly: prehistoric, medieval and modern. The medieval occupation involved the remodelling and adaptation of the prehistoric field

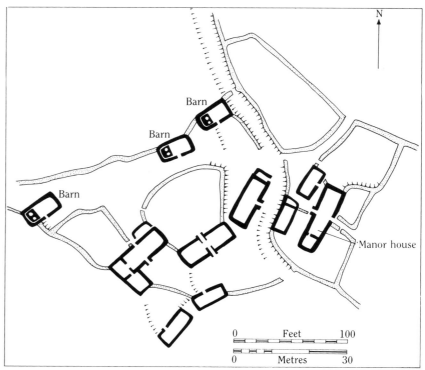

Houndtor medieval settlement (after G Beresford). EH

system. It comprised a number of arable fields of irregular size and shape which probably functioned as open-field furlongs. Several are subdivided into a series of strip lynchets, now mostly ploughed down. There is a further series of fields which are larger and more rectangular, bounded by ditches, not banks. Climatic deterioration began in the middle of the 13th century. It was gradual and led to the conversion of some abandoned houses for use as barns at Houndtor. By the middle of the 14th century, deteriorating conditions meant that settlements above the 1,000 ft (305 m) contour were untenable.

62

Kirkham House, Paignton
Late medieval

SX 888609. Paignton. In Kirkham Street
[A] EH

Kirkham House is a late-medieval house, which was later divided into two cottages and has since been restored to a unity with the removal of additions. It has the traditional three-room plan found in rural farmhouses but there are indications of a higher status as might be expected in its situation within an urban context, and not far from a palace of the bishops of Exeter.

The ogee-headed front doorway gives on to a passage, which has a well-preserved stud-and-panel screen with shouldered doorways. On either side of the passage are the hall and parlour, and there is another (unheated) room beyond the hall. The stone-hooded fireplaces in the hall and parlour have crenellated cresting and there are also stone basins in each room. Together with the moulded beams they give an impression of some degree of affluence. A characteristic feature of this type of building is an upper chamber jettied out over the cross-passage into the hall. The three chambers on the upper floor are entered from a gallery along the back of the house. The chamber over the parlour was the best room with a hooded fireplace. The room at the opposite end of the building has a plainer fireplace

but has its own garderobe. The kitchen was in a separate building to the rear and only foundations remain.

The house was furnished in the 1980s with modern craft furniture, textiles and ceramics.

63

Leigh Barton
15th–16th century

SX 721467. Churchstow. Turn off the A381 Totnes–Kingsbridge road to the B3194, then N by a lane at cross-roads ¼ mile E of Churchstow
[A] EH

This remarkable and puzzling group of late-medieval buildings constitutes an establishment of some style and pretension. It is associated with Buckfast Abbey but there is no evidence to show that the abbey had a grange here at Leigh, though it held lands in Churchstow. It has been suggested that it was built by the abbey on the land, and adjacent to the house, of a freeholder, John Leigh, as a residential retreat in which the abbot or other members of the abbey might stay from time to time on its Churchstow manor away from its direct tenants.

Fronting a lane leading from Kingsbridge to Aveton Gifford is a finely built gatehouse. A chamber over the nearly round-headed gate-arch has a fireplace and a garderobe. There are lengths of curtain wall on either side, but this is just a frontispiece, and there is no indication of the other boundaries of the property.

Opposite the gatehouse, across a courtyard, is a farmhouse and behind that on the other side of a small yard is an L-shaped two-storey range in the same fine masonry as the gatehouse. The ground floor contained a substantial kitchen whose massive chimney breast once occupied virtually the whole east wall. There is a serving hatch in the south wall underneath the external stair and gallery. The long room on the west may have been divided by a screen but there is nothing to suggest that this room was used for anything other than storage. The lodgings were on the first floor. The two in the south range were approached by an external covered stair and a gallery with an open timber arcade. The two rooms were of different quality. That to the west was the superior. It has a four-bay arch-braced collar roof, and the other a roof of four wider bays whose principals are joined by simple unbraced collars. A stud partition separates them; it divides the

Leigh Barton: the gallery to the lodgings range, before repair. EH

common entrance from the gallery and also the projecting garderobes. The main chamber had its own fireplace, the lesser chamber took its heating from the kitchen fireplace below. There was a third lodging in the west wing which may represent the quarters of a resident official. This was not entered from the farmhouse range originally, but by an internal gallery over the storage room below. The roof is modern but it was originally similar to that of the lesser chamber.

The farmhouse as it stands today is largely of the 17th century but it has medieval antecedents. There are visible elements from the earlier phases of its life. The earliest masonry is at the west or service end. There are fragments also of a richly decorated, early-16th-century screen for an open hall.

64

Old Post Office, Tintagel
15th–17th century

SX 056885. Tintagel. In main street
[A] NT

The best known of the small late-medieval hall-houses remaining in Cornwall, this was probably the

principal house of the manor of Trevena and built in the 15th century. It gets its present name from having served as a post office from 1844 to 1892. It was saved from demolition by the artist, Catherine Johns, and was among the first buildings to be acquired by the National Trust in 1903.

The house is built in local slate rubble with a few dressings in 'greenstone', a local igneous intrusion. Some of the smaller windows are narrow lights cut from this material. The roof covering is of heavy slate, which has contributed to the picturesque distortion of the roof line. The heavy, stepped, chimney stacks are a local vernacular feature, but the one beside the porch is a modern reconstruction.

The ground floor has a three-part plan; a central hall open to the roof whose construction is of raised cruck trusses with cambered collars. There is an integral porch on the east side of a cross-passage at the lower end of the hall which has a gallery over it. The window beside the fireplace forms a roughly built oriel. The low-end room to the north with a single central doorway conventionally might be expected to be the kitchen and service end and it has substantial fireplaces. Yet by analogy with other south-western houses of

higher quality it has been suggested that this may have been an 'inner room' or parlour rather than a service room. The room at the higher end of the hall may be an addition, although there are close similarities of construction with the hall. It could have served as a second parlour, though it does have an oven and therefore may have had a more functional use. It is now displayed as a Victorian post office. Each end-room has an upper chamber. The southern chamber is reached by a spiral stair in a turret, originally from the hall. The chamber was enlarged by a transverse roof and gable in the late 16th or 17th century. The northern chamber and the gallery are approached by a steep straight stair.

65

St Piran's Round
Late medieval

SW 779545. Perranzabuloe. On N side of the B3285, ¾ mile W of Goonhavern and E of Perranporth
[A]

St Piran's Round is a circular earthwork 154 ft (45 m) across. The bank stands over 8 ft (2.5 m) above the interior and there is an external ditch. The enclosure may originally have been one of a type of Iron Age settlement known in Cornwall as a 'round' occupied in the period between the 3rd/2nd centuries BC and the 3rd/4th centuries AD. This particular enclosure is traditionally regarded as a medieval *plen an gwarry* (literally 'plain of the play') or 'playing place' for the performance of Cornish miracle plays. The internal slope of the bank was adapted for seating although there is now no trace of this. There are opposed entrances, north-west to south-east.

The *plen an gwarry* was not an uncommon feature of medieval Cornish life and the place-name 'playing place' occurs occasionally even though actual examples are now few. The performance of miracle plays had widespread popularity in Cornwall. Most of the surviving Cornish texts emanated from the once famous centre of learning, Glasney College, Penryn. The

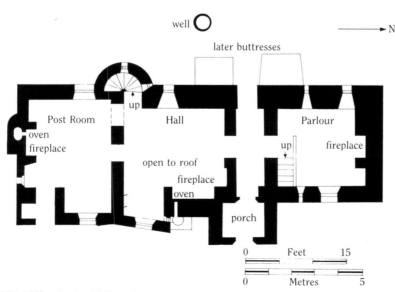

Old Post Office, Tintagel (after NT). EH

performances were of necessity in the open air. There is another fine example of a *plen an gwarry* in the centre of St Just in Penwith, and at Castilly, Luxulyan, excavation has shown that a Neolithic henge monument was converted to just such a use in the 13th or 14th century. The attribution to St Piran is not surprising in a parish dedicated to the saint, and where the remains of early religious sites associated with him may also be found.

Sanders, Lettaford. J COX

66

Sanders, Lettaford
c.15th–17th century

SX 702841. North Bovey. Signposted off the minor road to Chagford from a junction N of B3212, 3½ miles W of Moretonhampstead

[B] LT

Lettaford has been described as a typical Dartmoor hamlet with three long-houses and associated farm buildings around a small green. There is also a former Bible Christian chapel and school which were built in 1866. Of the long-houses the best preserved, and one of the best examples of its type, is Sanders.

Long-house is the name given to a fairly ubiquitous type of rural dwelling where the domestic house and the cattle byre shared a common roof but were separated by a cross-passage. At Sanders,

a central porch with massive jambs and shouldered lintel covers one end of a wide cross-passage. At the upper end of the building is a hall entered from the cross-passage. Beyond is an inner room. Three late-medieval roof-trusses survive, two on short raised crucks. The upper chamber, jettied into the hall, has an original closed truss. There is little left of the second chamber jettied out over the cross-passage because of the later insertion of the axial chimney stack and the stair projection.

At the lower end is the byre or shippon with a characteristic drain of stone slabs running centrally to an outlet in the end wall. The cattle were tethered with their heads facing the long walls, which have splayed ventilation slits, and tethering stakes were embedded in drilled stones sunk into the floor. The original roof of the byre has

gone but the early hay-loft cross-beams remain.

There are signs of later adaptations. What was probably a dairy was added to the back of the upper end in the 17th century, and entered directly from the hall. To the rear is a thatched, stone-built barn. The house was restored for the Landmark Trust in 1975–7.

67

Trowlesworthy Warren
13th–19th century

SX 575645. Shaugh Prior. By foot eastwards and S of the River Plym from Cadover Bridge which is on the minor road between Shaugh Prior and Meavy

[A]

The warrening of rabbits has long been a factor in the economy of Dartmoor. Rabbits were introduced into England by the Normans, and there is documentary evidence to suggest that they existed on Dartmoor in the 12th century. The earliest warrens were in the Plym valley, and of the five that are known there, Trowlesworthy is thought to be the oldest. It was granted by Baldwin de Redvers, Earl of Devon, to Sampson de Traylesworthy at some point in the 13th century. In 1551, it was leased by John Crocker of Lynham to William Woolcombe of Holland Farm and has remained with this family to the present day. By the 17th century, there were many private warrens, mainly on

St Piran's Round in 1896. RIC

Trowlesworthy Warren from the air. WEST AIR PHOTOGRAPHY

68

West Penwith Field Systems, Zennor

Bronze Age–present day

SW 454385. Zennor

[D]

The Land's End peninsula contains elements of Bronze Age, medieval and later field systems over a large area of farmland which give this treeless, stone-walled landscape a particular visual and archaeological character and importance. The farmland in the neighbourhood of Zennor provides good examples of this rare but still dynamic survival of early agricultural land apportionment.

Despite the effects of recent clearances of field walls enabling agricultural 'improvements', large areas of this palimpsest of ancient field patterns remain, often focused on present-day farms which frequently have medieval predecessors. Many of the field boundaries are Bronze Age in origin. The prehistoric system of small fields was more rectilinear in its layout than now appears, as subsequent boundary removal here and there has lent an irregular shape to many of the fields. Such is the historic importance of this landscape that West Penwith was among the first of the government-designated Environmentally Sensitive Areas.

uncultivated areas of waste land, where the rabbits were left to breed and were then trapped or shot as required for food on a commercial basis.

The construction of a warren involved three elements: the provision of a warrener's house and accommodation for dogs, the building of a boundary wall where a water barrier did not exist to restrict the movement of the rabbits, and the construction of long artificial burrows in which the rabbits would live and breed, known as 'buries' in Devon, pillow mounds elsewhere. The 'buries' were substantial structures. On Dartmoor the topsoil is peat which is usually wet and unsuitable for a burrowing animal. The 'buries' therefore had to be constructed above ground with piles of rocks covered with soil leaving holes for access, and with deep drainage ditches on either side. They vary in length from *c*. 5 yds (4.5 m) to over 80 yds (73 m) and are usually sited down the slopes of hillsides to encourage drainage, and often arranged in groups convenient for netting. Periodically the ditches were cleaned out and the soil and peat piled on top of the 'bury'. More than 160 'buries' have been recorded on

the Plym warrens alone. The rabbits were encouraged to breed during the summer and were caught in large numbers from September to March and sold in Plymouth. The practice of warrening continued until the mid-1950s.

A feature of the Dartmoor warrens, but not recognised elsewhere in Britain, are vermin traps since the warrens attracted predators such as stoats and weasels. On Dartmoor these are constructed from five extremely heavy stones and are perhaps 4 ft (1.2 m) long with trips which would allow slates above the entrances to drop and seal the trap.

At Trowlesworthy, the Warren House is comparatively modern, replacing an older building since demolished. In the vicinity of the house are a number of enclosed fields, one of them is named Kennel and was presumably used to keep the dogs. The field is enclosed by an 8 ft (2.4 m) high wall, capped by large inwardly projecting stones to prevent the dogs escaping. Nearly forty vermin traps have been recorded, the largest number for any of the Dartmoor warrens.

West Penwith from the air. NLAR

7

Castles and Later Fortifications

The full effects of the Norman Conquest on the south-west were probably not felt until after the quelling of an English revolt which centered on Exeter at the end of 1067. This provoked a siege lasting eighteen days, and a military campaign down the peninsula. A castle was built in the north-western angle of the Roman walls of Exeter and it is likely that castles were also planted in the other Devon *burhs* of Barnstaple, Totnes (32) and Lydford (19). The two Cornish castles mentioned in the Domesday Book of 1086 are at **Launceston** (72) and Trematon, both strategically sited to control the land access into Cornwall and the southern route from the mouth of the River Tamar respectively. The partition of Saxon estates among the Conqueror's supporters followed, and this too led to the erection of castles by leading magnates to control their fiefs.

There were about two dozen timber castles in both counties which had a limited life and now survive as earthworks, many of the motte-and-bailey type, others simple enclosures or ring-works. Kilkhampton (C), Bossiney (C), Week St Mary (C), Cardinham (C), Burley Wood (D), Loddiswell (D), Holwell at Parracombe (D), and Bampton (D) are particularly good examples. Some of these short-lived castles belong to the mid-12th-century conflicts of the Anarchy. The castles which enjoyed continuity of occupation and developed into more permanent masonry structures were generally those which were in the towns or were held by the major lordly families. Those pertaining to the earldom of Cornwall – Launceston, Trematon, **Restormel** (75) and Tintagel (23) – are particularly prominent, largely through the rebuilding campaigns of Richard, Earl of Cornwall in the mid-13th century. The Courtenay earls of Devon had a major role at **Okehampton** (73), Plympton and Tiverton. Exeter was in the king's hands for much of the Middle Ages. As many existing towns had castles planted upon them or were created as an economic base alongside a castle, town walls are an occasional feature. Exeter's (26) were inherited from the Roman town. Totnes and Barnstaple were walled and so was Launceston, the only town in Cornwall so protected. Apart from Exeter none have conspicuously survived.

A design feature, which by no means is confined to the south-west but is distinctive among Cornish and Devonshire castles, is the 'shell keep' – a masonry wall around the summit of a motte, or, in the case of Restormel, around the circuit of a ringwork – with residential and other structures built inside and against it, and serving in place of a tower. Launceston combines both with the insertion of a later round tower within the then-outdated shell keep. Plympton (D), Totnes (D) and Trematon (C) are the other exponents of this form. Of castles of this type, Restormel is the most instructive since the timber buildings against the inner face of the shell keep were replaced in stone at the end of the 13th century to create a residence. Castles which were adapted in later years into semi-fortified residences are best exemplified by Okehampton (73, D). Such fortified houses could still maintain a warlike function, as was demonstrated by the siege of Hemyock Castle (D) during the period of aristocratic feuding known as the Wars of the Roses.

While castles changed from being primarily fortresses into the defensible houses of the later Middle Ages, the effects of the Hundred Years' War with France increased the dangers of raiding and destruction for coastal trading towns. From the late 14th century and into the 15th century, the pressures to protect ports and harbours coincided with the increasing use of gunpowder weapons, and it is in the blockhouses at Fowey (28, C) and Polruan, in the early blockhouses at the water's edge at Plymouth (30, D) and particularly at the entrance to **Dartmouth** Haven (71, C) that provision for the early defensive use of artillery can be seen.

Coastal defence on a national and systematic scale was first undertaken in 1539 under the direction of Henry VIII. The years 1538–9 were a period of political crisis stemming from Henry's break with Rome and the first signs of Protestantism taking a hold in England. Invasion threatened from the Catholic powers. A map of 1540 shows how the south coast of Devon and Cornwall was protected with the blockhouses and forts already in existence, under construction or proposed. There are still remains of blockhouses of this period at Plymouth, Salcombe (D) and Fowey (C), but the principal forts were **Pendennis** (74) and **St Mawes** (77) castles defending the entrance to Falmouth Harbour. In the 1550s, the Isles of Scilly were given defences, and it is here at Harry's Walls on St Mary's that the first developed Italian style of angle-bastion fort in England can be seen. The south-west counties continued to be in the front line at the end of the 16th century as the likely threat was now from Spain, especially after the 1588 Armada. The defences of **Scilly** (78) were improved, the first fort was built on Plymouth Hoe, and Pendennis Castle was brought up-to-date in the latest fashion of military engineering.

During the Civil War, Exeter (26), Dartmouth (24) and Plymouth (30) were seriously fortified, but again it is in the Isles of Scilly where the Royalist batteries and breastworks can be traced. After the Restoration of Charles II, a splendid new bastioned **Citadel** (76) was built at Plymouth and from then on until the end of the 19th century coastal fortification was a spasmodic but necessary occupation.

The creation of the naval dockyard at Devonport made Plymouth the core of defensive preparation. The threat of invasion from Napoleonic France was very real in 1803–5. Scilly had mid-18th-century defences on the **Garrison** (78), and batteries and redoubts on Maker Heights, Cornwall covered the western approaches to Plymouth Dockyard. The anchorage of Torbay was similarly protected **Berry Head Batteries**, (69, D).

Dartmouth Castle. EH

Berry Head Batteries from the air. DCC/F M GRIFFITH

Devonport was ringed by a continuous bastion *enceinte*, now barely traceable. Additional defences were added in the 1850s but a popular panic in 1859 over an imagined French invasion attempt resulted in a prodigious feat of fortress building nationwide, lasting a decade, in which Plymouth ranked second in importance only to Portsmouth. The towns and dockyard were ringed with land forts as well as provided with modern sea batteries (**Crownhill Fort**, 70, D). Batteries were provided at ports like St Ives (C) and Dartmouth at the same time. The defences of Falmouth continued to be strengthened towards the close of the 19th century. The more recent invasion threat of 1940 has also left its mark in pillboxes and new gun positions, but with the ending of coastal defence in 1956, these modern fortifications have become as much part of the heritage as the Norman castles.

69

Berry Head Batteries, Brixham

18th–19th century

SX 946566. In Berry Head Country Park E of Brixham harbour. Signposted.

[A]

Torbay was a much used anchorage, and in the last decades of the 18th century it

was thought advisable to guard it. This became more imperative during the Napoleonic Wars. Batteries were in existence by 1783, and they, and the associated defended barracks, were substantially revised by Alexander Mercer between 1794 and 1804.

A drawing of 1807 shows the positions of individual batteries, but also the defensive works associated with them. An effective way of neutralising a coastal battery was for the attacker to put a landing party ashore and disable the battery from the rear. To prevent this, an earthwork cut off the tip of the headland from the beginning. This was formalised by Mercer with a revetted and angled earthwork from cliff to cliff. Inside were the barrack structures and associated buildings. In advance of this defensible line were two irregular-shaped redoubts and a separate shorter length of earthwork near the northern cliff edge. These three detached works were linked by a palisade. Such detached works of this date are of considerable interest, because they mark a shift in the thinking that continuous bastioned lines were the only answer to defensive problems.

The condition of this interesting defensive feature has been considerably improved in recent years, since falling within the bounds of a country park. The barracks are missing (they were prefabricated structures anyway) and only an artillery store and guardhouse remain, but the fortifications themselves including No. 1 redoubt survive substantially.

70

Crownhill Fort, Plymouth
19th century

SX 487593. Off the A386 N of the Crownhill interchange on the A38.

[A] LT

The Royal Commission on the Defences of the United Kingdom published its findings in 1860. Among the many recommendations were proposals for the better defence of Plymouth, which it considered to be the second great naval arsenal and port after Portsmouth in the United Kingdom. The Commission endorsed many of the recommendations that had been made in respect of Plymouth by the military two years earlier – that, as well as strengthening the batteries covering Plymouth Sound and the sea approaches, there should be full protection from attack from the landward side. This involved forts on the Cornish side of the Tamar to counter an assault on the dockyard at Devonport. The Commission also proposed a line of detached forts on the high ground behind Plymouth. These were termed the North Eastern Defences and, of the eleven forts and batteries between the Tamar at St Budeaux and the Plym near Laira, Crownhill Fort was at the centre and was the key to the whole position.

In common with nearly all British forts of the mid-19th century, the concepts of the bastion system of Vauban and his imitators had been

Entrance to Crownhill Fort, Plymouth. J COX

abandoned and Crownhill was designed on 'polygonal' principles. It was therefore self-contained, and had a mutually supporting role with Woodlands Fort to the west and Bowden Fort to the east. It is an extensive seven-sided earthwork surrounded by a deep ditch, 30 ft wide, each arm of which is flanked by a caponier and by scarp galleries for local defence. The main armament of 32 guns, including 4 in Haxo casemates and 6 mortars, was mounted on the ramparts. There were casemated barracks for 300 men. The North Eastern Defences were designed by the then Captain, Edmund du Cane. Work on the fort was completed in 1868. It has been continuously garrisoned until recent years so that it is in a very good state of preservation. It is now in the process of restoration and re-use.

71

Dartmouth Castle
15th–20th century

SX 887503. SE of town. Signposted from the B3205

[A] EH

Dartmouth Castle has a special place in the history of artillery fortification in this country, because it is here that we first see gunports for heavy guns in a purpose-built fort. The castle was begun by the townspeople in 1481 and completed by 1494, with royal subsidies, to protect the entrance to Dartmouth Haven and the prosperous merchant port from French and Breton raids. It was built immediately to the west of St Petrock's Church on the water's edge, and within an earlier fortified enclosure of the 14th century. A high curtain wall and the ruin of a tower belonging to this defence can be seen behind the car park on the other side of the church. In 1491, a companion fort to that of Dartmouth was begun on the Kingswear side of the estuary. There was, in addition, a chain boom which could be stretched across the estuary from Dartmouth Castle to a point further upstream.

The 'strong tower' is really a double tower. Work began on a small round tower but, after this had been taken to a

fair height, there was a change of plan and a rectangular tower was built alongside and then merged with the earlier. The main armament was placed in the basement with the guns in seven rectangular embrasures close to water level. To protect them from weather, external shutters were provided. There were also open batteries on either side of the tower. Garrison accommodation was in the upper two floors, which themselves had loops for handguns as well as windows, and more guns would have been mounted on the roof. In the 'round tower', at ground-floor level, is a large framed opening with slots for the axle of a pulley, and holes in the rock at the back of the room may have fixed the windlass for hauling in the chain boom.

Apart from repairs and minor alterations to the castle, the main improvements lay outside with the addition of new gun batteries. Lamberd's Bulwark, on the cliff edge where the 19th-century battery now stands, was referred to in 1547. Dartmouth was successfully besieged by the Parliamentary army of Sir Thomas Fairfax in 1646 and the castle was part of a ring of Royalist defences round the town. In the 18th century, Lamberd's Bulwark had become Maiden Fort with two tiers of guns and was rebuilt several times. The last major defensive transformation came in 1861 with the construction of a substantial granite-faced battery for five 64-pounder guns, three in bombproof casemates and two in an open battery above. In 1940, this battery was again pressed into active service and two 4.7 in quick-firer guns were mounted on the open battery.

72

Launceston Castle
11th–19th century

SX 331847. The castle occupies a dominant position on the western side of the town

[A] EH

Launceston Castle was one of two Cornish castles mentioned in the Domesday Book of 1086 when it was held by Robert, Count of Mortain. It was

Launceston Castle. EH

younger brother of King Henry III, was made Earl of Cornwall. The defences were remodelled with the insertion of the high tower within the shell keep, the gatehouses were reconstructed, and a continuous stone curtain wall was built round the bailey. Most of the visible masonry we see today belongs to this time.

As well as the defences, the bailey was completely reorganised. The Great Hall was rebuilt on a large scale with its own kitchen separated from it by a walled yard. A slightly earlier administrative hall was at right angles to the kitchen. These buildings have been excavated and their remains consolidated, though the Great Hall only survives in plan. It continued in use as the assize hall until the turn of the 17th century. The north gate, the constable's traditional residence, served also as a prison for the Catholic, Cuthbert Mayne, and the Quaker, George Fox. The 18th-century county gaol was removed when the castle was turned into a town park in the 1840s.

to be the principal castle of the future earls (later dukes) of Cornwall, and, although it lost much of its administrative purpose towards the end of the 13th century, it remained the centre for justice in the county. Even after its medieval buildings fell into ruin, it still contained the county gaol until 1840.

Launceston possessed great strategic importance. The castle controlled the whole of the country between Bodmin Moor and the western edge of Dartmoor. It overlooked the ford and later bridge at Polson nearby, which until the construction of the Tamar road bridge at Saltash was the chief landward entry into Cornwall. The earthworks of the castle are set on a ridge of high ground which falls sharply on the west and to the River Kensey on the north.

Towering over the roofs of the town, it is still a reminder of the authority of the earls of Cornwall. Yet very little of the castle survives other than its impressive defences: the high motte, crowned by its shell keep and tower, the ruined gatehouses and some lengths of stone curtain wall. The most obvious

features are the earthworks: the motte, half-natural and half-artificial, which formed the citadel of a rectangular embanked enclosure or bailey contrived on a steeply sloping ridge. It was a highly defensible site in terms of early-medieval warfare.

In recent years archaeology has added to what is known of the castle from historical sources. Excavation has revealed the sequence and character of the defences and given an insight into the sort of buildings that occupied the bailey throughout the Middle Ages. The first defences were clay and rubble ramparts fronted with timber. Inside were temporary huts of the initial garrison and, soon after, a substantial timber hall as the focal point of a crowded bailey. These buildings were soon replaced with more substantial timber constructions, and the defences were progressively remodelled, though still having timber breastworks. Only the great hall, the south gatehouse and the shell keep on the motte seem to have been built in stone during the 12th century. The greatest changes came in the mid-13th century when Richard,

73

Okehampton Castle
11th–15th century

SX 584943. One mile S of the town. Signposted from the A390 in the town centre

[A]   EH

Okehampton Castle was founded soon after the Norman Conquest, and was certainly in existence by the time of the compilation of the Domesday Book in 1086. It was held by Baldwin, sheriff of Devon. It later came into the hands of the Courtenay earls of Devon. Today, its compact bailey contains the well preserved remains, often to full wall-top height, of the essential components of a lordly residence of the early 14th century. It is in this respect the most complete and least altered example in Devonshire of the transformation which affected many early castles in the later Middle Ages.

The castle is located on a spur projecting into the West Okement river valley on the northern edge of

Okehampton Castle bailey from the motte. EH

Dartmoor, and stood beside an important route to Cornwall from the east. The lofty, part-natural motte must represent the earliest castle structure. The earthworks of a bailey remain in the wood to the west but it is the narrow bailey to the east which provides evidence of continuity of occupation. The masonry tower on the motte is of two phases. The first building was a small, square tower of the late 11th century, set towards the eastern edge of the motte. A rectangular block was added to the west side of this tower towards the end of the 13th century. This addition may be associated with the overall rebuilding campaign, which transformed the eastern bailey into a defensible residence.

The rebuilding of the castle is historically linked with Hugh Courtenay II, who died in 1340. The Great Hall lies on the north side of the bailey. It had a roof of base-cruck timber trusses set high in the wall in five bays, of which one bay covered the two-storey chamber block at the west end, one the screens, and the other three the open hall itself. Further west of the hall and chamber block was a detached kitchen with

additional service rooms extending southwards. At the western end, and added later in the 14th or early 15th centuries, are two well-preserved ovens. On the opposite side of the narrow courtyard was the chapel with a priest's lodgings attached. East of the chapel was a fine set of lodgings on two floors, the three grander apartments were on the first floor. The inner and outer gatehouses, which were attached by a long walled barbican, were all part of the same building scheme.

Archaeological excavation has shown that there were earlier phases of building beneath the hall, and there is a substantial length of thick curtain wall immediately outside the hall which belongs to the 12th century. For the later years of the castle's life there was much evidence of hunting parties during the 15th century. Life went on there into the 17th century when a late-medieval lodging west of the chapel was converted into a bakehouse and the barbican gatehouse seems to have been occupied. The castle, however, was in much the same ruined state as it is today when it was sketched by the brothers Buck in the 1730s.

74

Pendennis Castle
16th–20th century

SW 824317. Falmouth. Signposted from Castle Drive, Pendennis Head
[A] EH

The nucleus of Pendennis Castle belongs to the series of coastal forts built by Henry VIII to protect the more important anchorages from use by a threatened invasion force. Pendennis, together with St Mawes opposite, was intended to guard Falmouth haven. Building began in 1540 and was completed in 1545. The castle consists of a central tower, to which is attached a set of lodgings for the governor, and is surrounded by a low earth-backed polygonal curtain wall. The tower has a basement store and kitchen, a main gun-deck at entrance level and an upper floor also capable of mounting guns. The roof was another gun platform. The outer curtain is a later addition, and its parapet masks the circular embrasures in the main gun-deck of the tower. Nor were the governor's lodgings part of the original design. Early maps show a twin-towered gatehouse on the line of the curtain but there is now no trace of this.

Of much the same date as the castle, or slightly earlier, is a small blockhouse, called Little Dennis, on the tip of the promontory and at the water's edge. It too is matched by a similarly placed blockhouse below St Mawes Castle. Originally, it had three small gunports modified by the insertion of a much larger one of similar proportions to those in the castle.

The military significance of Pendennis continued thereafter. In view of the Spanish threat to the south-west in the years following the Armada, the defences were enlarged and brought up to date in 1597 to the design of an English military engineer, Paul Ive. The earlier castle was enclosed by an irregular but massive stone-faced earthwork trace including seven angle bastions and demi-bastions. There were additional outer earthworks cutting off the promontory and providing defence in depth for the vulnerable landward

Pendennis Castle keep from the west. EH

approach. The main granite gateway and associated buildings were not completed until 1611. Such was the castle which became a Royalist stronghold during the Civil War and held out for five months in 1646 before surrendering to Fairfax's army.

Pendennis continued to be maintained during the 18th century. The main batteries were now on the foreshore, principally at Crab Quay, to the north of Little Dennis and on the Half Moon Battery below the Tudor castle but outside the Elizabethan *enceinte*. At the time of the French invasion scare of 1803–5 there were 48 guns mounted here. Between 1894 and 1895, emplacements for three 6-in breech-loading guns were built and the guns mounted: two in the Half Moon Battery and the third in the south-east bastion of the fort. By 1898, Crab Quay Battery had been partially remodelled to mount two 6-pounder quick-firing guns to protect a minefield that was to be laid between Pendennis and St Mawes. These batteries, equipped with more modern armament, were manned throughout the Second World War and were not finally disarmed until 1956.

Within the fort there are few remains of early barrack and garrison buildings; the interior is now dominated by the extensive barrack block of 1901. Those buildings that do survive belong to the Napoleonic War period: the field train shed immediately behind the main battery and the building variously described as a 'store' and a 'hospital' between the barrack block and the gatehouse.

75
Restormel Castle
11th–14th century

SX 104614. 1½ miles N of Lostwithiel. Signposted from the A390

[A] EH

Restormel formed part of the large manor of Bodardle held, in 1086, by Turstin the Sheriff. It was he or his son, Baldwin, who constructed the first castle probably before 1100. This was an earth and timber defensive work, with the present circular bank and deep ditch a substitute for the common motte or castle mound, and with a bailey extending to the west. Perhaps the masonry gatehouse, the base of which still remains, was part of the original structure. During the 12th century, the manor passed by marriage into the

hands of the Cardinhams. It is generally thought that the stone shell-keep, which abuts the early gatehouse and replaced the timber defences, was the work of Robert de Cardinham *c*.1200. The internal residential buildings were still of timber.

In 1268, Richard, Earl of Cornwall, purchased Restormel from Isolda de Cardinham. It was probably Richard's son, Edmund, who became earl in 1272, who converted the castle into a great residence subsequent to his establishment of Lostwithiel as the earldom's administrative centre. A survey of the castle in 1337 lists the hall, a chapel, and three upper chambers with cellars below, within the keep, and also three chambers above the gate. Outside, in the bailey, were a great hall with two cellars beneath, a chapel, three upper chambers with cellars below, besides the kitchen, bakehouse and stables. An essential feature of the establishment was a large deer park which at the time of the survey contained 300 deer.

The ruins today have a most picturesque setting, and the view of the castle from the south looking up the valley of the Fowey is especially attractive. This is as it should be, for Restormel had ceased to be a true castle following the improvements of Earl Edmund at the end of the 13th century. It had been turned into something resembling a country house. There is no real defensive quality about its core. Immediately to the right on entering the gatehouse is the kitchen rising through

Detail from the Buck brothers' engraving of Restormel Castle, 1734.

two storeys. The principal rooms were on the first floor: the hall, chamber, an ante-chapel with the chapel itself projecting beyond the circuit, then two more high-status chambers. This was the house fit for earls and later, dukes of Cornwall, to stay when making occasional visits to their south-western estates.

76

Royal Citadel, Plymouth
17th–19th century

SX 481538. Plymouth Hoe
[B][D] MOD EH

Plymouth Citadel belongs to the period when the bastion system of artillery fortification was reaching its peak of development both in England and, more especially, in Europe. The Citadel was designed only a few years before the more famous achievements of the great French military engineer, Vauban, and his Dutch counterpart, Coehoorn, had perfected this highly scientific and geometrical system of defence in depth. The essence of the projecting angled bastions was complete flanking fire around the fortified area, and the

Main gateway to the Royal Citadel, Plymouth.
RCHME

application of this principle to an elaborate system of outworks which would keep an attacker at a distance.

The Citadel was the work of Charles II's chief engineer, Sir Bernard de Gomme. Work on the fort began in 1666 in recognition of the growing maritime importance of Plymouth and the Atlantic sea routes, and also for internal security, since Plymouth had held out for Parliament throughout the Civil War and had been a particular hurtful thorn in the side of the otherwise staunchly Royalist south-west.

There was an Elizabethan bastioned fort at the eastern end of the Hoe, designed by Robert Adams in 1592 to protect the entrance to the Cattewater and the main early harbour of Plymouth. It also included some of the gun-towers built at the water's edge in the time of Henry VIII. De Gomme's original scheme of 1665 was for an irregular pentagonal fort adjacent to, but independent of, the old Plymouth Fort. The two forts were, however, incorporated, and this makes the irregularity of the plan even more pronounced. In other respects the main body of the fort is a fine example of bastion fortification. The tragedy is that the outworks beyond the rock-cut ditch were levelled in 1880 as part of the landscaping of the Hoe and a road was taken through the ditch on the western side. The ghost of the northern ravelin, a detached work in the ditch masking the entrance, can still be made out.

The chief architectural feature is the fine baroque gate with pairs of Ionic pilasters on either side of the gateway, Corinthian columns above, and the whole crowned with a segmental pediment. The elevation is embellished with trophies and coats of arms. Celia Fiennes in 1698 was much impressed: 'the entrance being by an ascent up a hill looks very noble over 2 drawbridges, and gates, which are marble, as is the whole well carv'd, the gate with armory and statues all gilt and on the top 7 gold balls' (*The Illustrated Journeys of Celia Fiennes*, pp201–2).

The Citadel is still in military use and many of the internal buildings are modern and functional. The single-storey guardroom belongs to the early

18th century. The tall Governor's House to the right is late-17th-century. The chapel is an 1845 rebuilding of the 17th-century chapel. The much altered former Grand Store is another survival of de Gomme's scheme of barrack and other buildings arranged round a central parade. The dominant Officers' Mess was built in 1897 and many other of the substantial limestone buildings are of similar date. The lead statue of George II dressed as a Roman emperor, in front of the Mess, dates to 1728.

77

St Mawes Castle
16th–20th century

SW 841327. SW of the village on the A3078. Signposted
[A] EH

St Mawes Castle matches Pendennis Castle across Falmouth Harbour. Together they belonged to the series of coastal forts built by Henry VIII to protect the more important anchorages from use by a threatened invasion force. St Mawes was the first of the two forts to be started in 1540 and was completed in 1545.

Of all the dozen major forts built by Henry VIII, St Mawes is the most ornate and intricate in design. The plan of the fort is a neat exercise in geometry. It consists of a circular central tower with three lower semi-circular bastions clustered about it in clover-leaf pattern with space left for the entrance at the position of the 'stalk'. Each bastion had large embrasures for heavy cannon. They were also floored to provide a further tier of guns firing through the parapet. Guns were also mounted on the roof of the central tower. Archaic cross-loops for handguns protected the entrance approaches. For what was intended as a functional fortress, St Mawes has a surprising amount of surface decoration. On the face of each bastion there is a large shield which was intended to display the royal arms but which was left unfinished, and in the moulding below the parapets are inscriptions in Latin composed by the antiquary, Leland, at the request of

St Mawes Castle from the north. EH

Thomas Treffry of Fowey who was in charge of the construction.

Although the castle was well-sited to cover the entrance to the harbour, it was overlooked by higher ground to the rear and was virtually defenceless from the landward side. Like Pendennis, it also had a separate, low-level blockhouse at the water's edge. This is less well-preserved than Little Dennis but it does show a similar stage of updating in the form of the gunports, supporting the view that the blockhouses were slightly earlier in date than the main forts.

St Mawes did not have the same degree of involvement in the Civil War as Pendennis but it continued to be armed during the 18th and 19th centuries. A battery was built along the cliff edge during the Napoleonic Wars. In 1881, four 64-pounder guns were mounted but it was reported that the castle 'has little or no value as a work of defence against modern artillery, but it forms an object of great historical interest, and great local objections exist to its removal'. By 1898, the battery had been partially remodelled to mount two 6-pounder quick-firing guns. A little later, in 1903, a position for four 12-pounder quick-firers was completed on the hillside behind the castle. Finally, in 1941, a position for two twin 6-pounder guns was established. This was demolished with the abolition of coastal defence in 1956.

78

Star Castle and The Garrison, St Mary's
16th–20th century

SV 897105. Isles of Scilly. The Hugh, W of Hugh Town
Hotel [C]
Garrison Walls [A] EH

The Isles of Scilly contain a wide range of artillery fortifications, representing many of the changes that have affected British military engineering. From the mid-16th century onwards, the islands were recognised as a potential base for attacks on shipping, and defences were built to combat this in the 1550s. A century later, the islands were seized and held by the Royalists for just such a hostile purpose at the end of the Civil War, and were the object of a successful campaign by the Parliamentary forces to dislodge them. This military preoccupation has left its mark. Defences continued to be built fitfully during the 18th and 19th centuries.

The first fortifications centred primarily on Tresco to protect the anchorages there. By the 1590s, attention focused on St Mary's, and particularly on the Hugh. The concentration of defences here gave rise to a new name, The Garrison. The fort on Hugh Hill, now known as Star Castle,

was designed by Robert Adams in 1593, who was simultaneously engaged in building Plymouth Fort. It has an eight-pointed star trace with embrasures for guns mounted in the re-entrant angles to give complete flanking cover. The fort was little more than a blockhouse for a small garrison. The Captain of the Islands, Sir Francis Godolphin, who was well aware of their strategic significance, continued with other defensive measures, and the masonry-bastioned land-front across the neck of the promontory above Hugh Town was built by 1600.

Portions of the continuous breastwork thrown up by the Royalists on the edge of the cliffs round the islands still survive here. These and various batteries on headlands commanding the main shipping channels were later translated more permanently into stone during the first half of the 18th century. Between 1715 and 1746 the resident master gunner, Abraham Tovey, undertook this work and at the same time built a barracks, guardroom, storehouse, and a handsome house for himself. This barely-changed microcosm of an 18th-century garrison is now surpassed only by Berwick-upon-Tweed and Fort George near Inverness.

There were later additions. The Martello towers along the Kent and Sussex coasts, built to resist a Napoleonic invasion force, were anticipated by three 'Corsican' towers built by Major Lyman in 1803. One of them is on The Garrison. They were unlike the common form of Martello tower, being tall and thin, but they had a similar purpose and were intended to mount a 32-pounder carronade on the top. Later still, in 1881, a self-defensible battery was proposed to protect the principal anchorage, The Road, between St Mary's and Sampson. Nothing came of this immediately but Woolpack and Steval batteries, for four 6-inch guns, were constructed on The Garrison between 1898 and 1901. By 1906, there was a battery for two 12-pounder quick-firers as well, but in the same year the political situation had changed, France was no longer the principal threat, and all the guns were removed.

8

Country Houses and Gardens

It cannot be claimed that Devon and Cornwall are especially noteworthy for country houses. Remoteness from the Court and the centre of architectural fashion had much to do with it until communications improved during the late 18th and 19th centuries. Carew, in his assessment of Cornish gentlemen, alluded to other reasons. They 'can better vaunt of their pedigree than their livelihood' and, 'keep liberal, but not costly builded or furnished houses' (*The Survey of Cornwall*, p136).

Restormel Castle (75, C), in its late-13th-century internal re-ordering, shows the essential residential elements required for the occasional visits of an earl of Cornwall. Likewise, the 14th-century domestication of **Okehampton Castle** (73, D) illustrates how the former military functions of a castle could be softened. The same can be said of Tiverton and Powderham castles (D). One of the very few medieval houses to be built on a grand scale without overt defensive considerations was **Dartington Hall** (83, D). The houses of the Bishops of Exeter were primarily domestic too, but only fragments of these survive. At the turn of the 16th century is **Cotehele** (82, C), which is a substantial house but lacks architectural finesse. These late-medieval houses have in common a courtyard plan, and sometimes more than one. This was a feature which influenced many gentry houses of the 16th century.

In the 16th century prosperity increased dramatically in the south-west and led to the 'Great Rebuild' which had already affected churches, but the second half of that century, and the early years of the next, saw an extraordinary change in domestic architecture (**Trerice**, 89, C). It is a change recorded by Carew. Having earlier described traditional building design and practice in Cornwall, he goes on: 'whereas nowadays they seat their dwellings high, build their walls thin, lay them with earthen mortar, raise them to three or four stories, mould their lights large and

outward, and their roofs square and slight, coveting chiefly prospect and pleasure' (*The Survey of Cornwall*, p124). Carew probably had Mount Edgcumbe (1547–54) in mind, for it was a precocious house very far removed in design from Edgcumbe's Cotehele. This historically important house was burnt out in the Second World War. Another was Protector Somerset's unfinished addition to the domestic range at **Berry Pomeroy Castle** (79, D) with its loggia and early long gallery in the 1550s, reflecting the advanced Court taste of the time. Buckland Abbey (D) and Holcombe Court (D) possessed similar unconventional elements for houses of this period.

Architecture generally remained conservative in conception and detail, domestically as well as in church building, throughout most of the 17th century (**Lanhydrock**, 85, C). Godolphin (C) is an example of the marrying of Renaissance with Tudor tradition. Stowe near Kilkhampton (C) (built by John Grenville, Earl of Bath) was, however, exceptional; a baroque mansion of the 1680s on a grand scale and in the height of fashion. It was said to be the noblest house in the west of England but was demolished in 1739. Nevertheless, for all the lack of spectacular houses in this period, much care was lavished on interiors with high quality joinery and a passion for decorative plasterwork which extended well into the 18th century.

The country house, as understood elsewhere in England, was indeed slow in coming, and few landowners were interested in the grandest forms of display. The leading families more often preferred to improve or add to existing houses rather than build anew. This is the case at **Saltram** (88, D), one of the few examples of Palladianism applied to an earlier courtyard house. An example of a new Palladian house is Pencarrow (1765–75) near Bodmin (C). Country-house architecture in Devon began to develop towards the end of the 18th century with Robert Adams's work at

St Michael's Mount from the east.
A F KERSTING

Saltram and Ugbrooke (D). Ugbrooke (1763–6) is the start of a fashion for castellated mansions, which extended more notably to Cornwall, encouraged by various architects: Nash at Luscombe (1800)(D) and Caerhayes (1808)(C), Soane at Port Eliot (1802–6)(C), and Wilkins at Tregothnan (1816–18)(C). This was part of the movement towards the 'picturesque', usually denoted by 'Romantic Gothick'. Good rococo-gothick interiors may be seen at **St Michael's Mount** (87, C) and Hartland Abbey (D), and externally at Werrington Park (D). A stimulus towards the more frivolous building styles was the increasing popularity of the watering place. This came about with greater accessibility created by the turnpike trusts, opening up the south-west to the appreciation of romantic wildness or seaside cosiness. As well as the urban terrace, at Teignmouth (Den Crescent)(D) and at Sidmouth (Fortfield Terrace)(D), villas and *cottages ornés* sprang up particularly at Sidmouth (Elysian Fields) and Exmouth (**A La Ronde**)(86, D). The *cottage orné* was taken almost to country-house proportions by Sir Jeffry Wyatville at Endsleigh Cottage (D) for the 6th Duke of Bedford in 1810.

The development of garden design closely parallels this pattern of country-house building in the south-west. The formal, early-18th-century layouts of axial vistas and terraces can be seen at **Bicton** (80, D). A move away from formality survives at Saltram (D) where woodland walks and meandering paths connect carefully-disposed features such as temples and grottos. The picturesque landscape contrived by Capability Brown is exemplified at Ugbrooke (D), and his ideas were taken up at many other places. The activities of Repton in the 1790s with Red Books for Anthony and Port Eliot in Cornwall and at Endsleigh and Luscombe in Devon, brought a greater emphasis on the dramatic and exotic in the character of garden buildings. At Bicton, such buildings can be both romantic and practical as demonstrated by the superb Palm House. Mount Edgecumbe (C) was praised by Uvedale Price (1794) for its natural grandeur, impressive views and sudden contrasts.

The early 19th century saw the neo-classicism, so widely inspired by Foulston at Devonport and elsewhere in an urban or suburban context, extended to the country house at Buckland House, Buckland Filleigh (D) and at Arlington Court (D). Later came the impact of gothic, of which Bishop's Court at Clyst Honiton (d) is a fine example, and at Burges's **Knightshayes** (84, D), for the Heathcotes of Tiverton, where it achieved its apogee. Lower down the social and economic order are the Italianate villas, embodying on a smaller scale the themes endorsed so whole-heartedly by Prince Albert at Osborne. Gardens proliferated, the favourable climate encouraging the raising of exotic and semi-tropical species, especially magnolias, camellias, azaleas and rhododendrons from Asia. Formality returned with terraces and elaborate beddings, specialised gardens and arboreta. Mid-19th-century Bicton and the slightly later Lanhydrock represent this trend.

Towards the end of the 19th century came the reworking of Flete (D) by Norman Shaw to produce a Tudorish, castellated pile for a banker. Between 1910 and 1930, Sir Edward Lutyens created a 'medieval' castle for the founder of the Home and Colonial Stores at **Castle Drogo** (81, D). The country house came full circle in the 1930s with the restoration of the ruined Dartington Hall (D), and the incorporation within its grounds of houses of the International Modern idiom (some of the first successful examples in the country), to take the country house of more modest scale into the mid-20th century.

79

Berry Pomeroy Castle
15th–16th century

SX 836617. Berry Pomeroy. 2 miles NE of Totnes. Signposted from the A385 to Torquay

[A] EH

At first glance, Berry Pomeroy consists of the shell of a former castle with an early Tudor mansion, now in ruins, built inside it. It is, however, of much greater significance to architectural historians as an important step in the introduction into England of renaissance architectural forms and in the development of classical idioms.

There is little trace of the earlier medieval castle of the Pomerai family. The castle as it stands belongs to the second half of the 15th century. It was intended to be defended with gunpowder weapons and is of considerable interest in this respect. The gatehouse, with its angled turrets, has simple handgun loops. The provision for massive roof-timbers argues for the intention of placing heavy guns on top to command the high ground opposite. The gatehouse also contains, unexpectedly, a very fine fresco depicting the Adoration of the Magi. The Margaret Tower at the end of the curtain wall of the entrance front has considerable forward projection for flanking cover and very elaborate gun-loops. Behind the tower, and now enclosed within the later mansion, is an L-shaped domestic block of four storeys served by an internal square turret with access from an inner courtyard. This seems to have been refaced in ashlar on its west-facing elevation to a symmetrical three-storey composition with a central door in the early 16th century.

In 1547, Edward Seymour, Duke of Somerset, who was later to become Protector to Edward VI, bought the castle from the Pomeroys. He was already building Somerset House in London, Sion House and a great house at Bedwyn Brail in Wiltshire, yet he commenced a vast north range at Berry Pomeroy immediately. None of these works was completed before his execution in 1552 but they show great precociousness in the introduction of renaissance architectural styles, employing French and other craftsmen.

The north range was 230 ft (70 m) long and was intended for state rooms, adopting a plan and elevations which had not been seen before in the conventional great medieval house. On the ground floor was a great hall rising through two storeys, its dais marked by an enormous oriel and, opposite, a

Berry Pomeroy Castle. EH

doorway giving access to an ante-room and a parlour and grand stair. Above the kitchen and service end were an inner chamber and great chamber. Above the parlour was another great chamber. None of the cross walls are brought up into the second floor, which constitutes a vast undivided room the whole length of the building, a particularly long gallery, more familiar in great houses towards the end of the 16th century.

The most remarkable feature of Somerset's work was a loggia, another advanced piece of design probably derived from Serlio's *The Five Books of Architecture*, which had been published in France by 1547. Its foundations, in well-preserved Beer stone, were uncovered by archaeological excavation in 1982. The rusticated piers, pedestals, niches and mouldings are likely to be the work of Somerset's foreign craftsmen. They provide a rare glimpse

of the advanced Court styles that briefly flourished at the death of Henry VIII. Despite the unfinished design, the house was furnished and occupied, and only demolished early in the 18th century.

80

Bicton Gardens
18th–19th century

SY 074869. Bicton. Signposted from the A376 Newton Poppleford–Budleigh Salterton road

[A]

Bicton House was begun in the 18th century and completed in *c*.1800 by James Wyatt for the first Lord Rolle. It was remodelled in 1908–9 but behind the Edwardian facade the earlier form remains. It is now the Bicton College of Agriculture. The gardens are run

separately as a commercial pleasure ground with popular distractions sited more or less discreetly.

The ground at Bicton is undulating but slopes down generally towards the course of the River Otter. The 18th-century garden layout with its axial vistas is said to date from *c*.1735 when Henry Rolle had the formal garden (the Italian Garden) laid out south-east of the house. The design has been attributed to the influence of Le Notre. It involved a symmetrical terraced plan, descending to a rectangular pond with a central fountain and with an axial prospect over rising ground to the Obelisk (1743) beyond.

The present appearance of the gardens is largely due to John, Lord Rolle (d.1842) and his second wife, Louisa Trefusis, mostly from the 1820s onwards. The lake in front of the house is said to have been dug by French

Palm House, Bicton Gardens. RCHME

prisoners of war in 1812. The arboretum was created in 1830 with the advice of J C Loudon, the pinetum was begun in 1839 to the west and south-west of the Italian Garden, and the monkey-puzzle avenue was laid out (with a mound for each tree) from 1839 to 1869. Most of the buildings are also of this period.

The most exciting building is the Palm House (c.1820), a trefoiled, domed glasshouse against a wall. The side lobes are supported by thin iron columns. Its design is likely to have been inspired by the theories of Loudon who advocated curved glasshouse roofs. The Orangery (late 18th-century) is at the head of the Italian Garden. It has a central open loggia with two Ionic columns. The much delapidated Hermitage (1839) overlooks a smaller lake. It is wooden with an octagonal centre, complete with basketwork lining, rustic furniture and a

deer-bone floor. The Belvedere, or China Tower, of similar date is now outside the gardens to the north-west of the house. It is an octagonal, castellated tower in which a china collection was kept. East of the Italian Garden is the American Garden (1840–3), with the Shell House (c.1840) of cyclopian construction, intended to house a collection of shells.

South of the formal gardens, and separate from them, are the original but now ruined church, the mausoleum (1850) by Pugin, and the church of St Mary (1851) which form visual elements in the landscape scheme. The mausoleum was commissioned by Lady Rolle to commemorate her husband. It is a remodelling of an earlier chapel (possibly a chantry chapel) containing the baroque tomb of Denys Rolle (d.1638) as well as the memorial to Lord John Rolle. It has a severe, steeply

roofed and heavily buttressed exterior with 18th-century graffiti, including many representations of ships, on the south and east walls. Inside, are blue on yellow Minton tiles, a vaulted ceiling with decorated panels, and windows also designed by Pugin.

81

Castle Drogo
20th century

SX 721900. Drewsteignton, 4 miles S of A30. Exit A30 at Whiddon Down, or at Cheriton Bishop and approach via Crockernwell

[A] NT

'I do wish he didn't want a castle, but just a delicious loveable house with plenty of good large rooms in it,' wrote Sir Edwin Lutyens to his wife when Julius Drewe offered him a commission of £60,000 in 1910 to build Castle Drogo and its garden. Drewe was a successful tea merchant, co-founder of the Home and Colonial Stores, and had made a fortune by the time he was thirty, retiring soon afterwards. He had researched his ancestry and had identified a relationship with Drogo de Teign. Drewsteignton was interpreted as 'Dru-his-town-on the Teign'. So it was here, on a defensible promontory 900 ft (274 m) above sea level overlooking Dartmoor, that this castle was to be built. Every care was taken to achieve the correct siting and elevation by the use of full-scale timber mock-ups. There were to be no such things as cavity walls or bricks, only granite, quarried on Dartmoor, and walls 6 ft (1.8 m) thick.

Once Lutyens had reconciled himself that 'He wants to build a large keep or commemorative tower to commemorate the first Drogo and this will be over and beyond the £60,000 castle', the final scheme was agreed in 1911 for a U-plan, open to the north, with splayed outer wings enclosing a vast courtyard entered by a barbican and gatehouse. In fact, only part of this grand design was built. The east wing and the splayed service wing to the north, together with the basement of what was intended as the south range to house the principal living rooms, were all that was built. Even with this reduction, the work continued until 1930, the year before Drewe's death.

In its external style the house is more Tudor than medieval, with large rectangular mullion and transom windows with an idiosyncratic omission of hood-moulds above them, and an irregular crenellated parapet crowning the walls and turrets. The entrance tower is less austere with a heavily corbelled oriel between the corner turrets, and the Drewe lion and motto carved in relief below an eight-light window.

Most striking for the visitor is the interior with its bare walls of exposed granite and unpainted woodwork contrasting with the exotic, mainly Spanish, furnishings. Vaulted corridors and monumental stairs add to the dramatic and symbolic effect. The corridor linking the entrance hall, the main stairs and the drawing-room involves changes in both level and direction, and combines a tunnel vault with shallow domes. The planning is complex because the two ranges are at an angle to one another and are on different levels, a wing of three floors for family and servants and one of two floors for state rooms. A granite arch separates the billiard room from the library which has bookcases designed by Lutyens and were almost the last fittings built for the castle. Other family rooms are more modest in their design and furnishing. Particularly moving is Adrian Drewe's room, a memorial to Drewe's eldest son killed at Ypres in 1917. He had been closely involved with the design of the house. The chapel in the south-wing basement, groin-vaulted in granite below the abandoned great hall, represents an important aspect of Julius Drewe's life.

Much attention was paid to landscaping and to the formal gardens. Julius Drewe wrote to Lutyens in 1915, 'So far as the Drive is concerned . . . what I want is heather, bracken, broom, holly, brambles, foxgloves, etc.' Lutyens consulted his old friend Miss Jekyll who produced a planting scheme and also introduced circles of ilex. The formal gardens, including a circular lawn and a rectangular rose garden, were laid out in

the 1920s to the north-east of the house, replacing earlier plans for elaborate terraced gardens to the east.

82

Cotehele House
14th–17th century

SX 423685. Calstock. Signposted from the A390 and A388

[A] NT

Cotehele is the most extensive and grandest Tudor, or perhaps more accurately, sub-medieval house in Cornwall. It is relatively unaltered because, not long after its completion, the Edgcumbes shifted their interest to Mount Edgcumbe on the Cornish side of Plymouth Sound. The Edgcumbes had acquired Cotehele by marriage in 1353, and it is thought that the earlier house was a compact quadrangular building of red stone which forms the lowest courses of the walls surrounding the main inner court on its south and west sides. Certainly there was a substantial house here early in the 15th century since Peter Edgcumbe was granted a licence for a chapel in 1411.

The present building was shaped by Sir Richard Edgcumbe in the four years between his return from Britanny and his death in 1489, and by his son, Sir Piers, who had been a companion of Henry VIII in his youth, and who died in 1535. The only important addition has been the north-west tower in 1627, and refurbishings by a later Sir Piers after the Civil War, and for a dowager Countess of Mount Edgcumbe in the 1860s.

The original main entrance was from the west through an outer court called the Retainers court, where paired doorways in a range opposite the long, low, gatehouse suggest lodgings. The present entrance is through the site of a base-court containing a buttressed barn with, to the north, a stable with an upper room for storage or grooms' quarters. This entrance from the east was raised in status and design by adding a granite ashlar gate-tower above it.

On the opposite end of the courtyard is the Great Hall. Armorial glazing in the hall suggests that it was completed by Sir Piers before the death of his first wife, Joan Durnford, in 1520. The hall is lofty but not very large, with a great window lighting the high table, and a

Cotehele courtyard. RCHME

wall fireplace opposite. Its splendid roof, in conservative western fashion, has arch-braced collars and several tiers of purlins with crossed wind-braces. There is no screens passage. Of the three doors at the low end of the hall, one leads to a stair, the central door does not lead to a service room but to a low-end parlour, and the third to a lobby leading to a kitchen and to service rooms outside the main range. The square kitchen has one large fireplace with a huge oven behind it, and subsidiary hearths. At the high end of the hall, and unconnected with it, is the ground floor of a chamber block which functioned as a separate private residence. The ground-floor room has the name 'The Dining Room' which indeed suggests a private hall. This had direct access to the chapel, and, at the high end, is the three-storey residential tower added in 1627.

The chapel is to the north of the original entrance and projects into the Retainers court. It has a little bell-cote of granite with pinnacles. Internally, it has a typical west-country ribbed barrel roof. It is also notable for the contemporary screen, with delicate cresting, linenfold panelling, and, above all, the least-altered example in England of a late-medieval clock.

83

Dartington Hall
14th century

SX 798627. Dartington. Off the A385, E at the cross-roads beside the church

[A]

The survival of Dartington Hall and its subsequent restoration by Leonard and Dorothy Elmhirst in the 1920s and '30s as part of a 'centre for experiments in rural reconstruction and progressive education', together with accompanying buildings representing some of the first examples in this country of the fully developed International Modern Movement, must stimulate interest over a very wide range of architectural, social and economic questions. It is only possible to cover one aspect here and that must be the Hall which has been

Dartington Hall courtyard. J COX

the focal point of the whole enterprise. It has been said that, 'Apart from the Bishop's Palace at Wells, Dartington Hall is the most important major example of medieval domestic architecture in the west of England' (Anthony Emery, *Dartington Hall*, Oxford, 1970, p99).

The manor of Dartington was held by the Martin family between the early 12th and mid-14th centuries. It passed to the Crown in 1386 and was granted by Richard II to his half-brother, John Holand, Earl of Huntingdon and later Duke of Exeter, who, though a prominent Court figure, made Dartington his principal seat. Before his execution in 1400, for his part in an unsuccessful conspiracy against Henry IV, the majority of the Hall had been built.

The buildings are arranged round a large oblong courtyard with the hall at the south end. This is entered through a three-storey porch. The central boss of a ribbed vault over the entrance passage symbolically declared the political allegiance of its owner, with Richard II's white hart on a heraldic rose surrounded by the wheat-ears of John Holand. The hall was built on the grandest scale, but it must be appreciated that the magnificent five-bay roof is an early-1930s reconstruction by the architect William Weir, based on the ghost of the

medieval timbers left on the east wall after the old roof was taken down in 1813. An 1805 drawing of the original construction was discovered after the new roof was finished. It shows the combination of the newly fashionable hammer-beam with a more traditional crown-post system and windbraces, an experimental stage in the development of the full hammer-beam roof. Weir had omitted the crown-post, shortened the length of the hammer-beams and provided three tiers of windbraces.

Weir put back a screen, though modelled it on a local vernacular example. The central of the three service doors gives on to a passage which leads to a large square kitchen. This has also been restored. Buttery and pantry are on either side of the passage. Behind the dais end of the hall is the upper solar block with a large room at ground level, a great chamber above and probably another room on top. This private suite was much altered by later owners.

Of particular significance as an example of late-14th-century planning are the five groups of lodgings on the west side of the court. With the exception of that adjacent to the hall, each group consisted of four rooms, two on each floor, the upper being approached from a separate stair. Each room was a self-contained unit with its own entrance, window, fireplace and garderobe. The group at the north end is the best preserved. The east range was partly demolished in the 19th century, and the remainder converted into coachhouse and stables. This too was also an unfinished lodgings range.

There is no proper gatehouse and indeed it is surprising at this date that there is nothing in the way of defensive provision. To the west of the entrance is a two-storey range significantly less sophisticated in construction than the rest of the courtyard, and on the other side is a later barn of 14 bays.

South of the hall range is an isolated wall with seven, four-centered arches which, with evidence from archaeological excavation, seem to suggest the presence of a small second courtyard, intimately connected with the high end of the hall. Here is another example of Dartington being part of a transitional stage in the development of the greater late-medieval house.

84
Knightshayes Court
19th century

SS 960151. 2 miles N of Tiverton. Turn right off the A396 Tiverton–Bampton road at Bolham

[A] NT

Knightshayes Court was the home of the Heathcoat-Amory family who owed their fortune to John Heathcoat, a manufacturer of lace and textiles in Nottingham. Fearful that his machinery might suffer at the hands of the Luddites, he moved his operations to Tiverton which became the largest lace-making enterprise in the world during the 1860s. The textile factory, and the profound influence the Heathcoat-Amorys have had on the town of Tiverton, is still apparent today.

In 1869, John Heathcoat's grandson, Sir John Heathcoat-Amory, began to build for himself a grand country house on the high ground 2 miles north of Tiverton overlooking the town, and with its main axis aligned on his factory. For his architect, Sir John chose William Burges whose High Victorian Gothic idealism was already being applied at

Cardiff Castle for the immensely wealthy Lord Bute, and who was to achieve that landmark of visionary medievalism at Castell Goch, outside Cardiff, for the same patron. Was it just to obtain the services of a well-known and well-connected architect or did Sir John want a gothic masterpiece himself?

Looked at from the garden terraces, the main elevation seems a somewhat ordinary neo-Tudor composition with the central block flanked by gabled wings. It was said at the time to be 'stately and bold and its medievalism . . . not obtrusive'. On closer inspection,

however, one can see the tell-tale Burges fantasies: a corner oriel, plate tracery, quatrefoils and massive gargoyles. He planned a massive staircase-tower at the north-west corner but only the crenellated stump was built. The house is entered through the north porch beneath a hooded medieval figure acting as a lantern bearer over the door. By 1874, the house was structurally complete.

Burges intended his exuberant medievalism to be applied to the interior decoration. Fortunately, there exists in the house a set of his drawings which

Drawing room, Knightshayes Court. NT/J BETHELL

demonstrate what might have been. Some in fact were carried out before Burges was replaced by someone more conventional, J D Crace. It seems clear that Burges's schemes were too rich for the family's taste, and they were also very costly, and Sir John was not a millionaire like Lord Bute. Even some of Crace's brightly coloured rooms were later covered up. It is good that the National Trust, with the evidence of Burges's intentions, and of what did indeed previously exist, beside them, have made a number of very praiseworthy restorations of a number of rooms.

The Great Hall is one of the more important Burges survivals, although the magnificent screen was removed in 1914. At the high end is a gallery supported on marble columns from which Sir John might address his employees. The chimney-piece was not as elaborate as Burges intended but the carved corbels survive showing medieval figures engaged in various occupations. These, and other sculptures in the house, were the work of Thomas Nicholls. The Dining Room is now restored and the quotations from Burns once more revealed. The Library is largely the work of Crace.

The stables are very characteristic of Burges with a conical turret, triangular dormers and red painted woodwork. The gardens were largely created in the 1950s–1970s. The original scheme was by Edward Kemp, who had been a pupil of the great Paxton, but little of this survives.

85

Lanhydrock House
17th and 19th century

SX 085636. Lanhydrock. Signposted from the B3268 Bodmin–Lostwithiel road

[A] NT

In Pevsner's words Lanhydrock is 'the most rewarding of all Cornish mansions'. Before the Dissolution of the monasteries the estate had been the property of the priory of St Petroc at Bodmin. Richard Robartes, a Truro merchant who had grown rich from the tin trade and the sale of wood for smelting, was sufficiently prominent to be knighted in 1616 and had acquired the manor of Lanhydrock by 1620. By 1624, he had been created Baron Robartes (at a cost, it is said, of £10,000), and he then began to build a new house at Lanhydrock. On his death in 1634, his son completed the building in 1651 with the gatehouse.

It was originally built on a quadrangular plan with a second service court to the rear behind the hall. The east entrance range was removed about 1780, and much of the north and west ranges were reconstructed following a fire in 1881. The detached gatehouse was joined to the main building by flanking walls enclosing a forecourt. With its twin octagonal turrets on either side of a great round-headed carriageway, lavishly tricked out with ball-topped obelisks, columns, niches and pilasters, it attempts to show awareness of renaissance ornament but is half a century behind the times.

In 1857, the fashionable architect, George Gilbert Scott, was called in to carry out improvements. He built the low battlemented wall which links the gatehouse to the main house, and added the coach-house and stables to the south-east. The fire of 1881 gutted the whole house except for the north wing and the entrance porch. Richard Coad, a Cornish-born architect who had been in Gilbert Scott's practice in the 1850s, was brought in to rebuild the house with modern refinements such as central heating and an electric-lighting plant. It was also of fireproof construction, with wrought-iron girders, instead of timber joists, and an elaborate water supply. Work was completed in 1885.

The interior, in its planning and furnishing, illuminates the organisation and style of life in a late-19th-century country house. The Steward's Room, the various service quarters, and the servants' rooms demonstrate the workings of such a house. The main reception rooms are on the first floor presumably to associate them with the Long Gallery which survived the fire. Its

Stable courtyard, Lanhydrock. NT

remarkable barrel-vaulted plaster ceiling seems to have been finished before the outbreak of the Civil War in 1642 and is attributed to the Devonshire plasterers, the Abbots of Frithelstock, near Bideford.

The park and formal gardens are also of great interest. The avenue of sycamores which mark the ascent through the park to the gatehouse was planted in 1648. Within the gatehouse are formal terraces, plain parterres of grass, which were once interspersed with elaborately patterned beds laid out in 1857. The Higher Gardens to the north of the house are also mid-19th century. In the 1930s the gardens were extended to the rising ground up to the church of St Hydroc, which was rebuilt at the same time as the house in the 17th century and then heavily restored in 1888.

86

A La Ronde
1798

SY 004834. Exmouth. In Summer Lane between the A376, Exeter–Exmouth road and B3180, 1 mile SE of Lympstone

[A]

This house belongs to that phase of self-conscious antiquarianism around the turn of the 19th century which in its picturesque idiom produced the *cottage orné* so well represented in south Devon. A La Ronde is still in a rustic situation, with views across the estuary of the Exe and the Channel beyond.

The sixteen-sided house was built in 1798. It was the creation of two spinster ladies, Jane Parminter, daughter of a successful Devon merchant, and her younger cousin, Mary, and based on the plan of the 6th-century Byzantine basilica of San Vitale in Ravenna following their return from a lengthy 'Grand Tour'. The walls are of stone and the roof was originally thatched. It is now tiled, with dormer windows in addition to the central lantern. There are lozenge-shaped windows at the angles alternately positioned between rectangular windows.

A La Ronde. J COX

Internally, the cult of the 'picturesque' is taken to greater lengths. The eight rooms on each floor radiate from a top-lit central hall and are interconnected. There are sliding doors and hinged panelled benches as space-saving devices. Decoratively, the sitting-room still retains its frieze made up of feathers, and here and elsewhere, as well as portraits and conventional paintings in oils and water colours, there is an assortment of artwork in sand, seaweed, shells and paper. The climax for the visitor is the gallery within the central lantern. On the narrow, steep staircase one passes miniature grottos contrived with shells, and the gallery iself is lined with designs made from feathers and shells in amazing variety inspired presumably by the mosaics of San Vitale itself.

Jane Parminter died in 1811 and was buried below the small Congregational Chapel, Point in View, a little higher up Summer Lane. This, too, she had designed in the same spirit. The tiny chapel is surrounded by four single-storey almshouses with triangular-headed windows, and is lit by triangular roof-lights in a pyramidal lantern.

87

St Michael's Mount
12th–19th century

SW 515298. St Michael's Mount. By foot along a tidal causeway from Marazion

[A] NT

St Michael's Mount possesses both a picturesque situation and a wealth of legend. For many years it was believed this was the island of *Ictis* described by Classical writers as an entrepôt for the tin trade organised by Mediterranean (Phoenician) merchants. It now seems unlikely that the Mount was an island in pre-Roman times and there is no supporting evidence for a trading centre. The same uncertainties surround its place in Celtic Christianity and as an early monastery. It did, however, come into the possession of the abbey of Mont St Michel in Normandy around the time of the Norman Conquest. A church was built on the Mount and consecrated in 1135. There was also a monastic house for twelve Benedictine monks. The establishment was eventually suppressed as an alien priory in 1425 and was given by Henry VI to the Bridgettine Abbey of Syon.

After the Dissolution of the monasteries, the Mount remained in royal hands and took on military significance in south-western coastal defence. The fortifications were improved during the Civil War and it was garrisoned by the Royalists. In 1647, the Parliamentarian Colonel, John St Aubyn, was appointed Captain of the Mount, and he purchased it in 1659. The St Aubyn family remained owners until 1954 when it was given to the National Trust.

St Michael's Mount retains elements of its religious, military and domestic past brought together into a romantic country house by the architect member of the family, Piers St Aubyn, in 1850 and 1873–8. The rock, previously bare, was planted up in sub-tropical fashion in the late 19th century. The harbour, developed by the Brigittines in 1427, continues in use. Early religious life is evidenced by a cross of unusual design of three superimposed and contrasting crosses. For the military side, there are reconstructed gun batteries on the west, and unaltered defences of the Civil War period or earlier together with a sentry box. During the Second World War three pillboxes were erected as part of the continuing tradition of coastal defence.

The most prominent building is the much restored church of late-14th- and 15th-century date. On the crossing tower is a five-sided beacon. The original monastic buildings lay to the south and west. Chief among them is the refectory, now called the Chevy Chase Room from the remarkable plaster frieze of 1641 representing various hunting scenes. The ruined Lady Chapel was converted into the Blue Drawing Room and Boudoir between 1740 and 1750. The detail is very fine: pre-Strawberry Hill, rococo-gothic, with stucco vaults and pretty fireplaces. The Victorian wing by Piers St Aubyn is in a Tudor gothic castellated style. The north-west wing was added as late as 1927.

88

Saltram House
16th, 18th and 19th century

SX 521555. Plympton St Mary. 3½ miles E of Plymouth city centre. Take Plympton turn at the Marsh Mills roundabout on the A38 or from the A379 to the S

[A] NT

Saltram is the most impressive country house in Devon and one of the largest. To Fanny Burney, in attendance upon Queen Charlotte, visiting in 1788, it was 'one of the most magnificent houses in the country'. It has a certain Palladian character despite the fact that the house has grown piecemeal and with no clear architectural authorship until the later improvements and modifications of Robert Adam and John Foulston. Its setting on the east bank of the River Plym was on a grand scale, with views down the estuary towards Plymouth and the woods of Mount Edgcumbe beyond in the 18th century. These views were painted by Thomas Tomkins in the 1770s and are hung in the Garden

Venetian window in the saloon, Saltram. NT/J WHITAKER

Room. They contrast with the present setting which requires thick shelter belts and clumps of trees to screen the 20th-century landscape of expanded and industrial Plymouth.

The house is of considerable archaeological interest. Within its core is the four-storey, mullion-windowed, staircase tower of the 16th-century house of the Bagg family. This early house was built round a large courtyard which can be recognised in the plan. After the Civil War, Saltram passed to Sir George Carteret and the centre block of the west front appears to be a late 17th-century remodelling. The exterior today is essentially the mid-18th-century house of John Parker and his wife Lady Catherine Poulett, whose father was Secretary of State to Queen Anne. Between 1743 and 1749 they added the south front with its slightly projecting three-bay, pedimented centre, and the externally plain east range of reception rooms. They also extended the west front to incorporate the Carteret block.

The surprise comes with the lavishness of the interior decoration. The Parkers equipped the main rooms with elaborate ornamental plasterwork in the Devonshire tradition (it has been suggested recently that Bristol or Oxford stuccoists may have been responsible), fine chimney pieces and carved woodwork. In two of the first-floor rooms are Chinese wallpapers, one of them, in the dressing room, a very rare early-18th-century example. John Parker's son, the first Lord Boringdon, employed Robert Adam to refashion the house in 1770–2. The Saloon and Dining Room, originally fitted up as a library, are said to be 'two of the most complete and best preserved Adam interiors in the country'. Lord Boringdon's friendship with Joshua Reynolds, a native of neighbouring Plympton St Maurice, led to a remarkable collection of paintings by the latter, and there are still ten in the house. Of the next generation, the third John Parker was created Earl of Morley in 1815, and subsequently employed John Foulston to create the Library and the entrance porch in the south range between 1818 and 1820.

The 18th-century layout of the grounds exploited the situation of the house and the estuary beyond. The first scheme of the 1750s included formal features linked by winding paths. The Woodland Walk is part of this, together with the Amphitheatre beside the water and three small grottos. In the 1770s, Lord Boringdon employed a little-known landscape gardener called Richmond to plant in the 'new' informal manner. To this later period belong the Orangery, a garden temple and the Castle, which is an octagonal summerhouse in Kentian 'Gothick' style.

89

Trerice
15th–16th century

SW 845584. Newlyn East. SE of Newquay, signposted from the A3058 at Kestle Mill

[A] NT

Trerice is considered by many to be the most satisfying of the smaller Elizabethan houses in Cornwall. It gives an appearance of unity, arranged on an E-plan with a symmetrical south front, central three-storey porch and slightly projecting wings, as built by Sir John Arundell, Richard Carew's father-in-law, in 1572–4 and, as Carew described, 'offereth you the view of his costly and commodious buildings'.

The Arundells, who according to Camden were 'an ancient and noble family and also very numerous', had a house at Trerice since at least the 14th century. It is not therefore surprising that two earlier phases of building have been identified in the present house. The first perhaps belongs to the Sir John Arundell who died in 1471. This consisted of a hall, which was only identified by excavation during repairs in the 1950s, associated with a three-storeyed solar block, of which the lower part remains embedded in the west range. This simple plan was enlarged in the 16th century by the addition of a two-storey building on the south side of the solar block and now incorporated in the 1572–4 south front. This building may be attributable to Sir John Arundell (1495–1561).

The final version of 1572–4 was created by the addition of a new hall-house to the east of the phase-two structure. This new work was still medieval in conception with a central hall 24 ft (7.3 m) high rising through two floors, with the customary screens at one end approached through the central porch and chambers on the opposite side of the passage. A vast twenty-four-light window illuminates the high end of the hall. The fireplace has a scrolled plaster overmantel supported by caryatids and bears the date 1572. The plaster ceiling is

ornamented with medallions, strapwork and pendants with the initials of the founder, John Arundell, and those of his wife, Katherine. An enclosed corridor with unglazed window openings runs along the back of the hall giving access to the west wing and to a projecting half-octagonal stair tower. The lower eastern chambers were demolished in c.1860, and later were rebuilt maintaining the appearance of the old facade. On the western side of the hall, the great chamber on the first floor also has a magnificent plasterwork ceiling and an equally rich overmantel dated 1573. It has a great semi-circular bowed window looking south and west across the gardens.

The ornate scrolled gables, which are such a feature of the house, indicate a remarkably advanced architectural taste at this date. It is suggested that Sir John Arundell may have conceived this design for 'Dutch' style gables after soldiering in the Low Countries, but this claim is very tenuous. The excellence of the plasterwork suggests the employment of the same master craftsman who had worked at Collacombe Barton (D) and Buckland Abbey (D) at around the same time.

Front entrance, Trerice. NT/J BETHELL

9

Industry

Both Devon and Cornwall have a deep and varied industrial background. Monuments to this industrial past and present abound, nowhere more conspicuously than in Cornwall. Amidst today's pervasive replacement, the tourist industry, it is sometimes difficult to go beyond the evocative ruins of engine houses to the economic rises and falls that lay behind them, the invention and ingenuity that industry generated, and the emigration world-wide of the skills no longer required at home. Only the extraction of china clay maintains earlier traditions on any scale.

Cornwall, and also Devon, were in the forefront of the Industrial Revolution. Thomas Newcomen, inventor of the steam engine which, as early as 1712, enabled the draining of mines to greater depths than previously imaginable, was a native of Dartmouth. The engineer inventors and innovators, Richard Trevithick, Davies Gilbert, Sir Humphrey Davy and William Beckford, were all Cornishmen. John Rennie and John Smeaton carried out some of their most important work in Devon. William Cookworthy who initiated the china clay industry was from Plymouth. The manufacture of gas for lighting first began in Cornwall.

It is tin which lies at the heart of the area's industrial past. Its prehistoric antecedents cannot be denied, although hard evidence is difficult to demonstrate. The early exploitation of alluvial deposits, 'streaming', was a simple process not requiring much capital outlay or organisation. It was a part-time occupation combined with subsistence agriculture and farming. Proof that by the early Middle Ages there was a long-established set of customs and practices pertaining to tin working lies in the charter of the Stannaries issued by King John in 1201, which formalises that which had previously evolved. The Crown had for a long time taxed tin production, and in 1198, applied an administrative system to the separate stannaries of Devon and

Cornwall. This in fact gave a good deal of operating freedom to tinners, while at the same time regularising royal revenues through the coinage of tin. Convenient centres (stannary towns) were nominated for the assaying and taxing of smelted tin, courts and prisons were established, and tinners' parliaments were held. The Crown had an interest in other metals as well, including the silver/lead mines of Combe Martin (D).

Carew in 1602 gave a detailed description of the operation of stream works, primitive shaft mining and the smelting process in 'blowing-houses' (**Merrivale**, 96, D). It seems that Devon was the greater producer in the 12th century, but by the 13th century had been overtaken by Cornwall. By the end of the 15th century shaft mining was developed as the tin streams were followed back to their parent lode. Sir Francis Godolphin pioneered new methods of mining and processing with the help of German experts.

While tin remained the basic product, it was copper which made the most spectacular contribution to economic development in the 18th and early 19th centuries (**Botallack Mine**, 90, C). The richest copper mine in the world was, for a time, Devon Great Consols, above the Tamar near Tavistock. Fortunes were made and it was copper which stimulated the growth of ancillary industries like foundrys (such as the **Finch Brothers' Foundry**, 94, D) with the capacity to build the locally developed beam engines for pumping and winding, of which the most famous was that of Harvey's of Hayle (C), and the development of tramways and harbours (**East Pool Cornish Beam Engines**, 93 and **Charlestown**, 91, C). Copper had to be transported to the source of coal for smelting and this usually meant South Wales. An attempt to smelt the copper at its source, at Copperhouse, Hayle, was not a success.

The industrial history of the south-west is by no means all related to

Botallack Mine. E BERRY

metalliferous mining. At first a by-product of tin mining, china clay was a steadily developing industry in its own right during the 19th century. The technology of its extraction and processing have been totally transformed in the last generation. The lines of coal-fired dries are disappearing as are the distinctive conical sand tips, the 'white pyramids' (**Wheal Martin China Clay Museum**, 99, C).

Less immediately obvious today is the Devon cloth trade, although the monuments to its wealth – great churches, chantry chapels, town houses, schools, and almshouses – are many. By 1202, **Exeter** (26) was already seventh in importance among English cloth towns. The development of water-powered fulling mills in the 13th century, which was to revolutionise cloth production, was well suited to the rivers and streams of Devon. (Tucking is the name given to the fulling process in the south-west.) The early Devon cloth, known as 'straits' was rough and coarse. Its production lay to the north, and around Exeter. In the late-15th century east Devon had a reputation for finer 'kerseys', while the coarser cloths were limited to western Dartmoor and centred upon Tavistock (31). Towns like Tiverton (where there were to be as many as fifty-six fulling mills at work in 1730), Cullompton and Crediton were the main kersey producers. But by the 1570s, the New Draperies – worsteds, and later, serges – influenced by the movement of Flemish weavers to England, were beginning to succeed the kerseys. At the end of the 17th century Devonshire serge manufacture was the most important branch of the English woollen industry (**Coldharbour Mill**, 92). More concentrated industrialised methods elsewhere led to decline during the 18th century.

The lace industry was introduced during the 16th century and established itself in the Honiton and Ottery St Mary area (D). John Heathcote set up one of the largest machine-lace factories in Tiverton in 1815. The carpet manufactory begun in Axminster (D) in 1755 survived for only eighty or so years before the machinery was moved to Wilton near Salisbury. Paper-making

Wartime supplies at the Royal William Victualling Yard, 1942. RCHME

and a potting tradition in the region of Barnstaple and Bovey Tracey were other Devonshire industries. Cookworthy's Plymouth porcelain manufactory was very short-lived.

Seemingly timeless occupations, however, were fishing and quarrying. Structures associated with the great days of large-scale fishing in the 18th and early 19th centuries are the now-ruined fish cellars which provided the means for processing and packing large quantities of pilchards for export to Mediterranean countries (**Portquin Fish Cellars**, 97 and **Huer's Hut, Newquay**, 95, C). The production of free-stone for architectural details can be established from the 12th-century with stone from the Polyphant, Catacluse, and Pentewan quarries of Cornwall, and from Hurdwick and Beer in Devon. Roofing slate was a widely distributed medieval export, and quarrying of the material was also at its peak in the 1880s with the products of Delabole and the Tintagel area. Large-scale demands for granite for public buildings in London and elsewhere in the 19th century led to extensive quarrying, which required the means for transporting the product to ports by railway and canal.

The Royal Navy dockyards were among the first establishments to foster mass production, and monuments to the concentration of manufacturing processes have survived wartime bombing at Devonport and Stonehouse. As well as the **Royal William Victualling Yard** (98), the 18th-century smithery and sawmills are in the South Yard, Devonport, and the Quadrangle Building (1853) in the North Yard housed a variety of engineering functions under one roof.

Finally, it must be said that the industry which has left its greatest mark on the landscape of the south-west is tourism. The traditional hallmarks of the popular resort, the pavilions and piers, are few but the hotels and boarding-houses are legion. Many were the direct product of the railway, such as the Falmouth Hotel or the Metropole at Padstow. More recent are the caravan encampments and artificial theme parks.

90

Botallack Mine
19th–early 20th century

SW 362336. St Just. On cliff edge by track off the B3306 at Botallack village

[A]

To Thomas Spargo, author of *Mines of Cornwall and Devon* (1865),

Botallack Mine was 'probably the most remarkable in the world'. Certainly its dramatic situation, the fact that its workings went under the sea, and, for those visitors intrepid enough to venture into them, the awesome experience of hearing the ground swell of the sea above, made it the best known (outside Cornwall) of the county's mines. Queen Victoria made mention of 'the famous Botallack mine' in her Journal for 1846. Prince Alfred, some years later, made an underground visit, followed in 1865 by a celebrated visit by the Prince and Princess of Wales. A whole chapter was devoted by Wilkie Collins in *Rambles Beyond Railways* (1850) to his visit describing the mine and its workings in detail.

The mine was of considerable antiquity, tin being found in deposits close to the surface, and these workings are conspicuous today. By 1838, the mine was already over 150 fathoms deep, drained by a 30-inch (76-cm) engine, and it employed 172 people. By 1870, it was 240 fathoms deep and employed 530 people, with 11 engines in operation, and its workings extended half-a-mile beneath the sea. The mine produced both tin and copper and some arsenic. It was abandoned in 1895. There was an abortive attempt to rework the mine between 1906 and 1914, and much of the now fragmentary surface remains belong to this period.

The enduring features of Botallack, now and in the past, are the two engine houses perched on the cliff promontory of the Crowns section. The larger of the two is thought to have been built before 1816. The 30-inch (76-cm) engine built by Harveys of Hayle in 1823, as well as the masonry for its house, had to be manhandled down the steep cliff. The smaller engine house, a little higher up the cliff, was built about 1858–9 when the copper lodes were giving out and it was necessary to sink a new diagonal shaft to reach the tin. The engine operated a hoist both for the ore and the men.

In their present romantic isolation, the roofless engine houses give a false and partial impression of the former mine. This was best described by Wilkie Collins: 'Here, we beheld a scaffolding

perched on a rock that rose out of the waves – there, a steam-pump was at work raising gallons of water from the mine every minute, on a mere ledge of land half way down the steep cliff side. Chains, pipes, conduits, protruded in all directions from the precipice; rotten-looking wooden platforms, running over deep chasms, supported great beams of timber and heavy coils of cable; crazy little boarded houses were built, where gulls' nests might have been found in other places. There did not appear to be a foot of level space anywhere, for any part of the works of the mine to stand upon . . .' Robert Preston's photographic record of the Royal visit to Botallack in 1865 confirms that this description was no novelist's overblown conceit.

91

Charlestown
18th–19th century

SX 038517. St Austell. By the A3061 and signposted from the A390
[A]

Charlestown is a remarkable relic of Cornwall's development during the course of the Industrial Revolution and beyond. A harbour/industrial village promoted exclusively by Charles Rashleigh of Menabilly, near Fowey, it was built almost within a decade, beginning in 1791. So far, it has preserved its particular character, distinct from the commercial centre of St Austell and the cliff-top residential developments to the east. It is now, however, under threat from just such development.

Before Rashleigh's initiative, West Polmear consisted of a few cottages and fish cellars, and a population in 1790 of nine persons. It was then the practice to beach boats to unload lime and coal for the nearby tin and copper mines and take off metal ores and the newly appreciated commodity, china clay. This unsatisfactory state of affairs was changed by the building of a harbour, whose design is attributed to John Smeaton, together with all the necessary adjuncts and service industries of a commercial port.

An outer basin and pier protected a long narrow inner basin excavated into the rock and fed with water by adit from the neighbouring mines. This was capacious enough to admit vessels of 500 tons burden. A lock gate, modified in recent years, separated the two basins. In 1792, with work continuing on the harbour, a new pilchard seine was fitted out, a rope-walk constructed, and a hotel, houses and workshops begun. Lewis's *Topographical Dictionary* of 1840 reported: 'Here are yards and dry docks for building and repairing large ships, and a rope and twine manufactory: a great quantity of lime is burnt; but the chief trade of the place consists in its extensive pilchard fishery, for which several seans have been put on, and receiving-houses erected. Most of the china clay brought from St Stephen's is shipped at this port.' As well as a Methodist chapel, a National School for 150 children had been erected. One scheme which did not materialise during the 1790s was a proposal of Josiah Wedgwood to set up a 'pot-works' here close to the source of clay. It was no doubt cheaper to take the clay to Staffordshire than to bring coal to St Austell. For as long as the local mines were producing copper and tin, Charlestown served as their port but eventually china clay became the principal export.

Many of the surviving buildings relate to this period. The back-to-back cottages have been converted to suit modern health standards. The row of substantial cottages above the inner basin still have a Regency flavour. The chapel and hotel are still active. Fish cellars or palaces can be recognised though in some instances have been converted into residences. The remains of the lime kiln can be seen behind the estate office. Elsewhere there are businesses occupying the former coal and timber yards and cooperages, and there are still open areas which are identifiable as china clay and ore floors where these products were stored before shipment.

One industry that still remains is Charlestown Foundry which was established as early as 1827. It survived because it was able to diversify to serve the china clay industry. It built the last Cornish beam pumping engine in 1911 for the North Goonbarrow China Clay Company. The main intrusion into the original layout came in 1908 when John Lovering built a drying kiln for china clay which was run as slurry by gravity along pipes from his Carclaze pit some 1½ miles (2.1 km) away. This method overcame the problems involved in transporting clay by road in wagons. Here, the dry clay was placed in rock-cut storage bins and dropped into tram wagons in a tunnel which led to the top of the cliff above the inner basin, and then tipped down shutes into the ships at the quay below.

92

Coldharbour Mill, Uffculme
1797–20th century

ST 062122. Signposted from the B3391 SW of town

[A]

Devon's late-medieval woollen industry was based on kersey, a cheap, coarse-textured cloth whose principal manufacturing area was the Culm and Exe valleys, and serge, which took over from kersey in the 16th and 17th centuries due to the rise in production of worsted yarn from the longer fleeces

then available. The west-country woollen industry became nationally important as an exported commodity during the 17th and early 18th centuries, but declined thereafter. Coldharbour Mill, which, against the trend, was not established until 1797, continued production into the present century. It is now one of the few survivors of Devon's wool trade, and a little spinning and weaving is still carried out today.

Thomas Fox, together with his brother Edward, whose Cornish Quaker father had married into a Wellington serge-making family, changed the name of the business to Fox Brothers. They developed two factories at Wellington and Thomas Fox bought Coldharbour Mill in 1797 because of its reliable source of water. In the difficult conditions operating during the Napoleonic Wars, when the production of serge was hit by heavy export duties, Thomas Fox developed a flannel, a soft woollen cloth, which grew popular in the Americas. Following the British Army's switch from scarlet tunics to khaki uniforms in 1881, Fox Brothers successfully won a contract for the manufacture of 5,000 pairs of khaki puttees. They squared their Quaker consciences with the argument that not only would the new contract create employment but the new camouflage colour would help to save lives! Spinning worsted yarn for puttees became the main activity of the mill from then on.

The focus of the buildings that eventually composed the establishment is the three-storey stone mill of fireproof construction built by Thomas Fox in 1799. There are various brick additions and separate ranges of one and two-storey buildings, and a fine octagonal brick chimney 127 ft (38.7 m) high. The initial power source was water. The present 15 ft (4.6 m) by 18 ft (5.5 m) wheel is probably of 1885. Thomas Fox had investigated the possibility of steam power in the early 1780s but apart from the inherent cheapness of water, his other motive was to maintain levels of local employment. He wrote: 'I make it a point to spin all worsted I use by hand to employ as many of the poor as possible.'

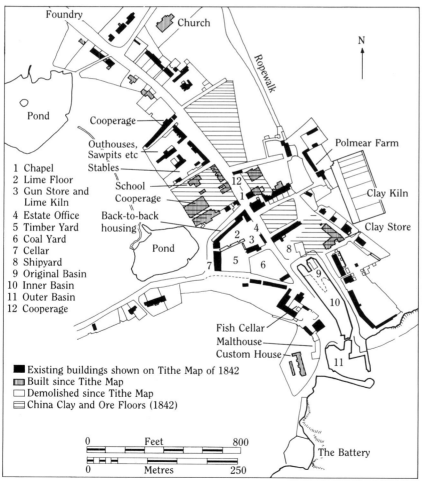

1 Chapel
2 Lime Floor
3 Gun Store and Lime Kiln
4 Estate Office
5 Timber Yard
6 Coal Yard
7 Cellar
8 Shipyard
9 Original Basin
10 Inner Basin
11 Outer Basin
12 Cooperage

■ Existing buildings shown on Tithe Map of 1842
▨ Built since Tithe Map
▢ Demolished since Tithe Map
▤ China Clay and Ore Floors (1842)

Charlestown industrial village (after J Stengelhofen). EH

Coldharbour Mill. J COX

Steam power did not arrive until 1865 when the factory changed to worsted production and new combing machinery was installed. Two beam engines were used over the years. The present Pollit & Wigzell horizontal cross-compound engine replaced the earlier equipment in 1910.

Close to the mill are cottages built for the workers at cheap rents on the philanthropic premise adopted by so many Quaker industrialists. The mill finally closed in 1981. Shortly afterwards the Coldharbour Mill Trust was formed to save the buildings intact together with the textile machinery and power sources, and to open them to the public as a working wool museum.

93

East Pool Cornish Beam Engines, Pool
19th century

SW 675416/679419. Camborne. Alongside the A3047 at Pool W of Redruth

[A] NT

While many ruined engine houses bear witness to the all-but-vanished metalliferous mining industry of the south-west, two Cornish beam engines are preserved in their engine houses at Pool.

The East Pool Whim is the more conspicuous. 'Whim' is the Cornish word for a winding device to raise men and ore up the mine shaft. It might employ horse, water or steam power. Here, the steam winding-engine is a late example of the beam type. Built in 1887 by Holman Bros of Camborne to the design of a local engineer, it was the last rotative engine to be made in Cornwall. It has a double-acting condensing engine. The cylinder is 30 in (76 cm) in diameter with a piston of an unusually long stroke of 9 ft (2.7 m), but is now impractical to work by steam and is driven by electricity on the occasions when it is in working order.

In the centre of the ground floor, or Bottom Chamber, is the cylinder encased with brick for insulation. Here was where the engine driver operated the wheel throttle valve and the brake on the massive fly-wheel outside. Signals could be transmitted to the driver by the men underground. The steel winding-ropes were wound round two drums in opposite directions so that while one 'cage' was raised the other was lowered. The Middle Chamber is at the top of the cylinder where the piston emerges to connect it to the end of the beam. The Top Chamber is at the level of the large cast-iron beam or *bob* as it was known in Cornwall. The boiler house was demolished following the closure of the mine in 1921. It has since been rebuilt. The new Taylor's Shaft was sunk as a replacement on the opposite (north) side of the road. This is partly concealed by houses but its stack has a prominent 'EPAL' (East Pool and Agar Ltd) picked out in white brick.

The Cornish Pumping Engine at Taylor's Shaft was one of the last of this type to be built by Harvey & Co. of Hayle in 1892 for the Carn Brea Mines. After their closure, the engine was re-erected at East Pool in 1924 and worked until this too closed in 1945. In fact, its active life did not end entirely since it was later used to assist the draining of the nearby South Crofty Mine until 1954 when new electric pumps were installed at South Crofty.

The internal arrangements are similar to the East Pool Whim. Here, the cylinder is 90 in (2.9 m) in diameter and its very large cast-iron bob is 33 ft 3 in (10 m) in length, one of the largest ever made. When installed, the engine pumped from a depth of 1,700 ft (519 m)

East Pool Whim and headgear, *c*.1895. NT

and raised 450 gallons (3,046 litres) of water a minute when running at the usual speed of about five strokes a minute. In order to balance the great weight of the wooden pump-rods there was a system of balance beams or *bobs* at stages in the shaft and at the surface. The surface balance-bob was unusual in being made of steel plates riveted together instead of cast-iron. It carries the date 1911, and was made by the Charlestown Foundry, St Austell. It originally formed part of the last Cornish engine to be built and later was re-used for the present engine.

94

Finch Brothers' Foundry, Sticklepath
19th–20th century

SX 642940. Sticklepath. On the former A30, now approached from Okehampton or from the Okehampton by-pass (A30T) at Whiddon Down

[A]

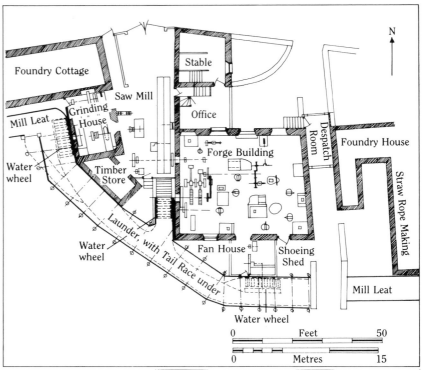

Finch Brothers' Foundry (after R A Barron). EH

The 'foundry' is really an edge-tool works founded in 1814 by William Finch and continued by five successive generations of the family until its closure in 1960. The works produced high quality hand-tools such as scythes, billhooks, picks and shovels for use in the farming, mining and clay industries of the south-west. The firm also had a sawmill on the site and a carpenters' and wheelwrights' business. Up to about 1940, between twenty and twenty-five men were employed.

At various times there were three or four watermills in the village powered by leats taken off the River Taw. The foundry was established in what was known in the early 1800s as the Manor Mills, comprising two distinct buildings, the easterly of which was a cloth mill. This was leased by William Finch and became the edge-tool works with a fan-room attached. A pair of tilt hammers and power-shears with their water-wheel were then installed. There were six or seven blacksmiths' hearths as well as two enclosed furnaces. Bellows were driven by a second water-wheel which

also provided blast to the forges. Two drop-forging hammers and a further set of power-shears were also driven by the wheel powering the tilt hammers. By the middle of the 19th century the lease of the old grist mill was obtained and a large grindstone installed driven by a third water-wheel. It is an overshot wheel, 12 ft (3.7 m) in diameter. The grindstone was about 5 ft (1.5 m) in diameter and 8 in (20.3 cm) thick. It was said that it would be reduced to half that diameter in about six months. About 1958, a water turbine was installed to drive the machinery by electric motors. The main trade in tools for the mining and china clay industries had, however, by then drastically declined through the closure of the tin and copper mines and increasing mechanisation of the clay pits and drys.

With the demise of the foundry in 1960, the buildings became derelict and the saw mill was demolished when the village street was widened. In 1966, an educational and charitable trust was formed to preserve the foundry as a

museum of industrial history. The three water-wheels can now be seen operating the machinery including the tilt hammers, as well as examples of the tools produced here and displays illustrating the development of the foundry.

95

Huer's Hut, Newquay
c.18th century

SW 807625. On the headland beyond Newquay harbour

[D]

The chief archaeological survival of the 18th- and 19th-century pilchard fishing industry is the fish cellar. The other, and now very rare, is the huer's hut or lookout tower. From it a lookout (huer), having spotted a pilchard shoal, would cry 'Hevva, Hevva' (the Cornish for shoaling) through long tin speaking horns (trumpets) to alert the local inhabitants, and the seine boats, who

Huer's Hut. E BERRY

would immediately put out in pursuit of the fish. From the tower, the huer would then direct the manoeuvring of the boats by semaphore signals, using 'bushes' consisting of wooden hoops covered with white bags. 'Hevva to the Lay [Cornish *legh*, a flat rock], the boats es gone to say' was an old St Ives saying. The bushes, trumpets and other paraphernalia from the St Ives balking-house have been preserved.

The huer's hut at Newquay is on the headland beyond the harbour. It probably belongs to the 18th century, and is therefore likely to be the earliest surviving building in the town. It is stone-built with mock battlements, whitewashed, with a little tower and external staircase. *Murray's Handbook* for 1859 describes Newquay as 'a small but rising watering-place where the pilchard industry is pursued on a considerable scale'.

96

Merrivale Blowing-houses
Medieval or later

SX 553754/553763. Walkhampton. N of the B3357 Tavistock–Princetown road, E of Merrivale Bridge. Stile opposite car park

[A]

Tin ore, usually obtained from alluvial deposits by the method known as 'streaming', was frequently smelted close to the streamworks where it was extracted in small masonry structures known as 'blowing-houses'. More than forty such buildings were recorded as

still surviving on Dartmoor by R Hansford Worth in 1940. It is argued that they represent an improved method of smelting which was introduced in the course of the 13th century and continued in use until the end of the 18th century. That the charcoal-fuelled blowing-house survived in competition with the coal-fed reverberatory furnace for so long was due to the superiority of the smelted tin achieved by this method especially that derived from streamworks.

The method of operation required a small, usually rectangular building, within which the crushed and prepared ore was smelted on the hearth of a granite furnace by a charcoal fire fed by the blast from a pair of bellows, which were worked by a water-wheel set in a pit to the side of the building and driven from a leat. The molten tin was then cast into granite moulds set in the floor to form blocks generally weighing around 200 or 300 lb. Carew (1602) describes how particles of tin could be driven into the thatched roof by the force of the bellows, 'for which cause the owners do, once in seven or eight years, burn those houses, and find so much of this light tin in the ashes as payeth for the new

building, with a gainful overplus' (*The Survey of Cornwall*, p95). For this reason, if no other, blowing-houses are likely to have been frequently rebuilt and may have had long intervals of use and disuse over many centuries. They therefore cannot be dated from their surviving structure alone.

The two blowing-houses above Merrivale Bridge, on the bank of rising ground above the eastern side of the River Walkham, are both well-preserved and readily accessible on moorland. The lower of the two measures 32 ft (10 m) by 15 ft 6 in (4.7 m) internally, and the walls nearly 3 ft (1 m) thick. The furnace is preserved with the sides standing to a height of over 4 ft (1.2 m). The hollowed 'float', into which the molten tin ran, still forms the bottom of the furnace though its level has been displaced. The mould stone is close to both the furnace and the door. The mould would have held 254 lb (115 kg) of tin. The position of the wheel-pit is not clear.

The higher blowing-house is about the same size as the lower. Its wheel-pit is well defined, suggesting a wheel of *c*.10 ft (3 m) diameter. There is also a mould stone close to the door which could hold 193 lb (87.5 kg) of tin.

Merrivale blowing-house. RCHME

97

Portquin Fish Cellars
18th–19th century

SW 971805. St Endellion.
Signposted from the B3314,
Wadebridge–Delabole road

[B] NT

The earliest documented place-name,
Porquin or *Porthguyn* meaning 'White
Harbour', goes back to the 13th century,
but the surviving buildings at the head
of a long narrow inlet in the north
Cornish cliffs belong to a small and
abandoned fishing settlement of the
18th and 19th centuries. The remaining
cottages are used as seasonal holiday
homes. John Betjeman quotes the story
that at the end of the last century all the
men of the village were drowned
together in the fishing boat owned by
the village and the settlement deserted
thereafter, but this is unconfirmed.

The most prominent structure here,
standing behind the tiny quay and slip,
is built about a rectangular courtyard.
The roofed range on the west has been
converted into holiday accommodation.
The outer face of the eastern wall has the

tell-tale line of rectangular holes for the
pressing-beams needed for processing
pilchards. It is in fact the remains of that
specialised type of building required for
the former pilchard fisheries – the fish
cellar. There is similar evidence for
another on the opposite side of the
valley.

Pilchards used to be smoked during
the 17th century but the practice of
pressing fish into hogsheads gained
ground and was the dominant
processing method during the 18th and
first half of the 19th centuries. The
pilchards were first laid in balks in the
cellars, the fish placed side by side with
salt between each layer, creating a wall
of fish 2–3 ft (0.6–0.9 m) thick and up to
6 ft (1.8 m) high. After thorough salt
impregnation the balk was broken and
the pilchards arranged in straight-sided
barrels. The fish were placed radially
until the barrels were full. They were
then pressed using a pressing-beam and
weights. The hogsheads were
deliberately leaky, and they were
arranged on a wooden platform or gutter
against the wall. The barrels were
pressed and refilled until they were
completely packed. The train oil was
sold for lighting and other purposes
such as the preparation of leather. In

1795, the industry employed some 3,500
men organised in over 100 concerns. In
good years vast quantities of pilchards
were exported to Italy and other Catholic
Mediterranean countries.

The primary requirement was a
'cellar' or 'palace', as it was known in
East Cornwall, to provide space for
balking and pressing, storing salt, and as
a place to keep nets, etc. A wide entrance
led into the courtyard. Sometimes
dwellings were provided. In many parts
of Cornwall the lower walls were built of
stone into which the sockets for the
pressing-beams were located, and the
upper walls were in cob. Particularly
around Falmouth and in St Austell Bay,
almost every cove had its cellar. With
the gradual disappearance of pilchard
fishing during the 19th century, this
common form of industrial building fell
into ruin or was converted for other
purposes.

98

Royal William Victualling Yard, Plymouth
1827–20th century

SX 462535. On the N side of the
Stonehouse peninsula from Cremyll
Street off Durnford Street

[B]

The chief industrial concentrations
during the 18th and early 19th centuries
were the Royal Navy dockyards. There a
number of processes were carried out on
a large scale, and the first signs of
mass-production techniques in Britain
have been recognised in the Block mills
at Portsmouth. If the dockyards were the
first industrial centres, 'the Victualling
Office was the country's first large-scale
food manufacturing and catering
organisation' (Jonathan Coad, *Historic
Architecture of the Royal Navy: An
Introduction*, London, 1983, p116). In
the 18th century the headquarters of
naval victualling was at Deptford but,
with the increasing importance of the
south-coast dockyards, their victualling
premises developed separately. After the
Napoleonic Wars, there was a move for
more centralised facilities at both
Portsmouth and Plymouth. The

Portquin fish cellars. E BERRY

Victualling Board began the process of modernisation at Plymouth, where the need was greatest, in 1822.

The site chosen was the Stonehouse peninsula below the Dockyard, where the Hamoaze meets the Sound. At this time, the engineer, John Rennie the younger, was completing the great breakwater in the Sound, and he was asked to take responsibility for the design and construction of the new victualling yard. The result was a compact and almost symmetrical arrangement of industrial buildings arranged around three sides of a square, tidal basin which acted as the focal point for an area of about 14 acres (5.6 ha). Here were a brewery, flour mill, bakery, cooperage, slaughterhouse, a large quadrangular storehouse (Melville Square), five houses for senior officers, porter's lodge and boundary walls. Rennie was also responsible for much of the machinery in the mill, brewery and bakery. The contracts for the first building, the Clarence Wharf storehouse, on the western side, and at forty-five degrees to the main complex, were let in 1827. The whole establishment was completed in 1831, and Rennie's design remains intact and, in the opinion of Jonathan Coad, 'is one of the most important groups of industrial buildings in the country'.

Architecturally, it is remarkably fine and has been described as 'by far the most impressive single architectural group in Plymouth' (Bridget Cherry and Nikolaus Pevsner, *Devon*, London, 1989, p653). Construction was in grey local limestone with granite dressings. The landward approach is from Cremyll Street through a monumental gateway crowned by a more-than-twice-lifesize statue of William IV. The main group of buildings has the quadrangle of storehouses of Melville Square at its centre with a tall central cupola over the entrance from the basin. Most of the supplies came in and out by water. On either side of the basin, and carried forward to the wharf edge to facilitate direct access by vessels, were the bakery and mill to the east and the brewery to the west. Each has a prominent chimney with entasis. The houses for the senior officers were just inside the gate behind

Royal William Victualling Yard. EH

the guardhouse on the south side of the main roadway.

99
Wheal Martyn China Clay Museum
19th–20th century

SX 004554. St Austell. Signposted from the A39 Bodmin–St Austell road at Carthew

[A]

Wheal Martyn is more than a museum. It is a clay and mica works which is now the most informative example of an early, small, family-owned works retaining the traditional essential elements of the industry. The museum in fact includes two old clay works: Wheal Martyn and the Gomm Pit, whose ancillary buildings were established in 1878 and closed in the 1920s, and in whose ruined remains the museum reception area has now been built. Gomm Pit itself lies behind the overgrown sand tip to the rear.

Wheal Martyn has a longer history, being part of the Carthew Estate bought by Richard Martyn in 1790. His son, Elias, probably started the china clay works in the 1820s. By the 1840s, Elias Martyn was working five pits producing 3,500 tons a year which, at the time, was about an eighth of the total annual production of Cornwall. His son, Richard Uriah Martyn, closed down most of his pits, including Wheal Martyn, in

1880. John Lovering then took a lease on it, and it was probably he who was responsible for the 'modernisation' of the works, which left them much the same as they are today. The pit continued working until 1931, just before John Lovering & Co. became part of English Clays Lovering Pochin. The works which form the museum site, however, continued in operation until 1969, processing low-grade clay from other pits in the area. In 1971, Wheal Martyn Pit was reopened but its clay is now piped up to modern treatment works elsewhere before going on to Par to be dried.

The museum's 'historic trail' broadly follows the traditional processes of refining, thickening and drying in their original sites and structures. The extraction of the clay can be seen half-a-mile away in the latter-day Wheal Martyn Pit while there are reconstructions in the museum area of a level of the kind to be found at the bottom of a 19th-century clay pit, and of an incline which carried waste up the tip. Beside the drive of the long-demolished Carthew House is a 35-ft (11-m) diameter water wheel originally used to pump clay slurry out of the pit, and it is the largest working water-wheel in Cornwall. It is a pitch-back wheel made at Charlestown Foundry and it operated a series of flat rods over a distance of about 1,000 yds (304.7 m) to the plunger pumps in a shaft half-way down the side of the Wheal Martyn pit. Elsewhere, is an 18-ft (5.5-m) diameter overshot water-wheel which, together with its balance box, has been restored to working order. It was also probably made at Charlestown Foundry and was erected on this site in about 1902.

The first stage of the refining process was to run the clay slurry through a sand trap in the bottom of the pit. It was then pumped to the surface and into sand and mica drags where fine quartz sand and mica flakes were deposited along U-shaped concrete channels. After passing through the blueing house, the slurry passed into settling pits and tanks for the start of the dewatering process. When the clay had drained and was air-dried sufficiently, it was moved to the pan kiln or dry to be dried over flues heated by coal firing. The long low building (dry), with a tall chimney stack at one end, is still the most obvious archaeological evidence in the 'Clay Country' of the former method of processing china clay. When the clay was dry, it was thrown out of the kiln into the linhay which formed the lower part of the dry. It was then ready for transporting either in blocks or in casks to the port or railhead.

Wheal Martin. The restored 18-ft-diameter overshot water-wheel. C BOWDEN

10

Communications

The geographical circumstances of Devon and Cornwall dictated that, while land communications with the rest of the country remained poor, the easiest means for transporting goods was by water. The arrival of the railway, and trunk roads in more recent years, have all but eliminated that remoteness which has long characterised the south-western peninsula.

The main Roman road into the peninsula, the Fosse Way, terminated at Exeter. The rudiments of a Roman road system have been traced west of Exeter. The principal route ran north of Dartmoor, and a recognisable stretch passed the fort near North Tawton. It may be assumed that, though there is now no physical trace, it continued roughly on the line of the present A30 past Okehampton to Launceston and Bodmin. A 'milestone' of the mid-3rd century found near Gwennap Pit (C) suggests its continuation westwards. Subsidiary roads are indicated from similar 'milestones' recording road maintenance at Breage and St Hilary in west Cornwall and by two more in the region of Tintagel. The only firm indication of a port in use in the Roman period, other than Exeter, is that at Mount Batten but the major estuaries are all likely to have been in use.

The pattern of local communication during the Roman period is unlikely to have changed much from that which had existed earlier. There are indications of the use of ridgeways along the higher ground and for cross-peninsula routes especially in Cornwall. A communication between the Hayle estuary and Mount's Bay can be expected, and so can links between the River Fowey and the River Camel at Padstow. With the consolidation of the settlement pattern during post-Roman times, and with Anglo-Saxon influence gradually affecting Devon and parts of east Cornwall, a network of roads and lanes connecting farmsteads and hamlets to local markets and with each other was implanted on the landscape.

The existence of bridges is alluded to in early charters and also in the Domesday Book. Kingsbridge (D) refers to the bridge linking two royal estates which led to the growth of a town of that name. The earls of Cornwall saw economic advantages from investment in bridge building. Their manor of Grampound (C) takes its name from the *grand pont* existing in the 13th century. Clapper bridges are impossible to date. They were principally intended for pack animals, which were the common form of transport during the Middle Ages, and indeed much later (**Postbridge**, 106, D). More substantial masonry bridges can be documented, notably at **Exeter** (101) by the end of the 12th century. Fine late-medieval bridges are numerous, with some of the best over the Tamar. A pioneering effort in poured concrete is the Seaton Bridge (D) built in 1877, the earliest surviving mass-concrete bridge in Britain.

In the early Middle Ages, the deeply indented coast enabled ships to serve markets well inland at places such as Tregoney (C), Lostwithiel (C) and Totnes (D). Natural causes and, particularly in Cornwall, the silting of rivers through tin-working debris, led to the progressive shift of ports to the mouths of estuaries where ferries were also a feature. The Kingswear Ferry is mentioned in 1365, Sherborne Abbey controlled the ferry between Exmouth (D) and Starcross (D), and others of importance were those across the Tamar at Saltash and Cremyll (C), and that between Appledore and Braunton Burrows (D).

In 1602, Carew wrote of 'the foulness and uneasiness of the ways', and more particularly the highways in east Cornwall 'by reason either of the mire or stones, besides many uphills and downhills' (*The Survey of Cornwall*, pp84, 125). During the Civil War, Fairfax's soldiers had to assault the defences of Dartmouth without artillery support because the condition of the south Devon roads did not allow the

movement of his guns. At the end of the century, Celia Fiennes complained of the deep pot-holes, having nearly come to grief in one west of Looe (C). Roads were however improving. A passenger coach took 4 days between London and Exeter in 1658, and 20 hours in 1828. Improvements came with the establishment of turnpike trusts. The first were formed in the mid-18th century in the region of Exeter, Honiton and Axminster (**Newton Poppleford Tollhouse**, 105, D). Cornish trusts were established from 1754. The laying of the first tarmacadam on the A30 was not until 1919, opening up the south-west to the motor car on an ever-increasing scale.

The topography of the region did not favour adoption of canals during the 18th century, and they were only successfully applied over short distances to serve particular needs. Tavistock to Morwhellham (D) and the **Bude Canal** (100, C) are examples. The Exeter canal was, however, crucial to the city's commercial development, and, in 1564, was the first canal in England to use a pound lock. The transport of the rapidly increasing mineral production in the south-west was better served by tramways and inclined planes. Novel solutions were adopted by Treffry in mid-Cornwall (**Treffry Viaduct**, 110). There was a network of tramways between Hayle and Portreath (C); at **Morwhellham** (104, D), there was a combination of canal, tramway and inclined plane, and there was the remarkable granite railway serving the **Haytor** quarries (103, D).

The experience in establishing mineral lines to the exporting ports had its influence on the development of railways proper. The first railway in Cornwall to use a steam engine, and the first passenger train, was the Bodmin & Wadebridge Railway in 1834. The line between Exeter and Bristol was opened in 1844. The eventual formation of the Great Western Railway sprang from a number of local companies, but the unifying influence was that of Isambard

Treffry Viaduct, 1844. RIC

Bude Canal sea lock. RCHME

Kingdom Brunel. There were failures such as his atmospheric railway between Exeter and Newton Abbot (**Starcross Pumping Station**, 109, D), but, more importantly, there was the **Royal Albert Bridge** (107, D) at Saltash and the engineering of his broad-gauge line through Devon and Cornwall. This was characterised by its many timber viaducts usually on masonry piers which still survive alongside later stone viaducts.

Communications with a wider world can be said to range from the Scillonian pilot gigs (some boathouses still remain on Tresco) to the Falmouth packet service to Iberia and beyond. Sea communications demanded lighthouses and navigational aids. The chapel of St Nicholas at Ilfracombe (D) which provided a light is a medieval example of this. The lighthouse on St Agnes in Scilly is one of the earliest surviving in Britain, dated 1680. Its brazier is preserved in Valhalla, Tresco Abbey. St Martin's navigational daymark was built only three years later. On such dangerous coasts the construction of lighthouses is epitomised by that of **Smeaton's Eddystone Lighthouse** (108, D). Finally, Cornwall's situation, projecting out into the Atlantic, has led to involvement in the fast-developing technology of long-distance

communications, first by submarine cables, then wireless telegraphy and radio, and now by satellite (**Goonhilly Earth Station**, 102, D).

100
Bude Canal
1819–1890s

SS 205064. Bude. The most accessible length runs from the harbour basin to Hele Bridge

[A]

The enthusiasm for canals in the 1770s as an effective means of bulk transport and an alternative to the inadequate road affected Cornwall as well as the rest of the country. In 1774, John Edyvean of St Austell advocated a canal link, 90 miles long between Bude Haven and Calstock on the Tamar. A canal from Bude did not, however, materialise until the turn of the 19th century with the support of the Molesworth family. Construction began in 1819 and it opened in 1823. It was the longest canal scheme in Cornwall and was the longest tub-boat canal in Britain. Its principal purpose was to transport quantities of sea sand inland as a dressing for the fields. It was remarkable for using inclined planes instead of locks and wheeled tub-boats. Thirty-five miles were constructed and it eventually extended to the Tamar at Druxton, 3 miles north-east of Launceston.

The canal depended on an embankment in the bay at Bude, constructed it was said in a manner similar to the Plymouth Breakwater, creating a sheltered basin for coastal vessels up to about 120 tons, and entered by means of a sea-lock. The widest stretch of the canal extends from this basin to Hele Bridge where the remains of a wharf still stand.

The feature of the canal which most impressed the author of Murray's *Handbook of Devon and Cornwall* (1859) was the inclined plane at Hobbacott Down near Stratton, 'which the stranger should visit . . . It is an ingenious substitute for a chain of locks, and consists of a steep roadway, about 900 ft in length, which is furnished with two lines of rails dipping at each end into the canal, and traversed by an endless chain. The barges, which are provided with small iron wheels, and are generally loaded with sand, are raised and lowered on this roadway by being attached to the chain, which is set in motion by two enormous buckets, each 8 ft in diameter, alternately filled with water, and working in wells 225 ft in depth. As soon as the descending bucket has reached the bottom of the well, it strikes upon a stake which raises a plug, when the water runs out in one minute, and finds its way through an adit to the canal below. This bucket is then in readiness to be raised by the other, which having been filled with water, descends in its turn . . . A steam-engine is also on hand should the buckets become unserviceable.' Four other shorter planes were powered by water-wheels. The outline of the Hobbacott inclined plane can still be seen above Coombepark Farm and defined by two hedgerows. There is the stone-built engine house and the single-storey house of the incline keeper.

The canal flourished for thirty years, but the coming of the railway and the substitution of alternative forms of fertiliser by the end of the century brought an end to its active life.

101

Exe Bridge, Exeter
c.1200

SX 914922. SW of the city, enclosed within the large roundabout formed by the Western Way ring road and the new crossings of the river

[D]

Devon and Cornwall possess a number of surviving late-medieval and 16th-century bridges. Charles Henderson listed twenty-four in Cornwall alone and drew attention to the fine examples crossing the Tamar. The remains of the Exe Bridge of *c*.1200, formerly the principal entry to the city from the west, have recently been revealed, if not overwhelmed, by the modern road system and river crossing.

The first stone bridge was due to the initiative of the mayor, Walter Gervase, and his wealthy merchant father Nicholas. There are documentary references to repairs and renewals during the Middle Ages. Leland's visit in about 1539 led him to mention the 'great stone Bridge of 14 arches over Ex River'. William of Worcester nearly a century earlier had given the number of arches as 16, and recorded that the length was '200 steppys meos computatos'. The original bridge may have been longer, about 650 ft (200 m) with 17 or 18 arches, probably crossing marsh land as well as the Exe itself.

Eight-and-a-half arches can now be seen and these are the survivors of one of the earliest long, stone bridges in the country. Two of the arches are pointed but appear to be of the same build as the four round arches. St Edmund's church was an integral part of the original bridge but the present ruins belong to the church of the 1830s. The bridge led directly to West Gate and Stepcote Hill.

102

Goonhilly Earth Station
20th century

SW 724213. The Lizard. Signposted from the B3293 Helston–Coverack road

[A] British Telecom International

The Lizard peninsula has a crucial place in the pioneering of wireless and the development of international telecommunications. It was from Poldhu, on the cliff-top, 2½ miles west of Goonhilly Downs, that the first wireless signal was transmitted across the Atlantic in 1901. Guglielmo Marconi chose the Lizard for pursuing his objective of long-range transmission because of its equable climate, the uninterrupted 'view' across the Atlantic, and the lack of interference from electric power cables. Here was built in 1900 the largest transmitter the world had seen (25kW). It continued in use until 1934 as an experimental centre, and it was

Exe Bridge. EAU

here that the short-wave beam wireless system and the coaxial system so essential for television were developed. There is a memorial on its site erected by the Marconi Company and foundations for the masts and the transmitter building are still to be seen.

Another of Marconi's coastal radio stations at the Lizard itself received the first wireless distress signal from a ship, the *Minniehaha*, aground off the Isles of Scilly, in 1909. As a result all the passengers were saved.

For more than half a century wireless was the principal means of long-distance telecommunication. The first experiments with satellites, the Telstar series, took place in 1962–3. Goonhilly Downs was chosen as the site for the British earth station for much the same reasons which had influenced Marconi sixty years before. Unlike the Americans and French, the Post Office engineers devised a 1,100-ton open-dish aerial which eventually was to prove the most effective design. Aerial 1's movements, or tracking, of the low-orbit Telstar, were monitored from the old control tower.

There are currently ten aerials arranged in an irregular circuit, with the operational controls and service buildings in the centre. Aerial 1, built in 1961, is still in use for British TV news distribution and other news services. Aerials 2 (1968) and 4 (1978) are used for transatlantic telephonic traffic. Aerial 3 (1972) gives support to Indian Ocean traffic. Aerial 5 (1983) provides services for maritime traffic using the Atlantic Ocean satellite. Aerial 6 (1985) has the largest reflector (32 m diameter) of all and provides further capacity for the transatlantic route. Aerial 7 (1983) is now used for trials to provide a telephone service to aircraft. Aerials 8, 9 and 10 are small-dish aerials used for research, testing and development. The nerve-centre of Goonhilly is the Operational Control Area where the positioning of all the aerials is checked and power supplies monitored. The old control tower now contains a scale model of the site and a view of all the aerials, together with the microwave tower which communicates with the London Telecom Tower. The station,

Goonhilly Earth Station. BOV/J MELVILLE

together with the site of Marconi's achievements nearby, represents the whole history of telecommunications over the past ninety years.

103

Haytor Granite Railway
1820–1860

SX 755775. Ilsington. Haytor Down N of B3387 at Haytor Vale
[A]

'On Saturday [16 September 1820] Mr Templer, of Stover House, gave a grand fête champêtre on Haytor Down, on the completion of the granite rail road' (David St John Thomas, *A Regional History of the Railways of Great Britain. Vol.1: The West Country*, Newton Abbot, 1966, p57). This was the first tramway in Devon, and unusual in that it was constructed from granite blocks 5–8 ft (1.5–2.4 m) in length, roughly 1 ft (0.3 m) square in section, cut with rebates 7½ in (19 cm) wide and 3 in (7.6 cm) deep on either side, with a gauge of about 4 ft (1.2 m) or a little more, instead of a system of iron rails. The flat-topped, horse-drawn trucks, which could carry up to 3 tons each, had flangeless iron wheels of 2 ft (0.6 m)

diameter which ran in the rebates of the blocks.

The tramway was a necessary adjunct to the Haytor quarries – which were the source of granite for, among other London buildings, London Bridge – and provided a means of transport to the Stover canal at Teigngrace, from where the granite was transferred to Teignmouth by barges prior to shipment. The cost of the granite was accordingly high but it was not until 1858 that the quarries here declined and the tramway fell into disuse.

The course of the tramway started near the Holwell quarry face and ran eastwards across Haytor Down for the first half of its length. Branches from the main quarries joined it before the line crossed the Widecombe–Bovey Tracey road. The single track was 8½ miles long and involved a climb of around 1,300 ft (396 m) without a steep gradient requiring extra horses. Nor were cuttings or embankments needed. At junctions, points were provided by the use of larger blocks with grooves set at an angle and numerous short, straight blocks were used for curves, their flanges being worn into shape.

Much of the tramway on Haytor Down and its granite slabs can still be traced, including 'points' and branch lines serving individual quarries.

Morwhellham Quay, c.1868, with Devon Great Consol's Quay in foreground.

104
Morwellham Quay
19th century

SX 446697. SW of Tavistock. Signposted from the A390

[A]

Morwellham served as the port of Tavistock and its neighbouring industries from the 12th century onwards. First it was the property of the Abbey of Tavistock until the Dissolution of the Monasteries, and then passed with much of the abbey lands to Lord John Russell, and so to the Bedford estate. In the early years of the 19th century it was greatly developed in order to cope with the expansion of mining in the Tavistock area, and in the 1840s new deposits of copper were found in Blanchdown above Gunnislake and formed the basis for Devon Great Consols. A new dock nearly 100 yds (91 m) long was needed in consequence, and begun in 1859. Near the quay, an inn, a chapel, and workshops, offices and cottages were built by the Bedford estate in the 1850s. The quay was the hub of an elaborate communication network in this part of the Tamar Valley. The port's prosperity, however, had declined by the end of the 19th century, along with that of the mines it served, its decline being further precipitated by the coming of the main railway line to Tavistock shortly after 1890.

In order to transport the copper ore cheaply and efficiently from the Mary Tavy mines, a 4-mile-long canal was constructed from Tavistock to a point 240 ft (72 m) above Morwellham Quay. At this point, the iron canal barges were put on trolleys which ran on grooved rails down an inclined plane controlled by a windlass and chain operated by a water-wheel to the quay. Copper ore and other minerals came down, and coal and limestone went up. Here on the east bank of the Tamar, vessels of 200 tons drawing 14 ft (4.3 m) of water could be moored. The canal was subject to an Act of Parliament passed in 1803, and the cutting of it, and the driving of a 2-mile-long tunnel below Morwell Down were the work of French prisoners of war to the design of the engineer, John Taylor. The canal was opened in 1817. In 1933–4 the canal was re-used to provide power for a local electricity supply.

In the early 1800s, manganese was mined locally and it was brought to Morwellham to be ground before shipment. The grinding stones were driven by a large overshot water-wheel. Elsewhere in the vicinity there are substantial lime kilns.

Since 1970 the derelict remains of the quay and its associated structures have been restored by the Dart Amenity Research Trust but are now overlaid with the trappings of the 'heritage industry'. The present water-wheel on the site was brought from china clay workings on Dartmoor. The re-excavated dock was served by an overhead railway, part of which has been reconstructed. The deep adit of the George and Charlotte mine has been made accessible.

105
Newton Poppleford Toll-house
1758

SY 079895. At the SE corner of the junction of A3052 Exeter–Lyme Regis road with A376 Budleigh Salterton–Ottery St Mary road

[D]

The Newton Poppleford toll-house is the oldest remaining in Devon. It was built in 1758 by the Lyme Regis Trust at the time when the network of turnpike trusts had just spread to Devon. It is a simple, single-storey thatched cottage and is therefore distinct from the more common, 'typical', toll-house which was a two-storeyed building with a three-sided front, having a door and porch on the front and windows in the angled

Newton Poppleford toll-house.

sides to give the toll collector visibility along the road from inside the house. There are in fact considerable differences among toll-houses, from the octagonal slate-hung building on the Tavistock–Launceston road to the single-storey cottage with pillars supporting the porch on the way to Two Bridges (D). Others have few distinguishing marks, apart from their situation and a tendency to have more windows than usual.

Turnpike trusts to administer and maintain particular roads or groups of roads, and empowered to levy tolls in order to raise the money to do so, date from 1663. Each toll-house had to exhibit its scale of charges usually on a painted board fixed beside the door. They did not spread to Devon and Cornwall until the 1750s, by which time large parts of England had already been covered. The earliest in Devon were the Exeter, Honiton and Axminster trusts. They reflected the increasing growth of traffic, particularly wheeled traffic, and were revolutionary in their effect, enabling enormous reductions in journey times through improvements in easier routes and surfacing. But they were expensive in their charges. They were first established on the main coaching roads, and were also a means of improving and establishing new roads. The heyday of the turnpike trusts was between 1815 and the development of railways in the 1840s. By about 1880, the trusts had almost entirely ceased to exist and the toll-houses were sold off, with new Highway Boards taking over road maintenance.

106
Postbridge Clapper Bridge
? Medieval–post-medieval

SX 647788. Lydford. B3212 at Postbridge E of the present road bridge over the East Dart

[A]

The clapper bridge is only a few yards below the present road bridge and was considered by Crossing to be the finest example, and among the largest, of these distinctive features of Dartmoor. It is

Postbridge clapper bridge. J COX

almost 43 ft (13 m) long and consists of three spans. The buttresses and piers are formed of large blocks of granite carefully fitted, and dry laid. The roadway consists of four enormous granite slabs, one laid over the western opening, another over the eastern, and two smaller slabs across the centre. One of these had been displaced early in the 19th century but later replaced upside down. It was not the only formal crossing of the East Dart as stepping stones still remain about 150 yds (137 m) above the clapper bridge.

Clapper bridges were intended for pedestrians and pack animals. While they are numerous on Dartmoor they also occur elsewhere in the south-west. Their date is uncertain. R N Worth believed that they were post-medieval and no earlier than 1400, but the number of well-attested medieval bridges in the two counties suggests that this simple form of construction could well go back to the earlier Middle Ages, and to the expansion of 13th-century settlement onto the Moor.

107
Royal Albert Bridge, Saltash
1859

SX 435587. View from the Saltash waterside below the station or from the Tamar Bridge

[D]

Brunel's railway viaducts in Devon and Cornwall (there were thirty-four on the line between Plymouth and Truro alone) were constructed in timber, springing from tall stone piers, and were a dramatic feature of the landscape. When the railway crossing of the River Tamar west of Plymouth had to be faced, the Admiralty required headroom for navigation of 100 ft (30.5 m) so that a timber construction was out of the question. Bridging the Tamar at a height of 100 ft was Brunel's last great achievement.

At Saltash, the river is 1,100 ft (335 m) wide and 70 ft (21.3 m) deep at high water. Brunel determined upon

Royal Albert Bridge. E BERRY

two main spans of 465 ft (141.7 m) each. There were also seventeen approach spans. The two great wrought-iron tubes enclosing the suspension chains were arched upwards into an oval in order that their breadth should be equal to that of the bridge platform below and the suspended chains would fall vertically. The formation of the deep central pier was the greatest problem requiring a cast-iron cylinder, 35 ft (10.7 m) in diameter at its base, as a coffer-dam within which a masonry pier could be built on the rock foundation 80 ft (24.5 m) below high-water level. The trusses were prefabricated complete on the Plymouth shore and floated into position on pontoons and from thence on to the piers. They were then raised by hydraulic presses as the masonry was built up beneath them. The first span was floated on 1 September 1857. The second was raised the following year and Prince Albert travelled down from Paddington to open the Royal Albert Bridge on 2 May 1859. Brunel was not present. As a dying man, he had his first and last look at the finished bridge sometime later, lying on a specially prepared platform truck drawn across for him.

108

Smeaton's Eddystone Lighthouse, Plymouth
1759–1882

SX 478538. Plymouth Hoe
[A]

So that ships could navigate coastal waters in safety, lighthouses and daymarks have been placed on cliffs, rocks and shoals at least since Roman times. The lighthouse built by John Smeaton in 1759 on the Eddystone reef, 14 miles off Plymouth, was also a landmark in terms of civil engineering.

Towards the end of the 17th century, Plymouth became increasingly important with the growth of the American trade and the establishment of a naval dockyard. Yet out in the English Channel, at the entrance to Plymouth Sound, was the terrible hazard of Eddystone, which regularly took its toll of shipping. The first attempt to place a lighthouse on these rocks was that of Henry Winstanley in 1696. He had lost one of his own ships there previously. His extraordinary structure, however,

lasted only three years when the tower, with Winstanley in it, was swept away in 1703. The next attempt in 1706 was initiated by John Rudyerd who was by background a silk merchant. His tower was finished in 1709, and remained in active use until 1755 when it was burnt down. For the third tower the established engineer, John Smeaton, was brought in without delay.

The earlier towers were of wooden construction since it was thought that the elasticity of timber would better resist the force of the enormous seas which could break over the reef. Smeaton decided on an entirely masonry structure. To give greater weight and stability, the lower half was solid with a wide base which then tapered towards the top in order to lessen wind resistance. The upper half of the tower contained four floors of residential space and was then crowned by the large lantern. Smeaton's novel ideas were also applied to the masonry. He devised a system of dovetailing the individual stones so that they not only interlocked but it was also impossible to remove any stone once set other than in the reverse order to the sequence in which it was laid. He used marble dowels as well as iron cramps to prevent horizontal shear and he also experimented with hydraulic cement which could set when wet. A further refinement was the creation of 'weather bars' to prevent water being driven through the joints. He used granite for the foundations and facings because he had observed the deterioration of limestone in the harbour works at Plymouth. The light was first shown in 1759, and so continued for another 123 years.

Smeaton's tower remained intact until the late 1870s when it became apparent that the rock on which it stood was itself being undermined by the sea. A new tower was designed by James Douglas, engineer in chief of Trinity House. It was built in four years and was first lit in 1882. Such was the feeling of the people of Plymouth for Smeaton's lighthouse that a fund was raised to dismantle the upper half and re-erect it on Plymouth Hoe.

Eddystone Lighthouse. A F KERSTING

109
Starcross Pumping Station
1846–1848

SX 977817. Starcross. Beside the jetty for the Exmouth ferry

[A]

Starcross pumping station, 1847. BRUNEL MUSEUM

Starcross is the best preserved of the pumping stations along the line of Isambard Kingdom Brunel's short-lived 'atmospheric' railway. Built in 1846, the engine house is Italianate in style with heavy corbels under the eaves and round-headed windows with large keystones. The tower, containing the chimney encased by a stair, was later reduced in height. The building now serves as a museum relating to the project.

Following the authorisation of the Bristol and Exeter Railway in 1836, some Plymouth businessmen proposed a railway to Exeter to meet it and Brunel surveyed the country in the same year. The plan was slow to catch on but the South Devon Railway was eventually authorised in 1844. From the start, the company adopted Brunel's recommendation for an atmospheric system for working the line because of the severe gradients west of Newton Abbot and Brunel's doubts over the capacity of steam locomotives to work the line economically. The use of compressed air, or employing the pressure of the atmosphere on a piston travelling in an exhausted tube, was not a new one and had been adopted with some success by the Dublin & Kingstown Railway. The system required stationary engines to pump air from a continuous iron pipe laid between the rails. The top of the pipe had a slot covered by a hinged flap-valve backed with iron, which could be opened and resealed to allow the passage of the piston arm which was connected to the leading vehicle and to a cylinder and close-fitting piston travelling inside the pipe. Air was let in behind the piston and its force rushing towards the vacuum in front propelled the train. The pipe was then resealed with pressure from a small roller on the vehicle and a fresh vacuum was then created by the pumping-house.

There were ten pumping-houses at intervals of about every 3 miles.

There were problems at first with the pumping-engines but the fundamental flaw lay with the sealing system of the longitudinal valve. The joint action of water on the leather, and chemical action between tannin and iron gradually caused the disintegration of the seal throughout the length of line between Exeter and Newton Abbot. The atmospheric trains began carrying passengers in September 1847; a year later, Brunel recommended the abolition of the system and the plant was sold. The 'Atmospheric Caper' was at an end.

110
Treffry Viaduct
1839–1842

SX 056573. Luxulyan. By minor road to Luxulyan from A390 at Penpillick

[A]

In the early 19th century, an outstanding figure in the engineering field was Joseph Thomas Treffry of Fowey. He was closely involved with the mines around St Blazey, particularly the highly profitable Fowey Consols at Tywardreath. He financed and built an entirely new harbour at Par nearby, and acquired, in 1838, the recently built harbour of Newquay on the north coast, both intended for the export of copper, granite and china clay. By 1849, he had, in the course of ten years, linked the two by a railway, later to be rebuilt as the Cornwall Minerals Railway. To Betjeman, 'with his eye for landscape and bold schemes of engineering he [Treffry] was a precursor of I K Brunel'.

The railway began in 1839 with the construction of the first great granite viaduct-aqueduct in Cornwall across the Luxulyan Valley. It is one of the great sights of Cornwall with its combination of natural and man-made beauty. It was designed by James Palmer and built in three years at a cost of £7,000. This magnificent monument is 660 ft (201 m) long, and carried both a railway and an aqueduct beneath the track on ten arches of 40 ft (12 m) span and at a maximum height of nearly 100 ft (30 m) above the valley floor. It also bears Treffry's coast of arms. There are still *in situ* granite sleepers which carried the rails. The water in the aqueduct eventually found its way by leat down the side of the valley for over a mile to Pont's Mill near Tywardreath Highway where it powered machinery to crush china stone. The railway ran from St Blazey and up the Carmears Incline across the viaduct to Luxulyan, Bugle and Indian Queens where it was joined by a tramway from Hendra Downs, St Dennis, then across to Newquay.

Select Bibliography

P Ashbee, *Ancient Scilly: From the First Farmers to the Early Christians*, Newton Abbot, 1974.

P M Beacham, *Devon's Traditional Buildings*, Devon County Council, 1978.

John Betjeman, *Cornwall: A Shell Guide*, London, 1964.

Frank Booker, *The Industrial Archaeology of the Tamar Valley*, Newton Abbot, 1967.

Bridget Cherry and Nicholas Pevsner, *Devon (Buildings of England* series), London, 2nd edn 1989.

V M and F J Cheshire, *The Cornishman's House*, Newton Abbot, 1968.

A Fox, *South-West England*, London, 1964.

Frances Griffith, *Devon's Past: An Aerial View*, Exeter, 1988.

L V Grinsell, *The Archaeology of Exmoor*, Newton Abbot, 1970.

F E Halliday, *Richard Carew of Anthony, The Survey of Cornwall etc*, London, 1953.

Helen Harris, *Industrial Archaeology of Dartmoor*, Newton Abbot, 1968.

R A Higham (ed.), *Security and Defence in South West England Before 1800* (Exeter Studies in History, No 19), University of Exeter, 1987.

W G Hoskins, *Devon*, Newton Abbot, 1954 (new edn 1972).

W G Hoskins and H P R Finberg, *Devonshire Studies*, London, 1952.

W Minchinton, *Devon's Industrial Past: A Guide*, Dartington Centre for Education and Research, 1986.

O J Padel, *A Popular Dictionary of Cornish Place-Names*, Penzance, 1988.

S M Pearce, *The Kingdom of Dumnonia: Studies in History and Tradition in South Western Britain AD 350–1150*, Padstow, 1978.

S M Pearce, *The Archaeology of South West Britain*, London, 1981.

R D Penhallurick, *Tin in Antiquity*, Institute of Metals, London, 1986.

Nikolaus Pevsner, *Cornwall (Buildings of England* Series), 2nd edn revised by Enid Radcliffe, Harmondsworth, 1970.

R A Stanes, *History of Devon*, Chichester, 1986.

G M Spooner and F S Russell (eds) *Worth's Dartmoor*, Newton Abbot, 1967.

Charles Thomas, *Explorations of a Drowned Landscape: Archaeology and History of the Isles of Scilly*, London, 1985.

Charles Thomas, *Celtic Britain*, London, 1986.

A C Todd and P Laws, *Industrial Archaeology of Cornwall*, Newton Abbot, 1972.

Malcolm Todd, *The South-West to AD 1000*, London, 1987.

Craig Weatherhill, *Cornovia: Ancient Sites of Cornwall and Scilly*, Penzance, 1985.

Index

Note: gazetteer entries are listed in bold, by their **page** number

Abbott, John (of Frithelstock)   41, 87
Abercrombie, Prof. Patrick   33
Adams, Robert (architect)   79, 89
Adams, Robert (engineer)   77
agriculture, effects of   1–2, 5, 16, 61, 63, 64–5, 68
Alfred, King of Wessex   16, 20
almshouses   38, 92
A La Ronde, Exmouth   80, **87**
Altarnun, St Nonna   45, **57–8**
Anglo-Saxon conquest   3, 61
Anthony House   80
Appledore   26, 101
Arlington Court   80
Armada of 1588   32, 71, 74
Arthur, King   23
Arundell, Sir John   89
Ashburton   26
Athelstan, King of Wessex   16, 53
Aveton Gifford   65
Avon, River   25
Axminster   92, 103

Babbacombe, All Saints   **47–8**
Baldwin, sheriff of Devon   73
Bampton Castle   69
Bant's Carn, St Mary's, Scilly   **13**
Baptists   47
Barnstaple   4, 16, 20, 25, 26, 27, 69, 92
    almshouses   38
    church   47
    Pannier Market   37
    Queen Anne's Walk   37
barrow/burial mound   6, 11–12
Bartholomew, Bishop   45, 53
Beckford, William   91
Bedford, dukes of   33–4, 80, 106
Beer stone   41, 81, 92
Benson, Bishop Edward   58
Berry Head Batteries   71, **71–2**
Berry Pomeroy Castle   34, 79, **80–1**
Betjeman, John   98, 110
Bible Christians   47, 67
Bicton Gardens   80, **81–2**
    American Garden   82
    arboretum   82
    Hermitage   82
    Italian Garden   81, 82
    Orangery   82
    Palm House   80, 82
    St Mary's Church   82
    Shell House   82
Bideford   87
Biscovey church   47
bishoprics   16, 17, 49, 53, 58
Bishop's Court, Clyst Honiton   80
Blackdown Hills   9

Blackmoor stannary   40
Blanchdown   106
Blore, William   56
blowing-houses   91, 97
Blundell's School, Tiverton   38, **39**
Bodmin   16, 25, 26, 31, 35, 101
    St Petroc's Church   53
    Courthouse   37
    Gaol   38
    Priory   86
Bodmin Moor   1, 2, 3, 5, 12, 25, 73
Bonaventure, Thomasine   44
Borlase, W Copeland   8
Boscastle   61
Bossiney   23, 69
Botallack Mine   91, **92–3**
Bovey Tracey   92, 105
Braunton Burrows   101
Braunton Great Field   61, **62–3**
Breage   101
Brewer, Bishop   49
Brewer, William de   58
bridges   3, 27, 101, 104, 107, 108, 110
Brixham   2, 71
Broad Down/Farway cemetery   6
Bronescombe, Bishop   49, 55–6
Bronze Age   6, 7, 8, 9, 12, 61, 68
Brunel, Isambard Kingdom   103, 107–8, 110
Bryher, Scilly   13
Buck, brothers   74
Buckfast Abbey   65
Buckland Abbey   79, 89
Buckland Filleigh   80
Buckland House   80
Bude Canal   **103–4**
Bugle   110
burh   16, 20, 25, 34, 69
Burges, William   80, 85–6
Burhwold, Bishop   53
Burley Wood Castle   69
Burnard, Nevill Northey   35, 58
Burne Jones   54
Burney, Fanny   88
Bury Barton, Roman fort   15
Busveal Chapel   50
Butterfield, William   47–8, 56

Caen, River   62
Caer Brane hillfort   7
Caerhayes   80
cairn, prehistoric   3, 5, 8, 11–12, 13
Callington   63
Calstock   83, 104
Camborne   6, 95
Camden, William   10
Camel, River   101
canals   29, 41, 92, 103, 104, 106
Capability Brown   80
Carclaze pit   94

Cardinham Castle   69
Cardinham family   75
Carew, Richard   4, 31, 44, 62, 79, 89, 91, 97, 101
Carey, Sir George   58
Carleton, Adam de   3
Carmears Incline   110
Carn Beacon, Veryan   6
Carn Brea   5, **6–7**
    Mines   95
Carn Euny Iron Age settlement   6, **7–8**
Carn Gluze, chambered cairn   5, **8–9**
Carnmenellis   1
Carteret, Sir George   88
Carthew   99
Castilly, Luxulyan   67
Castle an Dinas   6
Castle Drogo   80, **82–3**
castles   3, 7, 20, 23, 27, 28, 30, 31, 32, 35, 69–71, 72, 73, 75, 79, 80
Catacluse stone   92
cathedrals   28, 35, 45–7, 49–50, 58–9
causewayed camp   10
Cave, Walter   55
Celtic Christianity   3, 15–17, 18, 20, 23, 52, 53, 87
Celtic place-names   16, 18
Chagford   26
chambered tombs   3, 5, 8, 13–14
chapels   22, 47, 50, 62, 63, 87, 92
Charlestown   91, **93–4**
    Foundry   93, 96, 99–100
china-clay industry   1, 31, 62, 91, 92, 93, 96, 99–100, 110
chi-rho   16, 18
Cholwich Town stone row   5
Chun Castle   6, **9**
Chun Quoit   5
churches   3, 22, 28, 45–59, 92
Churchstow   65
Chysauster   15, **16–17**
cist grave   3, 8
Civil War   30, 32, 71, 72, 75, 76, 77, 83, 87, 88, 101
clapper bridges   101, 107
cloth manufacture and trade   3, 26, 29, 34, 35, 50, 85, 92, 94
Coad, Richard   86
cob   61, 98
Coldharbour Mill, Uffculme   92, **94–5**
Colebrooke   17
Coleridge, Samuel Taylor   57
Collacombe Barton   89
collegiate churches   16, 47, 49, 51, 52, 53, 55
Collins, Wilkie   93
Combe Martin   91
Come-to-Good meeting-house   **49**
Congregationalists   47, 87
Constantine, King of Dumnonia   15
Cookworthy, William   91, 92
Coombepark Farm   113
copper industry   4, 6, 34, 35, 91, 93, 106, 110

Copperhouse, Hayle   91
Copplestone Cross   16, **17**
Cornovii   15
Corringdon Ball   5
Cornish language   3
Cotehele   79, **83–4**
cottage orné   80, 87
country houses   79–89
Courtney earls of Devon   69, 73, 74
courtyard house   8, 15, 16–17
Crace, J D   86
Crediton   16, 17, 49, 53, 92
Cremyll Ferry   101
crosses   16, 17–18, 52, 54
Crownhill Fort, *see* Plymouth
Cullompton   26, 92
    St Andrew   45, **50–1**
        Lane Chapel   50, 56
        Moores Chantry   50
Culm Valley   94
custom houses   29, 37

Dalwood, Loughwood Baptist Chapel   47
Dart, River   25, 27, 34
Dartington Hall   79, 80, **84–5**
Dartmeet reaves   12
Dartmoor   1, 2, 5, 9, 10, 11, 12, 17, 20, 25, 34, 61, 62, 73, 74, 82, 92, 97, 101, 106, 107
    Forest of   26, 42
Dartmouth   25, 26, **27**, 62, 71, 72, 91, 101
    Bayard's Cove, fort   27
    Butterwalk   27
    Castle   69, **72**
    Cherub, Higher Street   27
    Church   27
    Lamberd's Bulwark   72
    Maiden Fort   72
    Newcomen engine   27
    Royal Naval College   27
    St Petrock's Church   72
    Townstall   27
Davy, Sir Humphrey   91
Dawlish   26
Daye, Robert   58
de Dunstanville, Lord   7
de Gomme, Sir Bernard   76
Defoe, Daniel   4, 29, 35
Delabole   92
Devon Great Consols   34, 91, 106
Devonport, *see* Plymouth
Devonshire Association   9
Domesday Book   3, 25, 33, 72, 73, 101
dovecotes   62
Douglas, James   108
Down St Mary   17
Dozmary Pool   2
Drake, Sir Francis   34
Drewe, Julius   82–3
Drewsteignton   82
Drogo de Teign   82
Druxton   104
Duchy of Cornwall   37, 39–40, 73
Du Cane, Captain Edmund   72
Duchy Palace, Lostwithiel   37, **39–40**

Convocation Hall   39
    Great Hall   39
Dumnonii   6, 15
Dunscombe quarry   55
Dupath Well Chapel   62, **63**

Early Christian period   9, 15, 17–18, 20, 22–3, 49
East Dart River   107
East Pool beam engines   91, **95–6**
    Taylor's Shaft   95
East Webburn River   12
Eddystone Lighthouse   103, 108
Edyvean, John   104
Edgar, King of Wessex   17
Edgcumbe family   83
Edmund, Earl of Cornwall   75
Eliot family   54
Elmhirst, Leonard and Dorothy   84
enclosures, prehistoric   3, 6
Endsleigh Cottage   80
entrance grave   5, 8, 13
Exe, River/valley   28, 29, 87, 94
Exeter   15, 16, 20, 25, 26, 27, **28–9**, 37, 69, 71, 92, 101, 103, 107, 110
    Assembly Rooms   29, 38
    Bowhill House   41
    Canal   29, 41, 103
    Cathedral   15, 28, 45, 47, **49–50**, 53, 56, 65
    city wall   15, 16, 28
    conduits   28
    Custom House   29, 37, **41**
    Devon and Exeter Hospital   29, 38
    Exe Bridge   28, 101, **104**
    Guildhall   28, 37, **41**
    Higher Market   29, 37
    Law Library   28, 41
    legionary bath-house   15, 28
    Pennsylvania Park   29
    Roman city   15, 28
    Rougemont Castle   28, 69
    Royal Albert Museum   29
    St Edmund's Church   104
    St Mary Major   49
    St Nicholas Priory   28, 51
    Sessions House   29, 37
    Tuckers' Hall   28
    Wynard's Almshouses   28
Exe Vale Hospital   38
Exmoor   3, 20
Exmouth   25, 26, 80, 87, 91

Fairfax, Sir Thomas   72, 75, 101
Fal, River   29
Falmouth   26, **29–30**, 71, 74, 98
    Arwennack   29
    King Charles the Martyr   30, 47
    Custom House   30
    Falmouth Hotel   92
    Haven   29, 71, 74, 75
    Marlborough House   30
    Packet service   103
    Royal Cornwall Polytechnic   30
    'The Moor'   30

fields, prehistoric   3, 7, 13, 14, 17, 64–5, 68
Fiennes, Celia   4, 27, 30, 31, 76, 93
Finch Brothers' Foundry   91, **96**
fishing   4, 27, 61, 92, 93, 96–7, 98
    cellars   92, 93, 96, 98
Flete   80
Foales Arrishes   12
Forrabury Stitches   61
forts, artillery   27, 31, 32, 69–70, 71, 72, 74–5, 76, 77
    hill   3, 6, 9–10, 13, 17
    promontory   3, 6, 13
fogou   6, 7, 17
Foulston, John   33, 34, 37, 38, 41, 80, 89
Fowey   25, 26, **30–1**, 77, 110
    blockhouse   69, 71
    church   47
    'King of Prussia'   31
    Old Town Hall   31
    Place House   30–1
    St Catherine's Castle   31
Fowey Consols   110
Fowey, River   10, 40, 75, 101
Fowler, Charles   38
Fox, George   49, 73
Fox, Thomas and Edward   94
fulling mills   92

gardens   79–89
Garrett, H A   43
Garrison, St Mary's, Scilly   71, **77**
    'Corsican' towers   77
    The Hugh   77
    Steval Battery   77
    Woolpack Battery   77
Geoffrey of Monmouth   23
geology   1, 2, 11
George and Charlotte Mine   106
Gilbert, Davies   91
Glasney College, Penryn   52, 66
Godolphin   79
Godolphin, Sir Francis   77, 91
gold extraction   6
Goonhilly Earth Station   103, **104–5**
Gorlois, Duke of Cornwall   23
Grampound   25, 101
Grandisson, Bishop John de   3, 49, 65–7
granite   1, 3, 5, 6, 14, 17, 20, 31, 35, 38, 43, 45, 50, 61, 63, 82, 92, 103, 105, 107, 108, 110
'Great Rebuild'   62, 79
Greenway Chapel, *see* Tiverton
Grenville, John   79
Grim's Lake   9
Grimspound   5, **9**
Gugh, Scilly   13
Gunnislake   106
Gwennap Pit   47, **50**, 101

Halangy Down, St Mary's, Scilly   13
Halse, James   63
Halestown   62, **63–4**
hall-house   61, 66
Halwell   16, 25

Hameldon   9, 12
Harlyn Bay Iron Age cemetery   6
Harry's Walls, St Mary's, Scilly   71
Hartland Abbey   80
Harvey's Foundry, Hayle   91, 93, 95
Hawker, R S   57
Hawley, John   27
Hayle   103
Hayle estuary   101
Haytor Down quarries   105
Haytor Granite Railway   103, **105**
Heathcotes of Tiverton   80, **85–6**, 92
Hedgeland, John   52–3
Hele Bridge   104
Helston   25, 26
Hembury   5, 6, **9–10**
Hemyock castle   69
Henderson, Charles   57, 104
Hendra Downs   110
Hensbarrow   1
Hobbacott Down   104
hogsback gravestones   18
Holand, John, Duke of Exeter   84
Holcombe Court   48, 49
Holcombe Rogus, All Saints   47, **48**
    Bluett Chapel   48
    Church House   38, 48
Holcombe Roman *villa*   15
Holman Brothers, Camborne   95
Holwell Castle   69
holy wells   62, 63
Honiton   92, 103, 107
Hookney Tor   9
hospitals   29, 32, 38
Houndtor medieval settlement   61, **64–5**
Huer's Hut, Newquay   92, **96–7**
Hugh Town, St Mary's, Scilly   77
Hundred Years' War   69
Hurdwick quarries   33, 92
Hurlers, The   5, **10**
huts/houses, prehistoric   3, 5, 6, 7–8, 9, 11, 12, 13, 17, 64

Ictis   6, 87
Ilfracombe   27
    Grecian Baths   38
    St Nicholas Chapel   103
Ilsham valley   11
Ilsington   105
Indian Queens   110
Innisidgen burial chamber   13
inscribed stones   16–19
Iron Age   6, 8, 9, 10, 11, 13, 15, 62, 66
Isca (Exeter)   15, 28
Ive, Paul   74

Jekyll, Miss   83
Jenner, Henry   63
Johns, Catherine   66

Kea   49
Kemp, Edward   86
Kensey, River   31, 73
Kent's Cavern, Torquay   11, **10–11**

Kilkhampton Castle   69
Killigrew, Sir John   29
King Doniert's Stone   16, **17–18**
Kingsbridge   45, 65, 101
Kingswear Castle   72
Kingswear Ferry   101
Kirkham House, Paignton   62, **65**
Knackyboy Cairn   13
Knightshayes   80, **85–6**

lace industry   85, 92
lan   16, 18
Land's End   61, 68
Lane, John   51
Lanhydrock House   79, 80, **86–7**
    St Hydroc's Church   87
Lanivet crosses   16, **18**
Lanyon Quoit   5
Launcells church   55
Launceston   25, 26, **31**, 44, 69, 101, 104, 107
    Castle   31, 40, 49, 69, **72–3**
    Eagle House   31
    King House   31
    Lawrence House   31
    Newport   31
    Priory   31, 47
    St Mary Magdalene   31, 45, 59
    St Thomas Church   31
    South Gate   31
    White Hart   31
Leigh Barton   62, **65–6**
Leigh, John   65
Leland   23, 76, 104
Leofric, Bishop   53
Lettaford   61, 62, 67
Lewannick inscribed stones   16, **18**
lighthouses   103, 108
Linkinhorne   10
Liskeard   25
Little Dennis, *see* Pendennis Castle
Lizard, The   16, 61, 104–5
Loddiswell Castle   69
long-house   22, 61, 64, 67
Looe, East   25, **27–8**
    bridge   27, 103
    grid plan   27
    Guildhall   27
Looe, West   25
Lostwithiel   25, 26, 39–40, 75, 101
    church   47
Loudon, J C   82
Lovering, John   94, 99
Lukis, W C   9
Luscombe   80
Lutyens, Sir Edwin   80, 82–3
Luxulyan   110
    Valley   110
Lydford   16, **20**, 25, 69
    Castle (prison)   20, 26, 37, **42–3**
    Norman castle   20, 42
Lyd, River   20
Lyman, Major   77
Lyme Regis   107

Lynmouth   20, 27

Madron   16
Madron workhouse   9
Magor Roman *villa*   15
Maker Heights redoubts   71
Manaton   9, 64
Marazion   87
   meeting-house   49
Marconi, Guglielmo   104–5
Mark, King   23
market houses   29, 35, 37
Martinhoe Roman fortlet   15, **20–1**
Martyn family   99
Mary Tavy   34, 96
Mawgan Porth settlement   16, **21–2**, 61
Mayne, Cuthbert   73
McEnery, Father J   11
Menabilly   93
menhir, *see* standing stones
Mercer, Alexander   71
Merrivale   5, **11–12**
   blowing-houses   91, **97**
   stone rows   **11**
Mesolithic   2, 10
Methodist chapel/meeting   9, 47, 49, 50, 58,
   64, 93
Metropole Hotel, Padstow   92
Middle Ages   1, 3, 21, 22, 27, 28, 35, 37, 42,
   44, 45, 52, 61, 62, 63, 69, 73, 91, 101, 104,
   107
milestones, Roman   15, 23, 101
Minniehaha wreck   105
minster churches   3, 16, 49
miracle plays   66
Molesworth family   103
monasteries   16, 23, 25, 28, 30, 31, 32, 34,
   47, 58, 87
Moretonhamstead Almshouses   **38**
Mortain, Count Robert de   3, 31, 73
Morvah   9
Morwell Down   106
Morwhellham Quay   103, **106**
Morwenstow, St Morwenna   45, **57**
Mount Batten   6, 31, 101
Mount Edgcumbe House   79, 80, 83, 88
Mount's Bay   101
mystery plays   52, 62

Nanstallon Roman fort   15
Napoleonic Wars   1, 71, 75, 77, 94
Nash, John   80
Neolithic   5, 9, 10, 11, 14, 66
Newcomen, Thomas   27, 91
New Draperies   92
Newlyn East   89
Newquay   27, 92, 96–7, 110
Newton Abbot   103, 110
Newton Poppleford toll-house   103, **106–7**
Nicolls, Thomas   86
Norden, John   14, 18
Norman Conquest   3, 25, 51, 52, 54, 69, 73,
   87
North Bovey   67

North Tawton Roman fort   15, 101

Ogham script   18
Okehampton   25, 101
   Castle   69, **73–4**, 79
   Roman fort   15
Old Burrow Roman fortlet   20
Old Post Office, *see* Tintagel
Otter, River and valley   9, 81
Ottery St Mary   92
   St Mary's Church   45, **55–7**
      Dorset Aisle   51, 56

Padstow   101
Paignton   65
Paignton Pier   38
Paleolithic   10–11
Palmer, James   110
Par Harbour   110
Parker family, Lord Borringdon   89
Parminter, Jane and Mary   87
Parracombe   69
Passmore Edwards libraries   38
Payhembury   9
Pearson, J L   47, 58–9
Pencarrow   79
Pendennis Castle   29, 30, 71, **74–5**, 76
   Crab Quay Battery   75
   Half Moon Battery   75
   Little Dennis blockhouse   74
Pengelly, William   11
Penryn   26, 29, 30
Pentewan   92
Penzance   37
   Egyptian House   38, **40–1**
   Market House   37
Perranzabuloe   66
Phillpotts, Bishop   47
Pilton   16, 25
Pipers, The   10
plasterwork   31, 34, 41, 43, 79, 86, 87, 89
'playing place', *see plen an gwarry*
plen an gwarry   62, 66–7
Plym River/valley   31, 67, 72, 88
Plymouth   4, 25, 26, 27, 30, **31–3**, 37, 62,
   68, 71, 72, 76, 88, 91, 92, 99, 107
   Barbican   32, 33
   blockhouses   69, 71, 76
   Bowden Fort   72
   Breakwater   26, 33, 99, 104
   Cattewater   31, 76
   Charles Church   33, 47
   Civil & Military Library   33, 41
   Crownhill Fort   71, **72**
   Devil's Point tower   32
   Devonport   4, 26, 31, 32, 33, 37, 41, 71,
      80
      Town Hall   33, 37
   Dockyard   33, 71, 72, 92, 99
   Doric Column   33, 37
   Drake's Island   32, 52
   Durnford Street   32
   Firestone Bay tower   32
   Fort   71, 76, 77

Guildhall   33
Hamoaze   32, 99
Hoe   32, 108
Ker Street   33
Laira   72
Old Custom House   37
Royal Citadel   32, 71, **76**
Royal William Victualling Yard   33, 92,
   98–9
St Andrew's Church   33
St Budeaux   72
Smeaton's Eddystone Lighthouse   103,
   108
Sound   26, 31, 32, 52, 72, 83, 99, 108
Stonehouse   31, 32, 99
Royal Naval Hospital   32, 38, **43**
Sutton Pool   31
Union Street   33, 37
Woodlands Fort   72
Plympton   26
   Castle   69
   Priory   32
   St Mary   88
   St Maurice   89
Point in View   87
Poldhu   104
Polmear almshouses   38
Polruan   31
   blockhouse   69
Polson Bridge   73
Polyphant stone   92
Polzeath   12
Ponts Mill   110
Pool   95
Port Eliot   53, 80
Porthellick Down   13
Portquin Fish Cellars   92, **98**
Portreath   103
Postbridge clapper bridge   101, **107**
pounds   3, 5, 9, 64
Poundstock church house   48
Powderham Castle   4, 79
Price, Uvedale   80
Prince Albert   108
Princetown (Dartmoor Prison)   42
prisons   31, 35, 37, 40, 42, 73
Pugin, A   82

Quakers   47, 49, 73, 94–5
quarries, axe-stone   3
quarrying   92, 105
Quiller Couch, Sir Arthur   31
quoit, *see* chambered tombs

railways   4, 27, 30, 31, 92, 101, 106, 110
   atmospheric   103, 110
   Bodmin & Wadebridge   103
   Cornwall Minerals   110
   Great Western   103
   South Devon   110
Raleigh, Sir Walter   29
Rashleigh family   31
Rashleigh, Charles   93
reaves   3, 5, 12

Redruth   50, 58
Redvers, Baldwin de   67
Rennie, John   33, 91, 99
Repton, Humphrey   80
Restormel Castle   40, 69, **75–6**, 79
Reynolds, Joshua   89
Richard, Earl of Cornwall   3, 23, 31, 40, 42, 69, 73, 75
Rillaton barrow   10
Rippon Tor reaves   5, **12**
roads   4, 101, 103
Robartes, Richard   86
Rolle family   81–2
Roman period   3, 6, 8, 9, 10, 15–17, 20–1, 28, 101
rounds   6, 15, 16, 66
Rovehead, Alexander   43
Royal Albert bridge, *see* Saltash
Royal Citadel, *see* Plymouth
Royal William Victualling Yard, *see* Plymouth
Rudyard, John   108
Rumps, The   6, **12–13**
Rysbrack   54

St Agnes lighthouse, Scilly   103
St Aubyn family   87–8
St Aubyn, J Piers   47, 87
St Austell   25, 93, 99
    Bay   98
    church   45
    Market House   37
St Blazey   110
St Boniface, Exeter   16, 28
St Cleer   14, 17
St Dennis   110
St Elidius, Scilly   22
St Germans Priory   16, 25, 47, **53–4**, 63
    almshouses   38
St Helen's Oratory, Scilly   16, **22–3**
St Hilary   101
St Ives   62, 64, 71
St Just in Penwith   67
St Kew   52
St Martin's, Scilly   13
    daymark   103
St Mary's, Scilly   13, 77
St Mawes Castle   71, 74–5, **76–7**
St Mawgan   21
St Michael's Mount   6, 80, **87–8**
    Blue Drawing Room   88
    Chevy Chase Room   88
    Lady Chapel   88
St Neot, St Anietus   47, **52–3**
    cross   16
    holy well   52
St Petrock, Lydford   20
St Piran's chapel   16
St Piran's Round   62, **66–7**
St Stephens (Launceston)   16, 25, 31
Salcombe   55, 71
Saltash   73, 101, 103, 107–8
    Royal Albert Bridge   103, **107–8**

Saltram House   79, 80, **88–9**
Sampson, Scilly   13, 77
Sancreed   7
Sanders   61, **67**
Saxon settlement   3, 16, 20
schools   38, 39, 44, 63, 67, 92, 93
Scillonian chambered tombs   5, **13–14**
    pilot gigs   103
Scilly, Isles of   1, 13–14, 16, 71, 77, 105
Scott, George Gilbert   47, 86
Seddings, E, J D and E H   47
Seaton Bridge   101
shell keep   69, 73, 75
ship building/repairing   30
Shaugh Prior   67
Shaw, Norman   80
Shovel Down stone circle   5
Sidbury, St Giles   16, 45, **54–5**
    Manor   55
    Saxon crypt   54
Sidmouth   26, 80
    Elysian Fields   80
    Esplanade   38
    Fortfield Terrace   80
silver/lead mining   91
slate   61, 66, 92
Smeaton, John   91, 93, 103, 108
Smeaton's Eddystone Lighthouse, *see* Plymouth
Soane, John   54, 80
Somerset, Duke of   80–1
Sourton inscribed stone   20
South Crofty Mine   95
South Molton   26
Spinster's Rock cairn   5
standing stones   3, 5, 11
stannaries   26, 34, 35, 37, 40, 42, 91
Star Castle   **77**
Starcross   101
Starcross pumping station   103, **110**
Sticklepath   96
Stone, John   55
stone axes   5, 6
stone circles   3, 5, 10, 11
stone rows   3, 5, 10, 11
Stonehouse, *see* Plymouth
Stover Canal   105
Stratton   104
Street, G E   47
Strode, Sir Richard   42

Tamar, River   20, 69, 72, 91, 101, 104, 106, 107
Taphouse barrow cemetery   6
Tavistock   16, 26, **33–4**, 37, 62, 91, 92, 106, 107
    Abbey   22, 33, 34, 47
    Bedford Hotel   34
    Betsy Grimbald's Tower   33
    Canal   103
    church   34
    Kelly College   38

Wheal Betsy   34
Tavy, River   20
Taw, River   25, 63, 96
Taylor, John   106
Tean Chapel, Scilly   22
Teigngrace   105
Teignmouth   26, 37, 105
    Den Crescent   80
telecommunications   103, 104–5
Telstar   105
Tennyson, Lord   23
tin industry   3, 26, 35, 40, 62, 64, 91, 92, 93, 96
tin streaming   1, 6, 25, 34, 35, 91, 97, 101
Tintagel   15, 20, 92
    Castle   **23**, 69
    church   23
    King Arthur's Castle Hotel   38
    Old Post Office   61, **66**
    Roman milestone   15, 23, 101
Tiverton   26, 62, 85, 92
    almshouses   38, 39
    Castle   69, 79
    Greenway Chapel   39, 45, 50
Tomkins, Thomas   88
Topsham   26, 29
Torbay   25, 26, 71
Torquay   10, 26, 47, 58
    Pavilion   38, **43**
Torre Abbey   47, **58**
Totnes   16, 20, 26, **34–5**, 62, 69, 101
    Bridgetown   34
    Butterwalk   35
    Castle   34, 69
    East Gate   34
    Guildhall   34
    Priory   34
    Royal Seven Stars   35
Tovey, Abraham   77
tourism   92
towns   25–35
    houses   62
Townstall, *see* Dartmouth
tre   16
Traylesworthy, Sampson de   67
tramways   103, 105, 106, 110
Trecarrel, Sir Henry   31
Treffry family   30, 77
Treffry, Joseph Thomas   110
Treffry Viaduct   103, **110**
Tregoney   25, 26, 101
Tregothnan   80
Trematon   25
    Castle   4, 69
Trerice   79, **89**
Tresco, Scilly   77, 103
Trethevy Quoit   5, **14**
Trevail, Sylvanus   38
Trevelgue Head, Newquay   13
Trevena   66
Trevithick, Richard   91
Trewint   58
Tristan and Isolde   23
Trowlesworthy Warren   61, **67–8**

Truro   26, 27, **35**, 50, 107
   Assembly Rooms   35, 38
   Boscawen Street   35
   Cathedral   35, 47, 53, **58–9**
   City Hall   35, 37
   Crown Court   35, 38
   Infirmary   38
   Lander monument   35
   Lemon Street   35
   Mansion House   35
   Prince's House   35
   River   35
   Royal Institution of Cornwall   35
   St Mary's Church   58–9
   Strangways Terrace   35
   Walsingham Place   35
tucking mills, *see* fulling mills
turnpikes   103, 106–7
Turstin the Sheriff   75
Two Bridges   107
Tyrwhitt, Sir Thomas   42
Tywardreath   110
   Priory   30

Ugbrooke   80
Unitarians   47

Vale of Lanherne   21
Valhalla, Tresco, Scilly   103
vermin traps   68
vernacular buildings   61–8
Viking raids   16, 20, 25, 49
   settlement   18

Walkham, River   97
Walkhampton   11, 97
Warelwast, Bishop William   49
watermills   62, 94, 96
Watson, J Paton   33
Week St Mary   43–4
   Castle   69
   College   38, **43–4**
Weir, William   84
Werrington Park   80
Wesley, John   47, 50, 58
Wessex, Saxon kingdom of   3, 15, 16, 20, 25, 53
West Okement, river   73

West Penwith   1, 2, 9, 10, 16
   field systems   **68**
West Polmear   93
West Webburn River   9
Wheal Martin China Clay Museum   102, **99–100**
   Gomm Pit   99
Widecombe-in-the-Moor   12, 105
Wilberforce, Bishop Samuel   48
Wilkins, William   80
William of Worcester   7, 104
wine trade   26, 27
Winstanley, Henry   108
wireless telegraphy   103, 104–5
Witney, Thomas of   50
Woodbury Castle   6
Worth, R N   107
Wyatt, James   81
Wyatville, Sir Jeffry   34, 80

Yellowmead Down stone circle   5

Zennor   61, 68

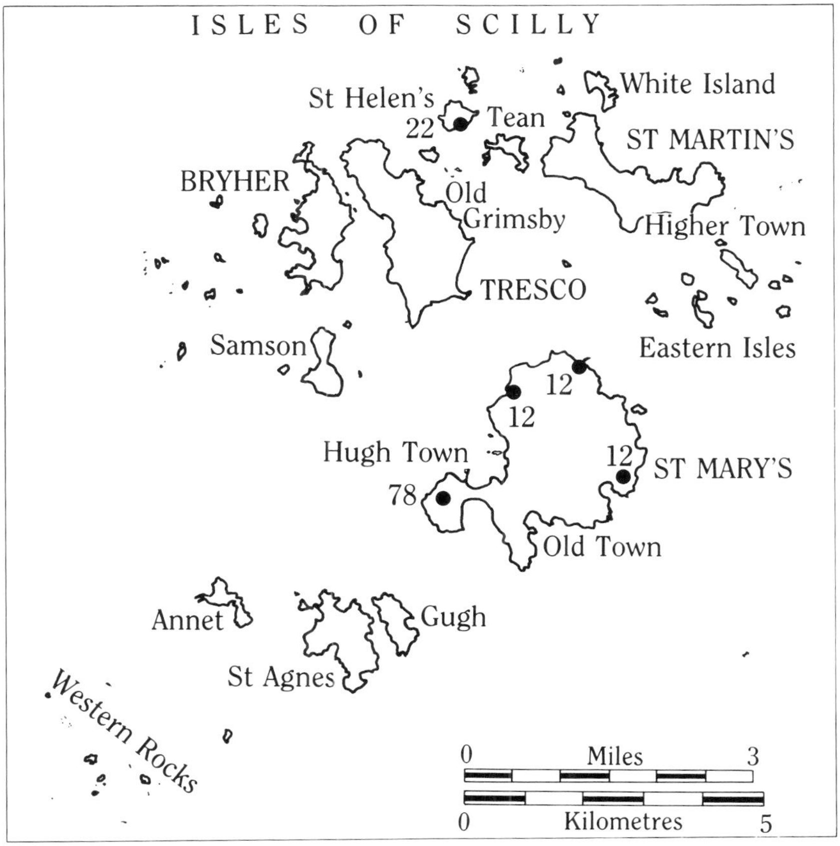

ISLES OF SCILLY

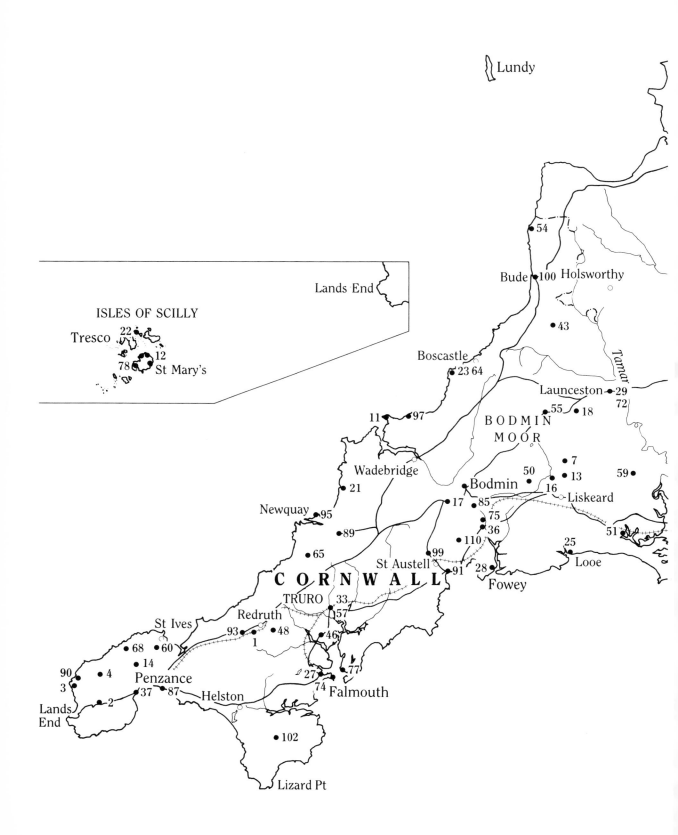

Lundy

ISLES OF SCILLY

Tresco 22
12
78 St Mary's

Lands End

54

Bude 100 Holsworthy

43

Boscastle
23 64

Launceston 29
72
55 18

BODMIN
MOOR

11 97

7
50 13 59

Wadebridge
16

21 Bodmin
17 85 Liskeard
75
Newquay 95 36
110 51
89
65 99 25
St Austell Looe
91 28
C O R N W A L L Fowey

TRURO 33
57
Redruth 46
St Ives 93 48
1
68 60
90 14 77
4 27
3 Penzance 74 Falmouth
2 37 87 Helston
Lands
End

102

Lizard Pt

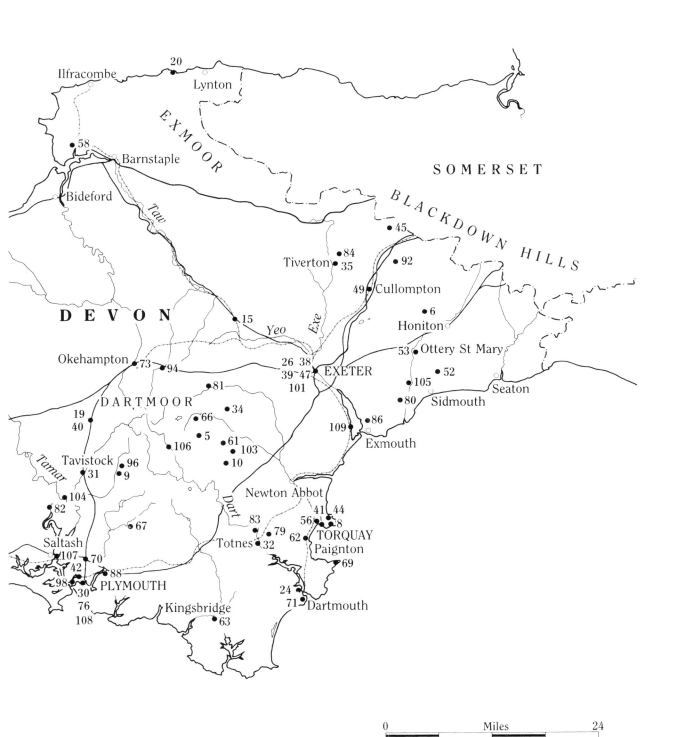

Ilfracombe
20
Lynton

EXMOOR

58
Barnstaple

Bideford

SOMERSET

Taw

BLACKDOWN

HILLS

45

84
Tiverton 35

92

49 Cullompton

15

DEVON

Yeo

Exe

6
Honiton

Okehampton 73 94

26 38
39 47
101

EXETER

53 Ottery St Mary

52

105

Seaton

81

DARTMOOR

34

80 Sidmouth

19
40

66

5

86

106

61
103

109

Exmouth

Tavistock 96
31 9

10

104
82

67

Newton Abbot

83

41 44
56 8

104

79

62

TORQUAY

Saltash
107 70

42

88

Totnes 32

Paignton

98
30

PLYMOUTH

69

76
108

Kingsbridge

63

24
71 Dartmouth

Tamar

Dart

0   Miles   24

0   Kilometres   30